NEW STUDIES IN BI

Hearing God's words

Titles in this series:

1 *Possessed by God*, David Peterson
2 *God's Unfaithful Wife*, Raymond C. Ortland Jr
3 *Jesus and the Logic of History*, Paul W. Barnett
4 *Hear, My Son*, Daniel J. Estes
5 *Original Sin*, Henri Blocher
6 *Now Choose Life*, J. Gary Millar
7 *Neither Poverty nor Riches*, Craig L. Blomberg
8 *Slave of Christ*, Murray J. Harris
9 *Christ, our Righteousness*, Mark A. Seifrid
10 *Five Festal Garments*, Barry G. Webb
11 *Salvation to the Ends of the Earth*, Andreas J. Köstenberger and Peter T. O'Brien
12 *Now My Eyes Have Seen You*, Robert S. Fyall
13 *Thanksgiving*, David W. Pao
14 *From Every People and Nation*, J. Daniel Hays
15 *Dominion and Dynasty*, Stephen G. Dempster
16 *Hearing God's Words*, Peter Adam

NEW STUDIES IN BIBLICAL THEOLOGY 16

Series editor: D. A. Carson

Hearing God's words

EXPLORING BIBLICAL
SPIRITUALITY

Peter Adam

APOLLOS

INTERVARSITY PRESS
DOWNERS GROVE, ILLINOIS 60515

APOLLOS (an imprint of Inter-Varsity Press),
38 De Montfort Street, Leicester LE1 7GP, England
World Wide Web: www.ivpbooks.com
Email: ivp@uccf.org.uk

INTERVARSITY PRESS
PO Box 1400, Downers Grove, Illinois 60515, USA
World Wide Web: www.ivpress.com
Email: mail@ivpress.com

 In some instances in the two sections for meditation on quotations, and in the chapter headings, I have adapted or slightly changed the words for convenience of presentation.

First published 2004
Reprinted 2005

British Library Cataloguing in Publication Data
A catalogue record for this book is available from the British Library.

UK ISBN 1–84474–002–1

Library of Congress Cataloging-in-Publication Data
These data have been requested.

US ISBN 0–8308–2617–3

Set in Monotype Times New Roman
Typeset in Great Britain by Servis Filmsetting Ltd, Manchester
Printed and bound in Great Britain by Creative Print and Design (Wales), Ebbw Vale

This book is dedicated to the students, faculty, staff and Council of Ridley College, my fellow-servants in the Lord Jesus Christ. May God continue his gracious work in and through us, for his glory. May the word of Christ dwell in us richly by his Spirit, and may God train us for gospel service in his world.

Contents

Series preface

New Studies in Biblical Theology is a series of monographs that address key issues in the discipline of biblical theology. Contributions to the series focus on one or more of three areas: 1. the nature and status of biblical theology, including its relations with other disciplines (e.g. historical theology, exegesis, systematic theology, historical criticism, narrative theology); 2. the articulation and exposition of the structure of thought of a particular biblical writer or corpus; and 3. the delineation of a biblical theme across all or part of the biblical corpora.

Above all, these monographs are creative attempts to help thinking Christians understand their Bibles better. The series aims simultaneously to instruct and to edify, to interact with the current literature, and to point the way ahead. In God's universe, mind and heart should not be divorced: in this series we will try not to separate what God has joined together. While the notes interact with the best of the scholarly literature, the text is uncluttered with untransliterated Greek and Hebrew, and tries to avoid too much technical jargon. The volumes are written within the framework of confessional evangelicalism, but there is always an attempt at thoughtful engagement with the sweep of the relevant literature.

In recent decades the notion of 'spirituality' has become astonishingly plastic. People judge themselves to be 'spiritual' if they have some aesthetic sense, or if they are not philosophical materialists, or if they have adopted a pantheistic view of reality, or if they feel helped or reinvigorated by the 'vibrations' of crystals. Even within a broadly Christian heritage, many writers appeal to 'spiritual disciplines' that are utterly divorced from the gospel and detached from the teaching of Scripture. Against the backdrop of these cultural developments, Dr Peter Adam encourages clear thinking: he traces the notion of spirituality through some of the turning points of Scripture, and finally grounds it in the gospel of Jesus Christ and its full-blown application to our lives. By appealing both to the Bible and to influential voices in the history of the church (notably John Calvin), Dr Adam manages to combine biblical theology and historical theology in an admirable synthesis. His academic training, years of pastoral ministry, and now principalship of a theological college, ensure that this book simultaneously informs the mind, warms the heart, and strengthens the will. And from the vantage of three decades of personal friendship, I gratefully attest that what Dr Adam writes, he also lives.

D. A. Carson
Trinity Evangelical Divinity School

Author's preface

My interest in Christian spirituality was first kindled by Harrie Scott Simmons, who not only converted and discipled me, but also introduced me to the spiritual writings of Ramon Lull, Gerhard Teerstegen, Samuel Rutherford and Amy Carmichael. He showed me the riches to be found in the devotional use of good Bible commentaries, and we also shared a passion for the Christ-centred Lutheran Pietism of the music of J. S. Bach.

My thanks are also due to John Cockerton, who, when Principal of St John's College, Durham, asked me to lecture on the history of Evangelical spirituality, and who inspired me by his own studies in spirituality.

I am grateful to God for both of these saints, and for the doors that they opened for me.

This is a wide-ranging book, as I use material from the history of Christian spirituality, and also from Old and New Testament, church history, and theology. I am well aware that I do not have specialist knowledge in all these areas, but I hope that this wide-ranging survey will be helpful for gaining an overall perspective.

In chapter six, the section on Word and Spirit in Puritan–Quaker debate is based on the St Antholin's Lecture for 2001. I am grateful to the Trustees of the St Antholin's Lectureship for their invitation to give that lecture.

I have used some modern reprints of older works, as they are more accessible to most readers.

The words quoted in the chapter headings are from John 8:47; Psalm 78:1; John 6:63; Romans 10:17; John 17:17; 17:6; and Psalm 119:130.

This book is a companion to my *Speaking God's Words* (IVP 1996), and reflects the truth that we must listen to God before we speak on his behalf.

My thanks are due to Don Carson for his encouragement and advice, and to Philip Duce and the staff of Inter-Varsity Press for their patience and professional assistance. Thanks too to Nicole Harvey for preparing the indexes.

I also want to thank all those who pray for me, and in this way support every part of my life and ministry, including my teaching and writing.

Peter Adam
Ridley College

The instructions of the LORD, sweeter than honey, and drippings of the honeycomb.

(Psalms)

It is written, 'One does not live by bread alone, but by every word that comes from the mouth of God.'

(Jesus Christ)

The words you gave me I gave to them, and they have received them, and believe that you sent me. Whoever is from God hears the words of God.

(Jesus Christ)

The Spirit searches the depths of God: we speak of these things in words taught by the Spirit. Faith comes by hearing, and hearing from the word of Christ.

(St Paul)

The crown is given for field-service (martyrdom) in time of persecution: in times of peace it is given to him who is certain of God's word.

(Cyprian of Carthage)

The Scriptures are the public oracles of the Holy Spirit: here the living words of God are heard.

(John Calvin)

The Scriptures are God's Voyce: The Church is his Echo.

(John Donne)

The Scriptures are one of the Church's greatest sacramentals.

(Thomas Merton)

God is love, but get it in writing.

(Gypsy Rose Lee)

Introduction: A strange silence

James Smart gave a haunting title to the book he wrote in 1970 – *The Strange Silence of the Bible in the Church*. It is one of the curious features of contemporary Christianity that at the very time when the Bible is most freely available in a multiplicity of versions and mediums, it is also effectively silent in many areas of church life. It is also strange when we realize that the increasing access to the Bible by ordinary church members in the Roman Catholic denomination has been matched by a decreasing attention to the Bible in much of Protestantism, as is evident in Christian bookshops.

This is especially obvious when looking for resources on spirituality. In secular bookshops it is easy to find books on every kind of spirituality, we might say from Aztec to Zoroastrian! In Christian bookshops books on spirituality will include many sources, including Catholic, Celtic and Orthodox. There is curiously little available on the Bible as a source of spirituality, or on biblical views on spirituality.

What an irony that the assumption that the Bible has little to do with spirituality is often found among Protestants. It is the Roman Catholic John L. McKenzie who has published *The New Testament for Spiritual Reading* (McKenzie 1969–71) following the long Catholic tradition of *Lectio Divina*, the reflective and meditative reading of Scripture. It is the distinguished Roman Catholic writer Lucien Joseph Richard who has written his moving account of the spirituality of John Calvin (Richard 1974).

Another common idea that has affected our assumptions about the status of biblical spirituality is that spirituality is only concerned with the exotic, the abnormal, the exciting, so the Evangelical preoccupation with the Bible means that it will have little to offer in the area of spirituality. The evidence for this idea is that Evangelical faith and practice is often now regarded as a good first step in spiritual growth, but that people must then grow up to maturity in other traditions: Catholic, Celtic, Eastern Orthodox or charismatic.

There are strange dilemmas and confusions in these modern

assumptions, but the result is clear and tragic: we pay little attention to the Bible as a source of spirituality, fail to enjoy the riches that it offers, fail to apply the biblical test to what other sources of spirituality offer, and fail to use the Bible as a guide and source of true spirituality. This is not the place for me to attempt to demonstrate the authority and sufficiency of the Bible, but I do hope to demonstrate its usefulness and effectiveness in the area of spirituality.

It is important for us to be confident in the model of spirituality taught in the Bible. It is important for all of us to recover biblical spirituality, and to test our spirituality by the Bible. It is important for those Christians who have left the Bible behind to recover the Bible and its spirituality.

While I disagree with David Yeago's claim that propositional revelation and verbal revelation are untenable, I agree with his plea for us to return to a passionate and careful study of Scripture:

> Such a project presupposes that we have reason to care about the judgements rendered in the biblical writings. The Fathers, scholastics and reformers had such reasons: they believed that when we conform our thinking to the pattern of judgements embedded in the prophetic and apostolic scriptures, our understanding is illuminated by a divine light (Ps. 36:9) and so we come to share in the *nous Christou*, the mind of Christ (1 Cor. 2:16).
>
> It is not at all clear that much of contemporary Western Christianity shares any longer in this motivation. Mainline theology has failed to replace the untenable early-modern doctrines of propositional revelation and verbal revelation with any account of scripture's role in the purposes of God which provide reasons for a passionate and attentive engagement with the texts. Indeed, such engagement would only hinder many contemporary theological and ecclesiastical projects; institutional interests of all sorts are best served by an instinctive tarring of any attempt to commend a posture of deference towards the scriptural texts with the dreaded fundamentalist brush. Anti-fundamentalism has become a powerful ideological tool in the mainline Western churches which almost guarantees the marginalization of any call to 'biblical seriousness', however clear its actual differences from fundamentalism. (1997: 97)

In this book I am trying to explain biblical spirituality because of what I believe about the significance of the Bible. If the Bible is God-given and therefore has God's authority, then biblical spirituality will express God's will. If the Bible is the sufficient word of God, then biblical spirituality will be sufficient spirituality. If the Bible is the effective Word of God, then biblical spirituality will be effected in us by those words.

I am writing

- to show how the Bible is a rich and fruitful resource for spirituality, that is, what we can learn from the Bible about spirituality, or what spirituality it contains;
- to show the fundamental shape and structure of the 'spirituality of the Word', or, how it works;
- to show the spirituality that the Bible teaches and encourages, or what spirituality results from using the Bible.

In *The Gagging of God* D. A. Carson ends with an appeal for Christian spirituality that has the following characteristics (1996: 566–569):

- *Spirituality must be thought of in connection with the gospel.* This means that the gospel itself must be the interpretative or heuristic device by which spirituality must be assessed. Spirituality must begin and end with the gospel, and not draw away from it or have an independent existence apart from it.
- *Christian reflection on spirituality must work outward from the centre.* The point here is that it is not good to assume the centre or heart of the Christian faith, and to develop peripheral matters and interests. If we avoid rehearsing the core of biblical faith then it will be lost in one generation. If it goes without saying, then it needs to be said!
- *At the same time we should be rightly suspicious of forms of theology that place all the emphasis on coherent systems of thought . . . but do not engage the affections, let alone foster an active sense of the presence of God.* Carson comments:

  > Sometimes this stance is simply an overreacting to the obvious excesses of the charismatic movement. But whatever its cause, it stands against both Scripture and the entire heritage of the best of Christianity, where men and women, by God's grace, know God. (1996: 568)

- *Nevertheless, what God uses to foster this kind of Gospel spirituality must be carefully delineated.* In order for us to receive the life that God gives, he has decided to use what the Puritans called 'means', such as the Bible, prayer, fellowship, the Lord's Supper and the created world. We should be careful to make full use of the means that God has given us. One of the neglected means in discussions about spirituality is the Bible. We need to recover the spirituality of the Word. This spirituality will come in various forms, including private reading, meditation and memorizing of Scripture, sermons and Bible studies, mutual exhortation and encouragement. This will also in turn lead to the spirituality the Bible commends, including the sacraments, fellowship, and enjoying the life and the wonderful world God has made and given us to enjoy.
- *Finally, such Word-centred Reflection will bring us back to the fact that spirituality, as we have seen, is a theological construct.* This means that as we continually check that our theology is being reformed by the content and shape of the Bible, so we will do the same with our spirituality. It will mean that there is no dissonance between our minds and our hearts, between what we know to be true and what we put into practice in our life with God.

I hope that this book will help to achieve these aims.

Meditation

Use the quotations listed before this chapter. Memorize a few that strike you, or write them on memory cards and carry them with you for a few weeks, looking at them when you get the opportunity.

Chapter One

Biblical spirituality: Whoever is from God hears the words of God

Biblical spirituality?

The words 'biblical spirituality' could mean using the Bible as a resource for spirituality, or could refer to that spirituality which the Bible commends and that results from using the Bible as a guide to spirituality. I intend both meanings in this book. I am writing about biblical spirituality in the context of the use of the Bible by different Christian traditions over the last 2,000 years, and I want to explain the Evangelical and Reformed traditions of spirituality. I also want to show the usefulness of biblical theology in forming a spirituality of the Word.

For the Bible is a great God-given resource and guide to true Christian spirituality. Its common neglect results in confusion about spirituality. One of the wonderful gifts of the Bible in every area of Christian life and practice is to clarify what is godly and what is not.

I also want to show something of the spirituality the Bible encourages and enables, which includes the right use of other resources of spirituality, including the creation, prayer and fellowship. Indeed we are likely to misuse these other resources unless we make good use of the Bible, which gives us spiritual discernment. Calvin uses the image of the Bible as glasses that help us see everything more clearly, that is, from God's perspective. Reading the Bible will help us assess all forms of spirituality.

Using another image, we can think of spirituality as being a kind of spiritual diet, in which the various resources provide necessary elements of that diet. Here are some examples: (1) A good dose of *the creation* reminds us of God's eternal power and greatness. (2) *Christian fellowship* provides personal encouragement, support, rebuke and correction. (3) *The Bible* gives us God's point of view on every area of our lives, and is the means God uses to speak to us.

It is easy to see what will happen if any of these three examples is missing from our spiritual diet: (1) If we neglect the great world God has made, which he sustains every moment, we may become overpressured by humanity, its needs and achievements, and forget God's greatness and that he does not need us or our achievements. (2) If we neglect fellowship, we may easily become erratic, unloving, unrealistic, self-centred, or hardened by the deceitfulness of sin: close Christian fellowship is a gracious provision of God to help us live in reality! (3) If we neglect the Bible as a spiritual resource, we will easily slip into confusion, error, imbalance, idolatry, lack of spiritual discernment, and be seduced away from the worship of Christ. We will not make the right use of the varied spiritual resources God has given us. To find God in fellowship but to neglect the Bible will leave us vulnerable to the pressures of the people around us, to be too concerned about the approval of other people rather than the approval of God, and subject to the spirit of our age and friendship group.

So I am not claiming that the Bible should be our only spiritual resource, because the Bible itself encourages the use of many other resources, including reflecting on God's creation, enjoying Christian fellowship and taking part in the Lord's Supper. If the Bible is not used, our spirituality will easily and quickly lose its moorings.

The Bible points beyond itself to God and to his Son the Lord Jesus, and results in more than Bible knowledge. I am not assuming that the Bible has some kind of magical quality, so that however it is used, true biblical spirituality will result. Any of us can misuse the Bible, or find ways of avoiding its message. Of course God is gracious, and often blesses us in the middle of our misuse or confusion, but we should not trade on God's grace. In the next two chapters we will study resources for spirituality from both the Old and New Testaments. I will now note the relationship between biblical spirituality, Evangelical spirituality and Reformed spirituality, note the usefulness of biblical theology in the study of spirituality, and then outline the shape and structure of biblical spirituality.

Evangelical spirituality?

Why is there a lack of confidence in the possibility of Evangelical spirituality? This lack of confidence is likely to be felt both by Evangelicals and by those of other traditions within Christianity.

The question is important for our subject, because it is Evangelicals who today are most likely to assert the unique and sufficient authority and power of the Bible under God. Does the doctrine of the Bible alone, *sola scriptura*, result in a deficient spirituality, or even no spirituality at all? Must biblical spirituality be supplemented with spirituality from other sources? Does the doctrine of the sufficiency of Scripture extend to spirituality? There is a popular assumption that Evangelicals, who in theory depend so much on the Bible, do not have any spirituality, and so they must take as much as they can from Eastern Orthodox or Roman Catholic spirituality, or even from the religions of the East.

In fact one of the distinctive features of Evangelical Christianity is its spirituality. The development of the habits of spiritual living is one of the characteristics of Evangelicalism, and personal Evangelical spirituality is one of the most important external signs of biblical truth. In Adam 1988 I attempted to indicate the rich and long heritage of Evangelical spirituality. Other recent studies include Stevenson 1979, the introduction to Pooley and Seddon 1986, Gordon 1991, McGrath 1993, Cockerton 1994 and Randall 1999.

It is also the case that many of the internal disputes within the Evangelical tradition over the past few centuries have been about appropriate expressions of spirituality. The debates about the possibility of Christian perfection, about a 'second blessing', the higher life, the Keswick movement, faith healing, and the charismatic movement are all debates about spirituality.

Another factor that complicates the subject is that many Evangelical Christians are wary of the word 'spirituality', fearing that it is far removed from authentic Evangelical faith and experience. In my opinion this attitude creates the problem it fears, and the best way forward is to state what is the nature of authentic biblical and Evangelical spirituality. John Newton had no such hesitations when he wrote of 'spirituality' as 'A spiritual taste, and a disposition to count all things mean and vain, in comparison of the knowledge and love of God in Christ, [which] are essential for a true Christian' (1831: 62).

For Newton, spirituality, a spiritual appetite and tendency to recognize the surpassing value of the knowledge and love of God in Christ is what distinguishes the true Christian from the person who merely professed Christianity, whom we would call a nominal Christian.

In fact Evangelicals have made a major contribution in the area of spirituality, often described as 'devotion', 'piety', 'the Christian life', 'the spiritual life'. For example, we find the traditional issues of

Evangelical spirituality expressed in the writings of Richard Baxter (1615–91), who illustrates the range and concentration of Puritan spiritual writing. In his *The Divine Life* he writes of 'The Knowledge of God', 'On Walking with God' and 'Of Conversing with God in Solitude' (1981: 125–748). In his *Christian Directory* (1838) he outlines the responsibilities of the Christian in four main areas of life, that of ethics (private duties), economics (family duties), ecclesiastics (church duties) and politics (duties to our rulers and neighbours). In this he covers a wide variety of cases, including such issues as friendship, taxes, gluttony, marriage, prayer, the sick and poor, fraud, trusts and secrets. His aim is to help those who profess to be Christ's disciples 'to learn of him, to imitate him, and be conformed to him, and to do the will of God' (1838: 7). He reflects the wide-ranging rigour and detail of Puritan spiritual writings.

Evangelicals have conveyed their spirituality by Christian biographies. These were first in the form of funeral sermons, some of which were later published. Books have included 'lives and letters' or biographies, which include those of Samuel Rutherford, David Brainerd, Hudson Taylor and Elisabeth Elliot.

Bibles published with devotional and theological comments have included the Geneva Bible of 1560, and those by John Bengel (*Gnomon Novi Testamenti* 1742), Matthew Henry (1708–10), Thomas Haweis (1765–6), Thomas Scott (1788–92) and J. C. Ryle's *Expository Thoughts on the Gospels* (1865–73); the modern equivalent is Scripture Union Bible reading notes. Sermons have been formative, especially when published (and more recently taped); for example those of Heinrich Bullinger, John Calvin, John Wesley, Charles Spurgeon and Martyn Lloyd-Jones. This reading of the Bible with heart and mind is the subject of a recent book by Tremper Longman III (1997), in which he develops the ideas of reading the Bible as receiving the life-giving seed of the Word, as seeing ourselves in a mirror, and as a life-giving encounter with God in Christ. This is a practical guide to the spirituality of Bible reading.

Books on the spiritual life have included Bayly 1714, Ryle 1956, Nee 1961, Murray 1962, Burroughs 1964, Bunyan 1965, 1966, Owen 1965, Wesley 1968, Schaeffer 1972, Packer 1975, Doddridge 1977, Arndt 1979, Lovelace 1979, Edwards 1986, Piper 1989, Wilberforce 1997, Veith 1999, Larsen 2001, Lowman 2001.

Earlier books that have been widely appreciated include Augustine's *Confessions* and *On the Imitation of Christ* by Thomas à Kempis. Christian leaders from Martin Luther, John Calvin, John and Charles Wesley, to Moody and Sankey and Billy Graham have used the words and music of hymns and songs to foster spirituality.

The use of the Bible as the definitive, authoritative and sufficient source of true spirituality was the rediscovery of the Reformation, though of course the use of the Bible as a spiritual resource is as old as the Bible itself. This contribution of the Reformation was then intensified by the Puritans and Pietists who followed up this work of reformation.[1] It was the Puritan ministers who were 'physicians of the souls' as they applied the Bible to their people in public preaching and private admonition. It was the German Pietists who pioneered the study of the Bible in home fellowship groups, each a little church within a church, *ecclesiola in ecclesia*. In the words of the Pietist Philip Spener:

> Thought should be given to a more extensive use of the Word of God among us . . . The more the Word of God is among us, the more we shall bring about faith and its fruits . . . It would not be difficult for every housefather to keep a Bible . . . and read from it every day . . . in addition to our customary services with preaching, other assemblies would also be held . . . several members of a congregation who have a fair knowledge of God . . . meet under the leadership of a minister, take up the Holy Scriptures, read aloud from them, and fraternally discuss each verse in order to discover its simple meaning and whatever may be useful for the edification of all. (Spener, in Erb 1983: 31–33)

Various Evangelical movements have contributed their own spiritualities, including the Pietists, the Puritans, the Methodists, and Keswick and other Holiness and Higher Life movements. The Puritans pioneered the practice of keeping a diary of one's spiritual life. The Moravian movement contributed such aids to spiritual life as the Bible text for the day (now secularized to become helpful thoughts on calendars!), the promise box, prayer meetings, heightened emotional response through music, and overseas missionary interest.

Indeed the missionary movements have had great effect on Evangelical spirituality, and have been significant promoters of it.

[1] Pietism was a movement for the renewal of Lutherans in the seventeenth century. It did not at that time imply introspection or lack of positive action in the world. In fact the early Pietists were very active in social concern.

Significant contributions have been made by lay people, and the lives of heroic men and women have had a profound effect. These special saints have set a standard for many.

The Evangelical strands of spirituality are clearly present in modern studies of spirituality, such as Senn 1986. He covers various strands of Evangelical spirituality, including Lutheran, Reformed, Anabaptist, Anglican, Puritan, Pietist and Methodist.

Some Evangelicals may feel that the word 'spirituality' is a dangerous one to use because it may be confused by association with other Christian viewpoints or New Age movements. Any word has its dangers. 'Devotion' places too much emphasis on our actions. The 'Christian life' becomes too easily a way of dividing life into sacred and secular. 'Piety' sounds pretentious and old fashioned. 'Holiness' sounds individualistic and elitist, and promotes a misunderstanding of the way the word is used in the New Testament (Peterson 1995). 'Spirituality' may sound introspective, too otherworldly, or as if it is in opposition to our physical existence, to matter. As 'spirituality' is a popular word in our society, I think the best communication strategy is to use it and fill it with biblical truth. 'Spirituality' is also a useful word to help us understand the Bible.

For a great need of our time is authentic gospel and biblical spirituality. The Bible also teaches us that as the gospel is easily distorted, so gospel spirituality is easily lost. J. C. Ryle explained it with his customary clarity:

> The Gospel in fact is a most curiously and delicately compounded medicine, and is a medicine that is very easily spoiled.
>
> You may spoil the Gospel by *substitution*. You have only to withdraw from the eyes of the sinner the grand object which the Bible proposes to Faith, – Jesus Christ; and to substitute another object in His place, – the Church, the Ministry . . . and the mischief is done . . .
>
> You may spoil the Gospel by *addition*. You only have to add to Christ, the grand object of faith, some other objects as equally worthy of honour, and the mischief is done . . .
>
> You may spoil the Gospel by *disproportion*. You only have to attach an exaggerated importance to the secondary things of Christianity, and a diminished importance to the first things, and the mischief is done. Once alter the proportion of the parts of the truth, and truth soon becomes downright error . . .

> You may completely spoil the Gospel by *confused and contradictory directions*. Complicated and obscure statements about faith, baptism, and the benefits of the Lord's Supper, all jumbled together, and thrown down without order before hearers, make the Gospel no Gospel at all. (Ryle 1964: 12–13)

What we describe as 'heresies' in the New Testament churches can more accurately be described as 'false spiritualities'. What happened at Corinth, Ephesus, Colossae and Galatia was not so much a clearly articulated 'heresy' as another spirituality, another way of living as a Christian, another way of praying, another way of relating to God. If this is the case, then the importance and relevance of studying the subject of spirituality will be obvious to all. Indeed people today also move from the purity of the Gospel because they adopt a different spirituality, more than because they adopt a different theology.

Another reason why Evangelicals may be reluctant to pursue the subject of spirituality is because they are single minded about primary evangelism. Their question is often 'What is the irreducible minimum of the gospel the unbeliever needs to hear?' rather than 'What is the fullness of the Gospel God has revealed?' Their preoccupation with initial conversion may have led them to neglect growth in the Christian life. If this is so, then there is room for repentance, for God's gospel is effective, not only to make new Christians, but also to produce mature Christians and mature churches.

Oddly enough, for many years Evangelicals have been accused of being too emotional and not intellectual enough, whereas now the accusation is more likely to be that they are too rationalistic, and not aware of the emotional and non-rational aspects of religion. This is relevant to our discussion because it is often assumed that spirituality is found more in the non-rational than in the rational.

The situation is further complicated by our common assumption that heart and mind are far removed from each other, that the emotional cannot be the intellectual, that passion and truth cannot exist together. This assumption forces us either into mindless passion or passionless truth! While mindless passion and passionless truth are certainly options, they are not the only possibilities. We will discuss this issue further in chapter five.

To say the same thing another way, one reason for the silence of the Bible in current discussion of spirituality is the assumption that spirituality functions at 'a deeper level' than words. This means that the wordy Bible is left behind in favour of dreams, sacred objects and places, visions, ecstatic experiences, miracles and feelings. It is the loss of the belief in the inspiration of the Scriptures that leads to a loss in expectancy in their impact on our spirituality. In the words of Austin Farrer:

> Anyone who has felt, even in the least degree, the power of these texts to enliven the soul and to open the gates of heaven must have some curiosity about the manner in which the miracle is worked . . . When verbal inspiration was held, men nourished their souls on the Scriptures, and knew that they were fed. Liberal enlightenment claims to have opened the scriptural casket, but there now appears to be nothing inside – nothing, anyhow, which ordinary people feel moved to seek through the forbidding discipline of spiritual reading. (1948: 36)

I am not assuming that Evangelicals have an exclusive claim on true spirituality. I am concerned about Evangelical spirituality because the growing tendency to discount or ignore Evangelical spirituality does damage both to Evangelicals and to those who are not Evangelicals. It should also be the case that if Evangelicals are those who are governed by the principle of *sola scriptura*, the Bible alone, then pure Evangelical spirituality ought to be pure biblical spirituality.

I do not believe in the infallibility of Evangelicals or of the Evangelical tradition, for in some areas of spirituality Evangelicals have missed the message of the Bible. Two main weaknesses in Evangelicalism are reflected in its spirituality: reaction and individualism.

Evangelical reaction reflects the reactionism that seems to be a characteristic of some forms of Protestantism. Here doctrine, theology or practice is shaped by a reaction against error in another tradition, such as Catholic or Liberal. So theology and practice are shaped by reaction against error, rather than by obedience to Scripture. This is sure to be wrong, and the situation becomes worse if it sets up a contrary reaction in the other tradition! The dynamic of reaction means that the agenda is still set by something other than the Bible. Evangelicals need their spirituality from the Bible, not from reaction against those they regard as in error.

Individualism was not a product of the Reformation, but of the Enlightenment. This individualism has meant that the gospel itself has been distorted into a message for individuals. Only one summary of the gospel in the New Testament comes in the form of Christ's love for the individual, and that is Galatians 2:20, where Paul writes of 'the Son of God, who loved me and gave himself for me'. In every other case it is corporate, as in God's love for the world (John 3:16), Christ's love for the church (Eph. 5:25), the gospel for all the Gentiles (Rom. 16:26), the need to make disciples of all nations (Matt. 28:19).

God's love for the individual is a consequence of the gospel, not the heart of the gospel. This has big implications for Evangelicalism, which has always prided itself on getting the gospel right! Here it has particular implications for spirituality, for it means that genuine biblical spirituality will reflect and express this corporate gospel. Many traditions of spirituality tend towards individualism: Evangelical spirituality, if it is biblical, will not fall into the same trap. Stanley Grenz tells us that spirituality for a postmodern age will need to be communitarian rather that individualistic, and Christianity that is lived as well as believed (Grenz 1996: 167–169). This is biblical spirituality.

There are other weaknesses in Evangelical spirituality. It is sometimes legalistic about matters of little importance. Simplicity can lead to superficiality. A focus on emotional response can lead to anti-intellectualism: a warm heart and a clear mind are not always found together! And despite its suspicion of the world, it easily and unconsciously adopts worldly ways, and is unable to critique its own society. As James Gordon writes:

> [T]he Evangelical spiritual tradition is a continuing witness to the power of the gospel and the mission of the Church in the modern world. John Stott, who stands as one example of the tradition at its best, has always insisted that Evangelical spirituality is by definition Christ-centred: 'The hallmark of authentic Evangelicalism has always been zeal for the honour and glory of Jesus Christ.' (1991: ix)

We all need to learn what true biblical spirituality is.

Reformed spirituality?

Because I believe the Reformed theology provides the pattern of thought that corresponds most closely with the theological structure of the Bible, I also believe that Reformed spirituality is most likely to reflect biblical spirituality. Of course one of the principles of Reformed theology is that of continual reformation by the Bible, and so it holds the corresponding principle of its own fallibility, as it needs continual reformation. So I do not think that Reformed spirituality always succeeds in reflecting the Bible, as I do not think the Reformed theology is always correct.

We do well to look at the shape of Reformed spirituality. Morton Kelsey, in his foreword to a book on *Reformed Spirituality*, comments, 'What puzzled me most as I read Rice's book was how this rich tradition was largely lost or neglected within the Reformed churches, and totally ignored and overlooked by writers outside that tradition interested in the spiritual life' (Rice 1991: 2). He then suggests that this may have happened because writers in the Reformed tradition used the word 'piety' rather than 'spirituality', though they cover much the same area of interest.

It is certain that the Reformation resulted in a rich spirituality. It was a spirituality firmly based on original documents, namely the Bible. It focused on Jesus Christ, and avoided the distractions of post-biblical inventions. It was grace-based, in that repentance is not the first step towards grace, but a response to grace. It was grace-based, and so produced a spirituality of grateful response and joy, rather than a spirituality of uncertainty. It was a spirituality for ordinary people, and not for a spiritual elite. It was open to the world and to what we call secular work and duties, and was able to engage the family as a unit of spiritual development. Because of the invention of the printing press, and a great commitment to education, it was a literate spirituality, and able to engage lay people in spiritual formation. Alister McGrath has written a helpful and positive account of general Reformation spirituality (1992).

Here I am referring to the Reformed tradition as one strand of the Protestant Reformation. This Reformed tradition is of course expressed in the Reformed and Presbyterian churches, but is also found within Anglican and Baptist denominations. It has been represented within Anglicanism by leaders like Nicholas Ridley, John Jewel, George Whitefield and John Newton, and within the Baptist Church by John Bunyan, John Gill and Charles Spurgeon. Whereas Ian Randall (1999), in his study of English Evangelical Spirituality 1918–39, studies such groups as the Keswick movement, the Anglican Evangelical movement, Wesleyan spirituality, the Oxford Group and the Pentecostals, there is no study of any Reformed tradition within Evangelicalism. Were he to write a complementary book covering the second half of the twentieth century, he would need to find room for such leaders as Martyn Lloyd-Jones, John Stott, Alec Motyer, J. I. Packer, R. C. Lucas and David Jackman, and the resolutely contemporary biblical and Reformed pattern of Evangelicalism they have promoted.

Rowan Williams tells us that one of the dilemmas at the end of the medieval period was the gap between the art of theology and the practice of spirituality:

> It was losing the sense of Christian experience as growth in direct encounter with God . . . there was less realization that the roots of theology lie in such experience and that Christian speculation is properly inseparable from engagement of a personal and demanding kind with the paradoxes of cross and resurrection. (1979: 137)

Reformed spirituality and theology was one movement that filled this gap. This tradition claims that the roots of theology lie in the revelation of God, rather than in experience. Or, to express the truth more completely, that the roots of all our theology and spirituality lie in the revelation of God in Christ, articulated by the Spirit in the Bible.

Howard Rice (1991) refers to the writings of Huldrych Zwingli, John Calvin and Heinrich Bullinger; the Scots, Heidelberg and Westminster Confessions; among the Puritans the writings of Lewis Bayly, Francis Rous, Samuel Rutherford, Richard Baxter, John Owen, John Bunyan and Henry Scougal; and, among later writers, Elizabeth Rowe, Gerhard Tersteegen and Jonathan Edwards.

The Reformed tradition employed the following methods in its use of the Bible, according to Rice:

- It paid close attention to the context of a text. According to the Puritan Thomas Goodwin, 'The right context of Scripture is half the interpretation' (1991: 101–102).
- It used the scholarly tools available. The Reformed tradition came out of the Humanist movement marked by careful scholarship, the use of original texts, the study of history and the use of language.
- It assumed the fundamental unity of the Bible, and treated it as a self-interpreting book.
- It knew that a right understanding of the Bible needs hard work, and the help of the Holy Spirit (1991: 101–104).

To which we can add:

- The Reformed tradition named and articulated its 'rule of faith',

which it used to interpret the Bible. This 'rule of faith' would be revised in the light of the Bible, but also helped interpret the Bible.
- It knew that the Bible is a book about God, and that our highest aim in reading the Bible is not to learn what we should do, but who God is and what God has done.
- It used the Bible as the major instrument of ministry, in reading, preaching, exhortation and meditation.

Other studies of Reformed spirituality include Wakefield 1957, Richard 1974, Battles 1978, Senn 1986, Ferguson 1987, Packer 1990b, McGrath 1991, Nuttall 1992, Whitlock 2000, Nunes 2002.[2]

The flavour of Reformed spirituality can be seen clearly in the following quotations from Calvin's *Institutes*:

> Nearly all the wisdom we possess, that is to say, pure and sound wisdom, consists of two parts: the knowledge of God and of ourselves . . . our very being is nothing but subsistence in the one God. (*Institutes* 1.1.1)

> God is not known where there is no religion or piety . . . I call 'piety' that reverence joined with the love of God which the knowledge of his benefits produces. (*Institutes* 1.2.1)

> Now, in order that true religion may shine upon us, we ought to hold that it must take its beginnings from heavenly doctrine and that no one can get even the slightest taste of right and sound doctrine unless he be a pupil of Scripture. (*Institutes* 1.6.2)

Wilhelm Niesel, a modern writer on Calvin, has described the centre of Calvin's theology as the mystical union between Christ and the believer:

> For Calvin . . . that joining of the Head and members, that indwelling of Christ on our hearts – in short, that mystical union is fundamental. We do not, therefore, contemplate him outside ourselves from afar in order that his righteousness may be imputed to us, but because we put on Christ and are engrafted into his body – in short because he deigns to make us one with him. (1962: 182)

[2] See also Toon 1987: ch. 7, and Mursell 2001a: 356–379.

In his study of the spirituality of John Calvin, the Catholic scholar Lucien Joseph Richard places him in the context of the *Devotio Moderna*, as expressed for example in Thomas à Kempis's *Of the Imitation of Christ*, and the Humanist movement in which Calvin participated. He points out the strong commitment to the power of words in the Humanism of Calvin's day: 'The renaissance writers believed in the power speech had to move the minds and hearts of men and therefore insisted on language that was both beautiful and pleasing' (Richard 1974: 137).

Whereas 'The *Devotio Moderna* reacted against scholasticism . . . by advocating an anti-intellectual spirituality' (1974: 136), on the other hand, 'The Humanists preferred a more affective type of theology, one that could double as spirituality' (1974: 139). Jacques Lefèvre d'Etaples, a leading Humanist at the University of Paris, aimed to bridge the separation between theology and spirituality:

> Lefèvre expressed his spirituality in his concept of *theologia vivificans* (theology that makes alive). This vivifying theology was a theological exegesis uniting spirituality and theology. It was based on an intuition of the primacy and sufficiency of the world [sc. word]. *Verbum Dei sufficit* (The Word of God is sufficient). (1974: 70)

The spiritual meaning of the scriptures illuminated by the Holy Spirit is the mystery of Christ himself (Richard 1974: 71). We find these ideas further developed in Calvin. Richard also makes the point that a common misunderstanding of Calvin is that of a cold logician. He quotes Theodore Roszak: 'He has no experiential sense of what it means to discover divinity dwelling within – a striking example of how remote head knowledge can be from visionary realization' (1974: 164). Richard comments, 'This is certainly a caricature. John Calvin affirmed many times in his writings the intensively experiential character of the knowledge of God' (1974: 164).

Richard demonstrates the important features of Calvin's spirituality in the following quotations from Calvin:

- The purpose of writing the *Institutes* is to promote piety:

> My intention is only to offer some basic rudiments through which those who feel some interest in religion might be trained to true piety. (*Institutes*: Prefatory Address)

- Piety is all that we owe God:

  Piety comes from the sure knowledge of God. From it we learn to humble ourselves, cast ourselves before God, seek his mercy. (1974: 99 = *Works* 1: 31)

- This knowledge is not merely conceptual, but is a doctrine of life, life-giving teaching:

  Doctrine is not an affair of the tongue but of the life; it is not apprehended by the intellect and memory merely, like the other branches of learning; but it is received only when it possesses the whole soul . . . The Gospel ought to penetrate the inmost affections of the heart, fix its seat in the soul, and pervade the whole man. (1974: 103 = *Works* 1: 1126)

- True worship or piety can only come from a true knowledge of God:

  We ought not to attempt anything in religion rashly or at random; because unless there be knowledge, it is not God that we worship but a phantom or idol. (1974: 119 = *Commentary on John* 4:43)

- The result is a mystical union between Christ and the church, and therefore Christ and the believer:

  We expect salvation from [Christ], not because he stands aloof from us, but because in grafting us onto his body he not only makes us partakers of all his benefits, but we also become one substance with him. (*Institutes* 3.2.24)

- So both sanctification and justification are the fruits of this God-given union:

  Christ lives in us in two ways. The one life consists in governing us by his Sprit and directing all our actions, the other in making us partakers of his righteousness, so that while we can do nothing of ourselves, we are accepted in the sight of God. (1974: 106 = *Commentary on Galatians* 2:20)

- This union with Christ is through the dynamic bond of the Spirit:

> The Lord by his Spirit bestows upon us the blessings of being one with him in soul and body and spirit. The bond of that connection therefore is the spirit of Christ who unites us to him, and is a kind of channel by which everything that Christ has and is is given to us. (*Institutes* 4.17.12)

- The purpose of this union is to restore us in the image of God:

> Christ is the most perfect image of God into which we are so renewed as to bear the image of God in knowledge, purity, righteousness, and true holiness. (*Institutes* 1.15. 4)

- Faith and prayer are two certain signs of the presence of true piety:

> The principal exercise which the children of God have is to pray; for this way they give a true proof of their faith. (1974: 121 = *Sermon on 1 Timothy* 2:1–2)

This faith must come from the hearing of the Word and from the work of the Spirit in sealing our minds and hearts. In these words Calvin distinguishes his view both from rationalism and fanaticism:

> Those who do not sufficiently know the darkness of human minds imagine faith is formed naturally by hearing and preaching alone; and there are many fanatics who disdain the outward preaching, and talk in lofty terms about secret revelations and inspirations. But we see how Christ joins these things together, and, therefore, though there is no faith unless the Spirit of God seals our minds and hearts, still we must not go to seek visions or oracles in the clouds, but the word, which is near us, in our mouth and heart (Rom. 10:8), must keep all our senses bound and fixed in itself. (Richard 1974: 147 = *Commentary on John* 15:27)

So God addresses us both by his Word and by his Spirit at the same time and by the same operation: 'God has therefore two ways of teaching; for first, he sounds in our ears by the mouth of men, and secondly he addresses us inwardly by the Spirit' (1974: 156 = *Commentary on John* 14:26).

Among the many of Calvin's contributions to spirituality, Richard points to the importance of his ideas of spirituality that involve service in the world, in contrast with the world-denying emphasis of the *Devotio Moderna*; his pursuit of a spirituality that was corporate and ecclesial as well as personal and individual; and his combination of spirituality and theology (1974: 174–192). Calvin's spirituality was expressed as much in his prayers and metrical translation of the Psalms for singing as it was in his theological writings (Battles 1978: 137–166). As we will see in chapter four, Calvin had a clear understanding of how the whole Bible functions as the word of Christ, and this too was a vital aspect of his spirituality.

Reformed spirituality attempts to be a true expression of pure biblical spirituality, and it deserves our attention for that reason. As Alister McGrath comments, Calvin's emphasis on the knowledge of God has been represented and made popular in recent years in the classic *Knowing God* by J. I. Packer (McGrath 1999: 170–173).

Whereas the Reformed and Evangelical traditions have generally been opposed to the use of sacred times, places, objects and actions, they have often been strongly 'sabbatarian', placing great emphasis on setting aside Sunday for worship, edification and meditation. In the words of *The Directory for the Public Worship of God*, 'There is no day commanded in scripture to be kept holy under the gospel but the Lord's day, which is the Christian Sabbath' (Westminster Confession 1958: 394).

Why is this so? The simple answer is that this spirituality regards instructions in the Bible as binding on believers, and is opposed to going beyond the Bible's instructions. This is because of the ideal of 'spiritual chastity', of faithfulness to God and his words. So the use of the means that God has ordained to express his care for us is a strong feature of Reformed and Evangelical spirituality. These means include the study, reading and preaching of the Bible; the use of Sunday to meet with God's people for worship and edification; the use of the sacraments of baptism and the Lord's Supper, mutual encouragement with other believers and receiving everything in life as a gift from God. These are the God-given means, and we should make full use of them and not distract or confuse ourselves with other man-made rules or practices. We are opposed to wrong means, not because means are unimportant, but because they are important. The wrong use of means will not only damage those who use them, but, more importantly, is an insult to God.

Richard Baxter gives a list of the means of grace in an Evangelical and Reformed spirituality:

> The reading of the word of God and the explication and application of it in good books is a means to possess the mind with sound, orderly, and working apprehensions of God, and of his holy truths.
>
> The same word preached with a lively voice, with clearness and affection, hath a greater advantage for the same illumination and excitation of the soul.
>
> Also in the sacrament of the body and blood of Christ, we are called to a familiar converse with God: Here there appears to us by a wonderful condescension in the representing, communicating signs of the flesh and blood of his Son, in which he hath most conspicuously revealed his love and goodness to believers: there Christ himself with his covenant-gifts, are all delivered to us by these signs of his own institution.[3]
>
> In holy, faithful, fervent, prayer, a Christian hath very much of his converse with God. For prayer is our approach to God, and calling to mind his presence and his attributes, and exercising all his graces in a holy motion towards him, and an exciting all the powers of our souls to seek him, attend him, and reverently to worship him. (1981: 195–196)

We should notice the importance of the Bible, the mixture of corporate and private activities, and the balance of Bible, sacrament and prayer. The use of means is also an issue in the debate between the Puritans and the Quakers, as we will see in chapter six. Reformed spirituality covers a wider range of thought and practice then we might expect. Puritan ministers served as spiritual directors, and that included the interpretation of dreams, the giving of advice about growth in spirituality, including how to pray, and how to deal with satanic attack.[4]

Even when Reformed theology found its most fervent intellectual defence, it was also marked by piety. Andrew Hoffecker shows the piety that marked the Princeton theologians and their influence, and has gathered evidence from their theological and devotional writings. He quotes Archibald Alexander's sermon to his congregation in Philadelphia in 1812: 'Two things I have consistently aimed at, first to inform the understanding, secondly to impress the heart' (1981: 1).

[3] For more on the Puritan use of the sacrament as a means, see Ferguson 1987: 211–233 on John Owen's view of baptism and the Lord's Supper.

[4] For more on this subject see Rice 1991: chs. 3, 5, Jensen 1995b, Gurnall 1964 and McGinnis 2002: 665–686.

Princeton Seminary was to be a 'nursery of vital piety as well as of sound theological learning' (1981: 1). Alexander contrasts dead with living faith:

> When Christ the special object of Faith is brought to the view of the soul, a living Faith always appropriates him, chooses him as a Saviour suitable to itself, receives him as its portion, trusts and depends on him alone for salvation, resigns itself up to him alone to be governed and directed agreeable to his will, and is pleased and delighted with him above all things. (1981: 13)

While the Princeton theologians warned on the one hand against dry and non-experiential Reformed theology, they also warned against the subjectivism of Schleiermacher and the emotionalism of some contemporary revivalism in America. But they also commended piety and devotion in the practice of Christianity. Hoffecker writes of Charles Hodge:

> Even more influential, however, was his personal religion, evinced especially in his famous Sunday afternoon conference addresses. His real and strongly emotional piety, the heart of which was vital apprehension of the love of God in Christ, wrought his most characteristic work upon students. (1981: 44)

This Reformed piety is based on meditation on the Bible. In the words of B. B. Warfield:

> You must taste its preciousness for yourselves, before you can apply it to others' needs. You must assimilate the Bible and make it your own, in that intimate sense which will fix its words fast in your hearts, if you would have those words rise spontaneously to your lips in your times of need, or in times of the needs of others. Read, study, meditate . . . until the Bible is in you. Then the Bible will well up in you and come out from you in every season of need. (Hoffecker 1981: 151)

A Reformed spirituality of the Word and election is perfectly expressed in Jesus' prayer in John 17 (vv. 6–8): '[These disciples] were yours, and you gave them to me, and they have kept your word . . . for the words that you gave to me I have given to them, and they have received them and know in truth that I came from you.'

In the light of these comments, it is disturbing to find that for many the Reformed tradition of spirituality is invisible. This is because they have already decided what spirituality will look like, that it will be represented by images, pictures, statues and certain kinds of rituals in liturgical practice, or else by a highly emotional internal and personal experience. They are then blind to other forms of spirituality. They are so aware of what Reformed spirituality does not include (statues, pictures, sacred places), that they miss the spirituality that is expressed. Indeed it is a mark of the great importance the Reformed tradition places on the expression of spirituality that it is so careful about its own practice.

The tradition of passionate Reformed spirituality is no novelty. It is also found in the Reformed Anglican Richard Sibbes (1577–1635), whom Mark Dever can describe as both 'Reformed' and 'affectionate' (Dever 2000: 99–160), because Sibbes believed that 'God has opened his heart to us in his Word' (2000: 156).

Reformed spirituality can also be destructive. In some cases it is merely verbose, its prayers have been 'sermons to the Almighty', and it has descended to legalistic and negative Christianity. But this is to see the movement at its worst. As Gordon Wakefield claims in his article on Calvinistic spirituality, at its best there is a delight in the creation and music and poetry, deep joy, and moral reformation (Wakefield 1983: 66). Clear theology is no enemy to deep spirituality.

There are some tensions between Evangelical and Reformed spirituality. Evangelical spirituality tends towards an intense personal relationship with God, is naturally egalitarian, and is suspicious of formality. Reformed spirituality is more concerned with our state before God than our relationship with him, depends more on the authorized minister, and tends to be more formal in style. Spirituality that is both Evangelical and Reformed can avoid the weakness and gain the strengths of both.

The strengths of Reformed spirituality include its focus on the glory and supremacy of Christ, its realization of the sinfulness of humanity, the priority of God's grace, the call to faith, the assurance of salvation and of God's persevering grace, its belief that all God's people have an equal share in his grace, and its commitment to the transformation of the world.

Of course theology and practice that do not follow the Reformed pattern also express spirituality. For example, John Wesley promoted

Christian spirituality through his own writings, his editions of the Christian classics, his published diary, his sermons, his hymns, and by setting up the class system of Methodism. Wesley's writings on spirituality included the controversial area of Christian perfection, and he had a profound influence in introducing Moravian spirituality to the English-speaking world, in promoting lay spirituality of regeneration, conversion, Bible study and prayer, small group as well as church, prayer meetings and above all songs.

I have focused on Reformed models of spirituality because I believe that they best reflect biblical reality, and because I want to correct the common impression that Reformed theology and practice have no possible connection with true Christian spirituality. Later we will see how Calvin's theology of the Bible as the Word of Christ lies at the heart of biblical spirituality. We will also discuss the complex issues of what expressions of spirituality the Reformed tradition will include, and what expressions it will exclude.

So biblical spirituality can be genuinely Evangelical and Reformed in its ethos. I do not think that it is only found within these traditions, or is limited to them. Genuine Christianity has always been marked by biblical spirituality. James Houston shows that the Desert Fathers incorporated the text of the Bible within their oral tradition:

> Scripture is interspersed within these sayings, not as the concentrated text we are habituated to in a writing culture, but diffused in the interplay of both oral and written traditions. As Benedicta Ward explains, 'The Language of the writings of the desert was so formed by the meditations of the scriptures that it is almost impossible to say when the quotation ends and the comments begin.' (1996: 157)

So too the medieval tradition of *Lectio Divina* referred to the meditative and prayerful reading of Holy Scripture that resulted in spiritual growth and transformation. Houston quotes the Carthusian Guigo II:

> Reading is the careful study of the Scriptures, concentration of one's powers on it . . . Reading seeks for sweetness of a blessed life, meditation perceives it, prayer asks for it, contemplation tastes it. Reading, as it were, puts food whole into the mouth, meditation chews it and breaks it up, prayer extracts its flavour, contemplation is the sweetness itself which gladdens and refreshes. (1996: 160)

Then from von Balthasar: 'Man is the being created as the hearer of the Word, and only in responding to the Word arises to his full dignity. He was conceived in the mind of God as the partner in dialogue' (1996: 173).

Such hearing of the Word lies at the heart of Christian faith and experience, and is universal among Christians. Biblical spirituality is not the discovery of a peripheral few, but the common heritage of all believers. Evangelical and Reformed spirituality lies within what Alister McGrath calls 'the Great Tradition' of mainstream orthodox Christianity (McGrath 2000: 139–158).

What is the shape of Evangelical and Reformed spirituality of the Word, in the light of other Christian traditions of spirituality? The best way to understand it is to realize that spirituality corresponds to revelation, both in content and form:

- Christ is the mediator of the revelation of God, so this spirituality is Christ-centred, responding with faith in Jesus Christ, and especially to his saving death and resurrection. Christ has revealed the Father, so this spirituality is that of trust in God our Father, his love and kindness in Christ, and his sovereign and providential rule over everything. Christ has sent the Spirit, so believers are sealed or anointed with the Spirit, the Spirit witnesses within them that they are the children of God, and they use the gifts of God in the service of God.
- The response of trusting Christ and obeying him, of loving God with heart, mind, soul and strength is common to all believers, so spirituality is not just an option for the advanced but is required of all the saints. It is a spirituality common to all the people of God. It is a spirituality of normal humanity, of daily life and duties, or work and play, of family and society.
- God's grace and acceptance of us in Christ means that we do not have to search for God, find him, ascend to him or journey towards him. God has come to us in his Son Jesus, spoken to us in the gospel, and welcomed us into his presence through Christ our High Priest. We stand now in God's grace, we are now at peace with God, we can now have assurance of final salvation, through trust in his promises.
- The great barrier to true spirituality is not the lack of technique in spiritual aptitude, but sin. Sin is the state of humanity in every aspect of life and personality, and the wages of sin is death. But God has dealt with our sin by the sacrifice of Christ, and has

accepted us as his children. His holiness and righteousness are demonstrated in the death of Christ, our sin is atoned for and we are forgiven. We stand in his grace, and he works in us by the death and resurrection of Christ and by his Spirit, to change us into the likeness of Christ. God gives us faith and obedience, God transforms us, and God does his good works through us.

- God has provided 'means' by which he works in us for his glory. We must make good use of the means provided by God, and not replace or supplement them with means that we devise. The means provided by God are explained in the Bible, namely the Bible itself, the fellowship of the people of God, prayer, baptism and the Lord's Supper, and a right use of the creation. We should not neglect these means, nor use other means, such as statues, pictures, icons, silence or impressions of God's will. We should not overvalue the sacraments, those visible words of God. While we will hear echoes of the Bible in our inner selves, the God-given and certain place to hear God speaking is in the Bible.
- The great means is the Bible, in which we find Christ clothed in all his promises. To love God is to love his words, and to be alert to the Spirit is to receive the words of the Spirit in the Bible. In the Bible we find God's self-revelation, God's character, God's will and God's plan. In the Bible God's mystery, Christ, is now revealed. A corporate and personal spirituality of the Word is at the heart of biblical faith and life. We do not know everything about God and his plan, but what we do know is found in the Bible.
- Prayer is an expression of our trust in God, and our dependence on him. It is gospel-shaped: we come to pray to God our Father through the power and goodness of Jesus' death on the cross. This is the means of our access to God. We pray in response to God's words in the Bible, so that we know the God to whom we pray, and what he has promised. As we read his Spirit-inspired words, the Spirit also works within us, prompting us to know that God is our Father, and that we may approach him with boldness because of Christ's death for us on the cross. We pray to God alone, and not to saints, because we pray as instructed by God in the Bible.

There are basically three schools of theology and of spirituality within Christian tradition:

1. *The Reformed and Evangelical view* is that all God's saving words and works are found within the Bible, and within that period of rev-

elation of the Old and New Testaments. So this spirituality of the Word will focus entirely on the Bible for the content of the knowledge of God. It also expects to find that biblical faith works, and so find corroborative evidence in the lives and ministries of the saints. It expects that the witness of the Spirit within the believer and within the church will correspond with his external witness in Scripture.

2. *The Roman Catholic and Eastern Orthodox view, and that held by some charismatics*, is that in addition to the Bible, God has continued to do his saving works and words over the last 2,000 years. He has revealed new truths, and supported them with new miracles. So this spirituality of the Word will include not only the words of the Bible, but also words given to the church since Bible times, whether recognized by Pope, Patriarch or Council of the Church, or given by a prophet in a local church.
3. *The Quaker and Liberal view* is that revelation comes direct from God today, by observation, reason, experience or emotion. It may include some ideas from the Bible and the tradition of the churches, but will find other parts obsolete and irrelevant. This is a spirituality of discerning what God is saying at the present time, in what is happening in the world around us or deep within our own consciousness. It is a spirituality of the contemporary words of God.

Views 2 and 3 both allow for new contemporary revelations, for hearing God speak today in the church, in individuals, or in society. View 1 holds to the notion that God's revelation is found in history, when he acted to save us, that God's word and works came together at the same time in salvation history.

Views 2 and 3 take the words of Jesus about the Spirit of truth, 'he will guide you into all the truth' (John 16:13), to mean that the Bible is less than all the truth that will be revealed, and that there is an ongoing work of the Spirit in new revelations, either throughout history, or especially today.

View 1 believes that Jesus' words 'He will guide you into all the truth' are in context a specific promise to his disciples, and that its fulfilment was in the apostolic witness to Christ that resulted in the formation of the New Testament. And the Holy Spirit continues to help us understand and receive the words of the Bible, given by that same Spirit so long ago. He does not guide us into more truth than is found in the Bible: we are to guard the good treasure *entrusted* to us 'with the help of the Holy Spirit living in us' (2 Tim. 1:14). In this view, as we look back in history for the work of God in Christ that saved us, so we look back to his work through the Spirit, the Bible, that tells us of our Christ and the salvation he won.

Biblical theology and spirituality?

If the Bible is a God-given resource for Christian spirituality, then the use of biblical theology will help us to derive as much spiritual benefit as possible from every part of that Bible.[5] The purpose of biblical theology is to treat every part of the Bible as contributing its particular riches to a full understanding of the gospel of Christ, both in promise in the Old Testament, and in fulfilment in the New Testament. For this reason it is entirely appropriate that a series of studies in biblical theology includes a volume on spirituality.

Biblical theology will help us to find a way to understand and find the coherent development of the practice of spirituality in the Bible. Why did Abraham set up altars? Should we do the same? Are there now places where God's name dwells on earth? Does the prohibition on graven images apply to pictures of Jesus in children's Bibles? Does God speak to us today? These are all questions about the practice of spirituality that arise from reading the Bible. Biblical theology will help us find a coherent answer.

Here are some definitions and descriptions of biblical theology. For Geerhardus Vos:

> Biblical Theology . . . discusses the form and content of revelation from the point of view of the revealing activity of God Himself. In other words, it deals with revelation in the active sense, as an act of God, and tries to understand and trace and describe this act. (1980: 7–8)

Or again it is 'that branch of Exegetical Theology which deals with the process of the self-revelation of God deposited in the Bible' (1948: 13).

J. I. Packer describes biblical theology as

> [T]he umbrella-name for those disciplines that explore the unity of the Bible, delving into the contents of the books, showing the links between them, and pointing up the ongoing

[5] According to Richard Gaffin, it was Geerhardus Vos who in modern times added the study of biblical theology to Reformed theology (Gaffin 1976), and who thus helped to uncover the flow as well as the structure of the Bible, the gradual revelation as well as its fundamental shape.

> flow of the revelatory and redemptive process that reached its climax in Jesus Christ. (1988: 8)

According to Graeme Goldsworthy:

> Biblical Theology is concerned with God's saving acts and his word as these occur within the history of the people of God. It follows the progress of revelation from the first word of God to man through to the unveiling of the full glory of Christ. It examines the several stages of biblical history and their relationship with one another. It thus provides the basis for understanding how texts in one part of the Bible relate to all other texts. (1991: 37)

The use of biblical theology is expressed in Peter Jensen's observation that our aim is to 'preach Christ so that every part of the Bible contributes its unique riches to his gospel' (Jensen 1995a: 64). So what is the relationship between biblical theology and spirituality?

Biblical theology enables us to make good gospel use of every part of the Bible; it has the potential to produce good and rich gospel spirituality, which reflects every facet and every stage of the biblical revelation. Christian spirituality needs biblical theology so that its use of the Bible is coherent, Christian, responsible, and reflects the full literary width and theological depth of the Scriptures. In particular, biblical theology enables the Old Testament to be used for true spirituality, that is, spirituality that expresses the gospel of Christ.

Biblical theology delivers spirituality from the irresponsible use of the Bible, and so delivers the Christian from an ultimately unsustainable gulf between heart and mind, between spirituality and understanding. Spirituality that is based on trivializing or psychologizing the Bible will not work. Sometimes we see in writings on spirituality a kind of 'spirituality fundamentalism', with texts taken out of context, proof texts universalized beyond their meaning, and a 'flat' use of Scripture that ignores its historical and theological context and development. The fundamentalism of spirituality is no more defensible than any other kind of fundamentalism. Biblical theology ensures a fully theological use of the Bible that reflects the way in which God has respected the human condition of the original writers, their use of language, historical context, place in salvation history, and their time within God's plan of gradual revelation of Christ and his gospel.

Biblical theology will also foster true spirituality because it takes account of the human and historical context of every part of Scripture. Because it recognizes the historical context of every part of Scripture, and its context in salvation history, it is less likely to produce a superhistorical and therefore superhuman use of Scripture, and is therefore less likely to foster a superhuman spirituality. Biblical theology respects the varied humanity of the Bible writers (Vos 1980: 14).

In the words of Walter Moberly, 'the primary and explicit purpose of a biblical theology should be to relate the Bible to the need and concerns of the spirituality of the Christian Church, that is, it should inform the corporate and individual living of the life of faith' (1992: 149). Indeed a reading of the Bible that does not consider spirituality is likely to miss the point: 'This is why biblical theology should focus on spirituality, because it is the dynamics of life under God that is the most constant factor running through the biblical material' (1992: 155).

Some may respond to this project by asserting that the Bible is only a limited resource for spirituality. Please read this book and learn more of the riches that are found in the Bible. Some may feel that frequent quotations from the Bible are a mark of fundamentalism. Please reflect on the fact that we owe a moral duty to let a book speak for itself, explain itself and defend itself. Some may feel that the Bible is an unlikely source for spirituality. Please suspend your disbelief, and find out more of what is in the Bible as you read this book. Some may think a defence of words necessarily implies a form of spirituality that is only cerebral, dry and rational. Please read this book carefully, and discover the total, holistic and relational effect that God intends and achieves in human lives through his words. John Goldingay quotes Fishbane's *The Garments of Truth*: 'One of the great contributions of Judaism to the history of religions is its assertion that the divine reality makes itself humanly comprehensible through the structures of language' (1994: 4). Goldingay then comments, 'it is through a written text . . . that God is known' (1994: 4).

The *shape* and *structure* of biblical spirituality

What then is the shape and structure of biblical spirituality? I hope to show the following shape in the pages that follow:

- *Its content and focus is God in Christ.* It shows us God's great plan of creation and salvation, how God revealed himself in his deeds and words, how he spoke through law, prophets and wisdom, as he pointed forward to Christ, and how Jesus Christ fulfilled God's plan by his saving death and resurrection, and will finally complete God's saving plan at his return.

- *Its practice is hearing the word of God by faith.* It is how God speaks to his people and his world today, as he addresses us with words he spoke long ago at the time of his revelation leading up to and in Christ and his messengers, and has preserved as his personal, powerful, effective, universal, relevant and sufficient word to us, to be heard and obeyed by faith.
- *Its experience is that of meeting God in his Spirit-given words.* As we read the Bible, we hear the voice of God. We are challenged to change our world view, our lives, our relationships and our desires and our action; we are comforted, enriched, enlightened, given hope, stretched, empowered and changed by the living and enduring words of the living God.
- *Its result is trust in Christ and our heavenly Father.* As we grow in trust, thanking and praising God for his grace in Christ, praying to him and obeying him, loving his truth and his people, growing in the fruit of the Spirit and in godliness, serving God in his church and his world, using the gifts he has given us, bringing glory to him and waiting for the return of Christ.

I have outlined the shape of biblical spirituality. Here is its theological structure within the Bible, a structure expressed in part or in whole in various books of the Bible:

- God speaks, and his words create and sustain life and blessing, and establish relationships. We hear, believe and obey God, receive that life and blessing, and are brought into relationship with God.
- If we do not hear God, but reject, neglect, disbelieve or disobey, then those words bring curse and death. We must receive the words of God, and also reject alien words that will seduce us away from God.
- We receive the Spirit-given words of God in Scripture, and are called to believe and obey them as part of our response to God.
- Jesus is both the Word of God, and also the one who hears, speaks and does God's words. Jesus' obedience to God's words leads him to death and resurrection, when he dies in our place because of our disobedience.
- We trust and obey God by believing his gospel word about his Son, Jesus Christ.

- We praise him according to his words, and speak words to others that bring blessing, not cursing. We pray to God in response to the words of truth he has spoken to us.
- We look forward to the new heaven and earth promised by God's word.

Chapter Two

The Old Testament: Hear my words, O my people

In this chapter we will study some books of the Old Testament to discover the spirituality they disclose and teach.

Genesis: Words of promise, words of power

From beginning to end the Bible is a book about God who speaks, about people who hear and respond to God's words, and about people speaking those same words to others. How people respond to God's words spoken personally to them or by the mouths of others is a measure of their response to God. If they obey God's words, they are obeying God. If they disobey God's words, they are disobeying God. Humans are measured by their response to the words of God.

The Bible opens with the God who speaks. The first chapter of Genesis rings with the refrain 'and God said' (1:3, 6, 9, 11, 14, 20). Words from God are powerful, creative, effective and successful. God speaks and the universe takes shape, and the God who says 'Let there be' also calls or names what he has made (1:5, 8, 10). The result of God's words spoken is that what God has made is 'good', even 'very good' (1:4, 10, 12, 18, 25, 31). God blessed the seventh day (2:3), and his blessing made it a blessing for humankind as well. This blessing of God is so powerful that it not only lasts for sabbaths on earth during the Old Covenant, but is also the foretaste of the rest of the people of God (Heb. 4:9–10). In the striking words of James Daane, 'The whole universe derived its existence and reality from the speech of God' (1980: 21). Or, in the words of Psalm 33:6,

> By the word of the LORD the heavens were made,
> and all their host by the breath of his mouth.

The God who speaks makes humans in his own image and likeness. Humans are made to speak and to hear. They relate to God by hearing and obeying his words, they express their responsibility for the world by naming the animals, and express their relationship with each other by speaking. So the man speaks words that express and establish his long-awaited and most significant human relationship:

> This at last is bone of my bones
> and flesh of my flesh;
> this one shall be called Woman,
> for out of Man this one was taken.
> (Gen. 2:23)

As humans are made in the image of the speaking God, so their relationships, like his, are expressed and established by words.

The creative power of the speaking God is also expressed by the word of light that God speaks to bring us to faith in Jesus Christ: 'it is the God who said, "Let light shine out of darkness", who has shone in our hearts to give the light of the knowledge of the glory of God in the face of Jesus Christ' (2 Cor. 4:6).

The way in which the man and his wife relate to God is expressed in their response to his words. The first question of the serpent begins, 'Did God say?', and this question is the first time in which God is misrepresented, as in the question his words are misquoted: 'Did God say, "You shall not eat from any tree in the garden"?' (Gen. 3:1). The words of question and misquotation are followed by words of contradiction: 'You will not die' (3:4). The words of the serpent bring about the first and primal sin, as the man and woman turn away from the truth of God to obey the first lie. By their disobedience they turn God's words of blessing into words of judgment. The words 'You may freely eat' (2:16) become for them an occasion of sin and therefore of judgment. They follow what a later writer will describe as 'the desire of the eyes' (1 John 2:16) rather than the words of God. They follow what their eyes desire rather than what their ears hear. They obey the suggestion of the serpent rather than the instruction of their God. They turn from the words of God to alien words.

God's address and search for Adam is by means of his words 'Where are you?' (Gen. 3:9). He uses words to pursue the man and to try to continue his relationship with him.

They have turned against God by denying his words, and the man uses words to blame the woman and to create distance between himself and the woman: 'The woman whom you gave to be with me, she gave me fruit from the tree, and I ate' (Gen. 3:12). Their words divide them from God and from each other.

If God's words of blessing bring life and health, then his words of judgment and curse after the fall bring suffering, toil, exclusion and death. If God's words of blessing are powerful, his words of curse are powerful as well, and there is no escape from them: 'cursed are you . . . cursed is the ground' (Gen. 3:14, 17).

Yet from the beginning God's judgment is tempered with mercy in the words to the serpent speaking of the descendant of the woman:

> he will strike your head,
>   and you will strike his heel.
>
> (Gen. 3:15)

The judgment and mercy of God on humankind are also expressed in subsequent events. In Genesis 4 God's question of the murderer Cain leads to God's words of judgment: 'now you are cursed from the ground, which has opened its mouth to receive your brother's blood from your hand' (4:11).

The only recorded words of Lamech are words of revenge and separation:

> I have killed a man for wounding me,
>   a young man for striking me.
> If Cain is avenged sevenfold,
>   truly Lamech seventy-sevenfold.
>
> (Gen. 4:23–24)

Words no longer convey God's gift of life, but are now weapons of death.

In the story of the flood, we read of the words of the Lord, 'I will blot out from the earth the human beings I have created' (Gen. 6:7), and yet he also warns Noah with words of instruction about the building of the ark of salvation (6:13ff.). Noah, warned by the words of God, becomes a herald of righteousness to others (2 Pet. 2:5). Noah becomes the first speaker for God, as he passes on the message the Lord has given him.

In the story of the tower of Babel, the words of the people express their sin and are the means of encouraging others to participate in that sin. 'Come, let us build ourselves a city, and a tower with its top in the heavens, and let us make a name for ourselves' (Gen. 11:4). God's determination to bring scattering judgment is expressed in the contrasting words 'Come, let us go down, and confuse their language there' (Gen. 11:7). Now the people are no longer able to encourage each other in corporate sin against God, and God's limiting of their power to speak intelligible words is both judgment and mercy.

Until now God has been limiting the effects of sin, as people have used words against God and each other. Now God speaks the words of covenant promise, the words that will express and achieve his saving will for the human race, and also inform others of the shape and method of his saving purpose. Into the chaos and disorder of the judged and scattered human race, God speaks words to Abram, the one he has chosen. By these words God will bring his blessing, and that blessing will be the means of bringing a divided humanity together. The words are the blessing, and also an invitation to Abram to believe and obey:

> Go . . . from your father's house to the land that I will show you. I will make of you a great nation, and I will bless you, and make your name great, so that you will be a blessing. I will bless those who bless you, and the one who curses you I will curse; and in you all the families of the earth shall be blessed. (Gen. 12:1–3)

When we read 'So Abram went, as the LORD had told him' (12:4), we are encouraged to find a man who hears and obeys the word of God, and who thus becomes an example of faith to all believers. As we read in Hebrews, 'By faith Abraham obeyed when he was called to set out for a place that he was to receive as an inheritance; and he set out, not knowing where he was going' (Heb. 11:8).

In addition to the promise of land, that he would become a great nation and he would bring blessing to all the families of the earth, God's covenant with Abraham in Genesis also includes a promise of an offspring or seed (Gen. 13:15). The rest of Abraham's life is spent looking for the fulfilment of these promises of God. We read that Abraham 'believed the LORD; and the LORD reckoned it to him as righteousness' (15:6).

But the trial of Abraham's faith in the words of God is evident, as he stayed for a time 'in the land he had been promised, as in a foreign land' (Heb. 11:9), and there only 'in tents' (Heb. 11:9). Isaac, born to him and Sarah in their old age, is the son of promise. Abraham must believe the word of God, and Sarah will find her laughter of disbelief turn to laughter of joy in the birth of her promised son Isaac (Gen. 18:9–15; 21:1–7).

We discover in the New Testament that when Abraham looked at the Promised Land, he saw beyond it to 'the city that has foundations, whose architect and builder is God' (Heb. 11:10). He was like all the believers in his day, as they died in faith 'without having received the promises, but from a distance they saw and greeted them', as they waited for 'a better country, that is, a heavenly one' (Heb. 11:13, 16).

We also discover in the New Testament that Scripture declared the gospel beforehand to Abraham, that the descendant of Abraham is Jesus Christ, that in Christ the blessing of Abraham has come to the Gentiles, and therefore that all who believe in Jesus Christ are 'Abraham's offspring, heirs according to the promise' (Gal. 3:29).

Faith in the word or promise of God marks us as the true descendants of Abraham. If we believe the word of God as he believed, and if we believe the word of God that he believed, then we can rightly call Abraham our father. He believed in the God who could raise from the dead to fulfil his word and promise. We believe in the same God. He fulfilled his promise to Abraham not only by giving him Isaac when Abraham's body was as good as dead (Rom. 4:19), but also giving Isaac as it were back from the dead to Abraham on the occasion of his sacrifice (Heb. 11:19). He also fulfilled that word and promise to Abraham and to us when he 'raised Jesus our Lord from the dead' (Rom. 4:24). God's affirmation of Abraham is recorded in the words 'because you have obeyed my voice' (Gen. 22:18).

Abraham, who lives by faith in the word and promise of God, is called to be a man of words. He is a teacher of righteousness, 'that he may charge his children and his household after him to keep the way of the LORD by doing righteousness and justice' (Gen. 18:19). He is also a prophet whose words of prayer are powerful and efficacious: 'he will pray for you and you shall live' (Gen. 20:7). As God's words bring blessing, so do his words through Abraham. Those who hear and receive God's words are blessed.

The remainder of Genesis is about how God fulfils the promise he has made to Abraham. All this is slowly worked out in the stories of Isaac, the birth of Esau and Jacob, of how God's blessing goes to Jacob the younger son; and then how God's blessing goes to Jacob's son Joseph, through whom God preserves his people in Egypt. The God of Abraham, Isaac and Jacob is a God who keeps his covenant word of promise. The promise of God is found in words, and those who believe those words live by them, and enjoy the blessing of God. Those who are blessed by God can also speak words of blessing to others, and by these words the blessing of God is passed on. We see this happening as Isaac unintentionally blesses Jacob, and cannot recall the blessing once he has spoken it (Gen. 27). We see this too in Jacob's blessing of the twelve tribes, blessings that form the nature of their subsequent history (Gen. 49). Words convey the blessing of God.

Genesis ends with the story of the death of Joseph, who still believes on his deathbed the word and promise that God made to his forefathers: 'God will surely come to you, and bring you up out of this land [Egypt] to the land that he swore to Abraham, to Isaac, and to Jacob' (Gen. 50:24). In the words of Hebrews, 'By faith Joseph, at the end of his life, made mention of the exodus of the Israelites and gave instructions about his burial' (Heb. 11:22). Faith in the promise of God lives on in Joseph's final words, which end the book of Genesis.

Here is a spirituality of the Word, of the covenant promise of God. The people of God believe the words of God, even when that is all they have. Patriarchal and matriarchal spirituality is a spirituality of the Word. That is why the fundamental biblical assessment of Abraham is that he believed what God the Lord had spoken, and it was 'reckoned' to him 'as righteousness' (Gen. 15:6; and also Rom. 4:5; Gal. 3:6; Jas. 2:23). Being the people of God means living and dying in the sure hope that God's words are true. God's plan for a new creation is revealed in his words of promise and of power.

Deuteronomy: Hear, O Israel!

It is difficult to avoid the spirituality of the Word found in Deuteronomy. The book begins, 'These are the words that Moses spoke' (1:1), and is in the form of four sermons given by Moses on the plains of Moab before the people of Israel enter the land promised to them by God. The first sermon, given in chapters 1 – 4, is based on a summary of the history of the people after they left Horeb/Sinai. The second sermon, given in chapters 2 – 26, is a reiteration and application of the law given on Sinai. The third sermon is the covenant blessings and curses of chapters 27 and 28. The fourth sermon is the appeal for covenant faithfulness in chapters 29 and 30. These are followed by the commissioning in chapter 31 of Joshua to be Moses' successor, and then Moses' song and final blessing in chapters 32 and 33. Moses' role is that of mediator of the words of God to the people, as it was at Horeb: 'The LORD spoke with you face to face out at the mountain, out of the fire. (At that time I was standing between the LORD and you to declare to you the words of the LORD . . .)' (Deut. 5:4–5).

These sermons were not only spoken but also written down, so that Israel could continue to hear God's words through Moses even after his death: 'Then Moses wrote down this law and gave it to the priests . . . Moses commanded them . . . you shall read this law before all Israel in their hearing . . .' (31:9–11).

So the basic structure of the theology of Deuteronomy is that God has spoken, and given his words to Moses to pass on to the people. The people must hear, believe, obey and preserve these words for future generations.

Israel must 'give heed' to the instructions Moses is teaching them, 'neither add anything . . . nor take away anything . . . but keep the commandments of the LORD your God with which I am charging you' (4:1–2). So the command 'Hear, O Israel' is characteristic of Deuteronomy (Craigie 1976: 169). This command is the basis of the Shema: 'Hear, O Israel: The LORD is our God, the LORD alone. You shall love the LORD your God with all your heart, and with all your soul, and with all your might' (6:4–5). What is it to love God according to the Shema? To love God is to value his words: 'Keep these words . . . Recite them to your children and talk about them . . . Bind them as a sign on your hand . . . fix them as an emblem on your forehead, and write them on the doorposts . . .' (6:6–9).

'Hear, O Israel' is followed by instructions to remember, teach, discuss, meditate on and practise these words of God. Here is the verbal spirituality at the heart of Deuteronomy.

Some writers point out some similarities between Deuteronomy and the Hittite suzerainty treaties (e.g. Craigie 1976: 38–45). Treaties are words that establish and explain relationships between nations. Similarly words in Deuteronomy establish and explain the relationship between God and his people. God has created this relationship in the past, by his promises to the ancestors of the present generation; and it is words that recall and communicate those promises. This relationship has also been established by God's actions and words at the time of the exodus. For the generation at the time of Deuteronomy, this history can be communicated only by using spoken words. It is written down so that future generations can also learn what God has spoken and done in times past. The words of God to his people are central to the spirituality of Deuteronomy. The sequence 'hear . . . learn . . . revere . . . teach' reflects this spirituality of the Word.

We can also see the power of God's words in the blessings and curses of chapters 27 and 28: 'If you will only obey . . . all these blessings shall come upon you . . . if you will not obey . . . all these curses shall come upon you' (28:1–2, 15). The response of the people to the words of God will determine the effect of the covenant on them, and God's blessings and curses are powerful words that will achieve their purpose among the people.

What is the response of the people to these words of God? At the original giving of the law their response was 'All the words that the LORD has spoken we will do' (Exod. 24:3). Here on the plains of Moab their response is not recorded. There are signs in the text that indicate the expected response. For example, in chapter 1, when Moses recites the history of the people he reminds them of their refusal to enter the land: 'But you were unwilling to go up. You rebelled against the command of the LORD your God' (1:26). Moses adds, 'When the LORD heard your words, he was wrathful' (1:34). And when they did try to enter the land and failed, 'the LORD would neither heed your voice nor pay you any attention' (1:45).

In their past they have refused to obey God's words, so he has refused to listen to their words. What of the future? There is an ominous sign in the blessings and curses in chapters 27 and 28. In 27:11–26 curses are declared from Mount Ebal, and no blessings are declared from Mount Gerizim. In the account of the blessings and curses in chapter 28, although the blessings come first, much more space is given to the curses that follow. In chapters 29 and 30 these conditional curses and blessings have become 'future facts' (Barker 1995: 179–180). Here is also the solemn prediction of the scattering of the people from the land to live in exile, even being sent back to Egypt (28:58–68). Finally there is Moses' instruction to put the book of the law beside the ark of the covenant, 'as a witness against you' (31:26). If the theology and spirituality of Deuteronomy are simply that obedience to God's words lead to blessing, and disobedience leads to cursing, then the expectation is that finally none will obey and none will be blessed.

There is more to the words of God than instructions about how to live. God's words also reveal his character, as they explain who he is and what he has done. There is more to Deuteronomy than words to obey. So the basis of God's choice was not the strength of the people, but it was 'because the LORD loved you and kept the oath that he swore to your ancestors, that the LORD has brought you out with a mighty hand, and redeemed you from the house of slavery, from the hand of Pharaoh king of Egypt' (7:8). God's words include his covenant oath or promise that he made to Abraham: this comes from his electing love, and is expressed in his redemption of the people from

Egypt. God's expressed purpose will be achieved, despite the weakness of the people.

There is also the reminder that ' the LORD your God is not giving you this good land . . . because of your righteousness; for you are a stubborn people' (9:6). They must not say to themselves 'it is because of my righteousness that the LORD has brought me in to occupy this land' (9:4). The basis of what has happened and is to happen is not the implicit goodness of the people, nor is it their tendency to hear and obey God's words. It is the character and grace of God, who has decided to choose this people, has made a covenant with them, and will achieve his purpose with them.

We also read of the certainty of the curses coming on the people, in their being sent into exile. Yet cursing is not the last word, and the blessing of their God is promised to them. In Barker's words, 'The curse is inevitable because of Israel's iniquity; the blessing because of Yahweh's promise' (1995: 181). Part of the promise of the restoration of the people to close covenant relationship with their God is his promise that 'the LORD your God will circumcise your heart and the heart of your descendants, so that you will love the LORD your God with all your heart and with all your soul, in order that you may live' (30:6).

For the goal of Deuteronomy is 'the transfer of [the] law into the heart', for a proud heart leads to disobedience and lack of faith (Barker 1995: 210). In the wilderness God was testing what was in their heart, and humbling them so that they might understand that 'one does not live by bread alone, but by every word that comes from the mouth of the LORD' (8:3). This is why in chapter 10 they are instructed, 'Circumcise, then, the foreskin of your heart, and do not be stubborn any longer' (10:16). So in chapter 30 it is hoped that the people will call the blessings and curses to mind (literally 'heart'), that they will turn and obey God with all their heart (30:1–2). Part of God's promise is that he will circumcise their heart, that is, remove from their hearts their rebellion against him, so that they will love him (30:6). As God has acted for his people, so now he will act within his people, to change them by changing their heart:

> Yahweh will act on Israel's stubborn heart to enable it to do what it is otherwise unable to do, namely that which is required to keep the covenant . . . Only Yahweh can change the heart. The circumcision of the heart by Yahweh in 30:6 is therefore the resolution to the problem of Israel's inability and infidelity to the covenant. (Barker 1995: 194)

We will see in Jeremiah that the prophet adds that circumcised ears are needed in order to have circumcised hearts. Radical change is needed for people to hear and obey God's words.

So the spirituality of Deuteronomy is 'Hear O Israel'. Moses calls the people to believe God's words and so to know God's grace. God invites them to continue to be his people, and promises to change and restore them so that they can continue to enjoy his blessing.

Job: Words of revelation, words of faith

Words are the key to the book of Job. Of course the book is made up of words, but words are also the structure of the debate and the means of its resolution.

For Job is blameless and upright (Job 1:1), but Satan tells God that if trouble comes, 'he will curse you to your face' (1:11 and 2:5). This is the sin of using words to curse God. Satan uses words to accuse Job to God. Satan wants Job to commit a sin of speech, to curse God, an act that would show a deep rebellion against God: 'Sin may at times be purely interior (1:5; 31:1, 7). But out of the abundance of the heart the mouth speaks. The speech of a man betrays his sin' (Dhorme 1967: cxxvii).

Job's response is that he 'did not sin or charge God with wrongdoing' (Job 1:22), despite his wife's advice to 'Curse God, and die' (2:9). He did not commit the sin of speech. Job's continued integrity is described: 'In all this Job did not sin with his lips' (2:10). Job does complain and lament, he does question God and challenge God to respond, but he does not curse God. He does not understand what God is doing, but he will not accuse God of being evil. The agonizing trial of Job's faith does not result in Job cursing God.

The drama of the book of Job unfolds by means of words spoken by Job, his friends and finally the Lord.

Job begins to speak, not to curse God, but to curse his own existence: 'After this Job opened his mouth and cursed the day of his birth' (3:1).

Eliphaz begins his first speech with the question 'If one ventures a word with you, will you be offended?' (4:1), and includes an account of a vision with words that he received at night:

> Now a word came stealing to me,
> my ear received a whisper of it.
>
> (4:12)

Nevertheless Job continues in his words of complaint:

> Therefore I will not restrain my mouth;
> I will speak in the anguish of my spirit;
> I will complain in the bitterness of my soul.
> (7:11)

Next Bildad accuses Job:

> How long will you say these things,
> and the words of your mouth be a great wind?
> (8:1)

Job's reply includes the words

> How then can I answer him [God],
> choosing my words with him?
> (9:14)

Zophar begins his address

> Should a multitude of words go unanswered,
> and should one full of talk be vindicated? . . .
> But O that God would speak,
> and open his lips to you,
> and that he would tell you the secrets of wisdom!
> (11:1, 5–6)

Job wants to argue his case with God:

> But I would speak to the Almighty,
> and I desire to argue my case with God.
> (13:3)

He warns his friends not to speak lies about God:

> Will you speak falsely for God,
> and speak deceitfully for him?
> (13:7)

As the debate continues, Job replies:

Have windy words no limit?
  Or what provokes you that you keep on talking?
(16:3)

Then the three friends cease to answer Job, and Elihu begins his words:

I am young in years,
  and you are aged;
therefore I was timid and afraid
  to declare my opinion to you . . .
See, I waited for your words,
  I listened for your wise sayings,
  while you searched out what to say.
I gave you my attention,
  but there was in fact no one that confuted Job,
no one among you that answered his words.
(32:6, 11, 12)

He continues:

But now, hear my speech, O Job,
  and listen to all my words.
See, I open my mouth;
  the tongue in my mouth speaks . . .
Hear my words, you wise men,
  and give ear to me, you who know;
for the ear tests words
  as the palate tastes food.
(33:1–2; 34:2–3)

As we seem to be drowning in a sea of words, the Lord finally answers Job out of the whirlwind:

Who is this that darkens counsel by words without
  knowledge?
Gird up your loins like a man,
  I will question you, and you shall declare to me . . .
Shall a fault-finder contend with the Almighty?
Anyone who argues with God must respond.
(38:2–3; 40:1–2)

Then Job answered the Lord:

> See, I am of small account; what shall I answer you?
> I lay my hand on my mouth.
> I have spoken once, and I will not answer;
> twice, but will proceed no further.
>
> (40:4–5)

In Job's final words, he confesses:

> I have uttered what I did not understand,
> things too wonderful for me, which I did not know.
> Hear, and I will speak;
> I will question you, and you declare to me.
> I had heard of you by the hearing of the ear,
> but now my eye sees you;
> therefore I despise myself,
> and repent in dust and ashes.
>
> (42:3–6)

But what does Job mean by the crucial words 'I had heard of you by the hearing of the ear, / but now my eye sees you'? Dhorme explains, 'The meaning here is: "by hearsay". Audition is opposed to vision' (1967: 646). Atkinson comments, 'Job is satisfied. He has not received a direct answer, but he has seen the Lord' (1991: 156).

Job has not seen a vision, nor has he heard a description of a vision of God. However before he has heard the words of the Lord from the whirlwind, and those words have expressed the power of God reflected in the creation. He has 'seen', by receiving the words of the Lord. In Fyall's words, 'Truly to hear God is to see God' (2002: 179).

Finally the Lord speaks to Eliphaz and accuses him of words that are wrong: 'My wrath is kindled against you and against your two friends; for you have not spoken of me what is right, as my servant Job has' (42:7). The sin of Job's friends is the sin of heresy, in this case the subtle heresy of saying what is true in other situations, and wrongly applying it to Job. It is the painful heresy of right truth wrongly applied.

God's grace extends to heretics, for he further promises Eliphaz, 'My servant Job shall pray for you' (42:8); then we read, 'and the LORD accepted Job's prayer' (42:9). At the beginning of the book we find Job praying for his family in case 'they cursed God in their hearts' (1:5); now at the end of the book we find Job praying for Eliphaz, because he has not spoken what is right about God (42:8).

The book of Job turns on the use of words: the temptation to curse God, Job's refusal to commit this sin with his lips, the well-intentioned but wrong words of Job's friends, Job's verbal defence of himself and his speech, the revelation of the Lord by the words he speaks, Job's verbal response to the Lord, the Lord's condemnation of Eliphaz, and Job's prayer for Eliphaz, accepted by the Lord.

To understand the book of Job, we can adapt some words from 1 Peter: 'for a little while you have had to suffer various trials, so that the genuineness of your faith may be tested: but after you have suffered, the God of all grace will himself restore, support, strengthen, and establish you' (from 1 Pet. 1:6–8 and 5:10).

The resolution of the book hangs on the words of God, for it is God's presence and reply that remind Job of the relationship that continues, whatever happens. The 'endurance of Job' (Jas. 5:11) is the endurance of faith under trial, waiting, however impatiently, for God to speak. The long-awaited words of God are the blessing and restoration of God. Words of revelation are answered by words of faith.

Psalms: O that today you would listen to his voice!

While most books of the Bible are made up of narrative, instruction or teaching, the moving characteristic of the book of Psalms is that it is mostly made up of words of response to God. In the Bible we are told who God is, what he has said, what he has done: in this book verbal response to God is also articulated and described, that our verbal response to God may echo these inspired words. As Jesus teaches the disciples how to pray by giving them the Lord's Prayer, so in this book all believers are taught how to respond to God in praise, prayer, lament and thanksgiving. Here we are shown the shape of our spirituality. Here the words of our response are articulated for us. Here are words that resonate with our own humanity formed by God's grace.

Here is the spirituality of the Word in the book of Psalms.

Psalm 1

Here is the happiness of those who delight and meditate in the law of the Lord (1–2). People are influenced by words; the Psalm notes that those who delight in the teaching of the Lord will not be influenced by the wicked, the sinners or the scornful, but will meditate on the teaching of the Lord day and night. If they do this, they will be fruitful, secure and prosperous (3), and will stand in the day of judgment (4–6). The song of this psalm is the joy of delighting in and meditating on the teaching or instruction of the Lord. It is a most appropriate introduction to the book of Psalms, as it makes clear that the religion of this book is a response to the verbal revelation of God.

Psalm 19

This is a moving comparison of the revelation of God in the creation and the revelation of the Lord in his law or teaching. In the creation the glory of God is proclaimed (1–6); in the law the instruction that the Lord has provided for his people is revealed (7–14). As nothing is hidden from the heat of the sun (6), so nothing can be hidden from the perfect law of the Lord (7, 11–13).

We can also notice the significant equivalents in the latter part of the psalm. The law is the same as the decrees, the precepts, the commandment, the fear and the ordinances. This law or instruction is perfect, sure, right, clear, pure, true and righteous. This law or instruction revives the soul, makes wise the simple, rejoices the heart, enlightens the eyes, endures forever, and is desirable and sweet (7–10).

The significant response to this twofold revelation of God in his two creations, the heavens and the law, is a prayer that 'the words of my mouth and the meditation of my heart' will be 'acceptable to you, / O Lord, my rock and my redeemer' (14). The shape of responsive obedience to the revelation of the Lord is clear and articulated, and is the response of trusting prayer about spoken words and personal meditation.

Psalm 115

Here is a telling comparison between the Lord our God who is in the heavens and who does whatever he pleases (3) and the idols of the nations. This invisibility of the Lord is a matter of reproach for the other nations, who ask, 'Where is their God?' (2). But their too-visible idols are only the work of human hands, and they cannot speak, see, hear, smell, feel, walk, or make any sound (4–7). What a contrast with the Lord, who can rescue, be a help and shield, and effectively bless his people (9–15).

It is the silence of the idols that is so telling: the list of their weaknesses begins and ends with their inability to speak or make any sound. The steadfast love and faithfulness of the Lord (1) is revealed in his words, and seen in history.

The response? 'We will bless the Lord. . . Praise the LORD!' (18).

Psalm 119

This psalm is a celebration of the verbal revelation of God. The same themes sound again and again through the varied language of the psalm.

The verbal revelation of the Lord is described as his law, decrees, ways, precepts, statutes, commandments, ordinances, word, ways, works, the way of faithfulness, promise, truth, steadfast love, righteous promise, words, judgments, the truth, and, commands.

The varied response to this revelation is as follows: to walk in, keep, seek him with the whole heart, treasure, do no wrong, have the eye fixed on his commandments, learn, observe, delight in, meditate on, behold wondrous things in, long for, cling to, trust in, hope in, keep continually, speak of, love, revere, take comfort in, watch for, seek, consider, fear, not forget, and, rejoice at.

In addition the writer finds that this spirituality of the Word is happiness, delight, reverence, song, better than gold or silver, sweeter than honey, a lamp and light to feet and path, inheritance, the joy of the heart, wonderful, light-giving, and, the truth.

What is the richly varied verbal response to God's revelation? Here are some prayers:

- Do not let me stray from your commandments. (10)
- Teach me your statutes. (12)
- Open my eyes, so that I may behold / wondrous things out of your law. (18)
- Do not hide your commandments from me. (19)
- Revive me according to your word. (25)
- Make me understand . . . [and] strengthen me according to your word. (27–28)
- Graciously teach me your law. (29)
- Give me understanding, that I may keep your law / and observe it with my whole heart. (34)
- Turn my heart to your decrees. (36)
- Confirm your word to your servant. (38)
- Do not take the word of truth utterly out of my mouth. (43)

- Remember your word to your servant. (49)
- Be gracious to me according to your promise. (58)
- Keep my steps steady according to your promise. (133)
- Redeem me from human oppression, / that I might keep your precepts. (134)
- My lips will pour forth praise, / because you teach me your statutes. (171)

And though this is strongly personal religion, it is not self-centred religion, for the psalmist also prays:

- I will also speak of your decrees before kings. (46)
- Hot indignation seizes me because of the wicked, / those who forsake your law. (53)
- I am a companion of all who fear you, / of those who keep your precepts. (63)
- My eyes shed streams of tears / because your law is not kept. (136)

And the psalmist suffers for his tenacious commitment to God's words. Note these prayers:

- I live as an alien in the land. (19)
- The arrogant smear me with lies, / but with my whole heart I keep your precepts. (69)
- The arrogant have dug pitfalls for me; / they flout your law. (85)
- I am severely afflicted, / give me life, O LORD, according to your word. (107)
- My zeal consumes me / because my foes forget your words. (139)
- I am small and despised, / yet I do not forget your precepts. (141)
- Trouble and anguish have come upon me, / but your commandments are my delight. (143)
- Those who persecute me with evil purpose draw near; / they are far from your law. (150)
- Princes persecute me without cause, / but my heart stands in awe of your words. (161)

Psalm 119 provides a model spirituality of the Word. Are the prayers of this psalm in our mouths?

What other spirituality can we learn from the Psalms?

The spirituality of the whole book of Psalms includes the following points:

- Praising God the creator:

> You set the earth on its foundations,
>   so that it shall never be shaken.
> You cover it with the deep as with a garment;
>   the waters stood above the mountains.
>
> (104:5–6)

- Praising God the redeemer:

> Bless the LORD, O my soul,
>   and do not forget all his benefits –
> who forgives all your iniquity,
>   who heals all your diseases,
> who redeems your life from the Pit,
>   who crowns you with steadfast love and mercy.
>
> (103:2–4)

- Remembering the great acts of God in salvation:

> When Israel went out from Egypt,
>   the house of Jacob from a people of strange language,
> Judah became God's sanctuary,
>   Israel his dominion.
>
> (114:1–2)

- Remembering the oracles of God:

> The LORD says to my lord,
>   'Sit at my right hand
> until I make your enemies your footstool.'
>
> (110:1)

- Praising God in the congregation:

> Praise the LORD!
> I will give thanks to the LORD with my whole heart,
>   in the company of the upright, in the congregation.
>
> (111:1)

- Hoping that God will redeem his people:

O Israel, hope in the LORD!
  For with the LORD there is steadfast love,
  and with him is great power to redeem.
It is he who will redeem Israel
  from all its iniquities.

(130:7–8)

- Lamenting the past:

By the rivers of Babylon –
  there we sat down and there we wept,
  when we remembered Zion.
On the willows there
  we hung up our harps.

(137:1–2)

- Praying for justice and vengeance:

O that you would kill the wicked, O God,
  and that the bloodthirsty would depart from me.

(139:19)

- Lamenting the present:

I pour out my complaint before him;
  I tell my trouble before him.
When my spirit is faint,
  you know my way.

(142:2–3)

- Rejoicing in God's revealed character:

The LORD is gracious and merciful,
  slow to anger and abounding in steadfast love.
The LORD is good to all,
  and his compassion is over all that he has made.

(145:8–9)

- Meditating on God's words, works and character:

Oh, how I love your law!

It is my meditation all day long.
(119:97)

I will meditate on all your work,
  and muse on your mighty deeds.
(77:12)

We ponder your steadfast love, O God . . .
(48:9)

- Pleading his covenant promises:

Remember your congregation, which you acquired long ago,
  which you redeemed to be the tribe of your heritage.
(74:2)

- Praying for the prosperity of God's anointed King:

May he have dominion from sea to sea,
  and from the River to the ends of the earth.
May his foes bow down before him,
  and his enemies lick the dust.
(72:8–9)

- Teaching others the way to live to serve God:

Keep your tongue from evil,
  and your lips from speaking deceit.
Depart from evil, and do good;
  seek peace, and pursue it.
(34:13–14)

- Lament in times of overwhelming disaster:

O LORD, why do you cast me off?
  Why do you hide your face from me?
Wretched and close to death from my youth up,
  I suffer your terrors: I am desperate.
(88:14–15)

- Calling on all people to praise God:

Let everything that breathes praise the LORD!
Praise the LORD!

(150:6)

The psalms speak of both the character and works of God, and also articulate the varied human responses to God. In speaking of both divinity and humanity they point forward to the coming and character of God's incarnate Son: 'The word of God is full of the Word of God. Christ is conceived in human language through the Holy Ghost, as He was conceived in human flesh, of the Holy Ghost' (Merton 1953: 68).

Clement of Alexandria also comments on the connection between the book of Psalms and the Lord Jesus Christ:

> Thus did the Word of God, who is David's son yet David's Lord, play the song of the Spirit, not on a lifeless harp, but on the body and soul of a man.
> Thus did He make His music heard through all the world.
> On these living strings
> He makes melody to God.
>
> (Whelan 1994: 5)

Proverbs: Every word of God proves true

Walter Brueggemann describes the kind of preaching that works in our modern age. He claims that the preaching that is appropriate now is not patriarchal, hierarchical, authoritarian, monologic, flat or universal, but is marked by ambiguity, playfulness, openness, irony and contradiction (1997: 29, 43–44). He writes of the need for a rhetoric that conveys a countertruth subversive of dominant, commonly accepted givens, and which has a different style or mode of articulation (1997: 57). This rhetoric will be 'not excessively solemn or rationalistic or final or given with too much sobriety. Rather it is an utterance that is playful, open, teasing, inviting, and capable of voicing the kind of unsure tentativeness and ambiguity that [the people of God] must always maintain' (1997: 57).

If this is right, then the spirituality of the book of Proverbs must be very appealing to many people today. For the content and method of communication of Proverbs are both subversive, though we should also note that a kind of metanarrative is also present, namely that fear of God which is the foundation of wisdom.

The content is described in chapter 1:

> For learning about wisdom and instruction,
>   for understanding words of insight,
> for gaining instruction in wise dealing,
>   righteousness, justice, and equity;
> to teach shrewdness to the simple,
>   knowledge and prudence to the young.
>
> (1:2–4)

And the method is also described:

> [L]et the wise also hear and gain in learning,
>   and the discerning acquire skill,
> to understand a proverb and a figure,
>   the words of the wise and their riddles.
>
> (1:5–6)

In Proverbs God speaks through the voice of Wisdom, the personified mediator of God's words. In Wisdom God created the world; in his Wisdom he delights in the human race and calls us to live according to his words of Wisdom (8:22–36). The words of Wisdom are not alien words, because Wisdom is created by God and is his mouthpiece. That is why

> Long life is in her right hand;
>   in her left hand are riches and honour . . .
> She is a tree of life to those who lay hold of her;
>   those who hold her fast are called happy.
>
> (3:16, 18)

The fear of the Lord is the basis of knowledge and wisdom (1:7; 9:10; see also Estes 1997: 35–39). Because he is the creator of the world in which we live, fearing or honouring the covenant Lord must be the foundation of all true wisdom. Wisdom comes through words.

In speaking through Wisdom, God takes the initiative in relating to human beings. Wisdom 'cries out in the street; / in the squares she raises her voice' (1:20). She speaks through others, especially parents and teachers, as she summons people to learn from her:

> Listen, children, to a father's instruction,

and be attentive, that you may gain insight . . .
(4:1)

Daniel Estes shows the variety of rhetorical styles used by the human teacher who is communicating the words that come from Wisdom, and therefore from God (Estes 1997: 101–134). For, 'proverbs at times illuminate the hearer, and at other times use ambiguity and enigma to tease the learner into deeper understanding' (1997: 103). These rhetorical styles include the following (1997: 104–123). Notice the varied range of motivations Proverbs uses to encourage people to adopt a spirituality of wise words.

Address:

Trust in the LORD with all your heart,
  and do not rely on your own insight.
(3:5)

Description:

A scoundrel and a villain
  goes around with crooked speech,
winking the eyes, shuffling the feet,
  pointing the fingers,
with perverted mind devising evil,
  continually sowing discord;
on such a one calamity will descend suddenly;
  in a moment, damage beyond repair.
(6:12–15)

Condition with command:

My child, if you have given your pledge to your neighbour,
  if you have bound yourself to another,
you are snared by the utterance of your lips,
  caught by the words of your mouth.
So do this, my child, and save yourself,
  for you have come into your neighbour's power:
go, hurry, and plead with your neighbour.
(6:1–3)

Command with reasons:

My child, do not despise the LORD's discipline
or be weary of his reproof,
for the Lord reproves the one he loves,
as a father the son in whom he delights.
(3:11–12)

Command with reasons and illustrations:

[M]y child, do not walk in their way,
keep your foot from their paths;
for their feet run to evil,
and they hurry to shed blood.
For in vain is the net baited,
while the bird is looking on;
yet they lie in wait – to kill themselves!
and set an ambush – for their own lives!
(1:15–18)

Command with consequences:

Therefore walk in the way of the good,
and keep to the paths of the just.
For the upright will abide in the land,
and the innocent will remain in it.
(2:20–21)

Command with rhetorical questions:

Can fire be carried in the bosom
without burning one's clothes?
Or can one walk on hot coals
without scorching the feet?
So is he who sleeps with his neighbour's wife;
no one who touches her will go unpunished.
(6:27–29)

Incentive:

Happy are those who find wisdom,
and those who get understanding,
for her income is better than silver,

and her revenue better than gold . . .
She is a tree of life to those who lay hold of her;
those who hold her fast are called happy.
(3:13, 14, 18)

Invitation:

Wisdom has built her house,
she has hewn her seven pillars . . .
'You that are simple, turn in here!'
To those without sense she says,
'Come, eat of my bread
and drink of the wine I have mixed.
Lay aside immaturity, and live,
and walk in the way of insight.'
(9:1, 4–6)

These are all different ways in which the word of God is brought to those who hear. It is important to notice that this style of communication is not propositional, and that to read individual proverbs as eternal and universal propositions is to miss the point of them. God's words come in a variety of rhetorical styles, including propositions such as 'the fear of the LORD is the foundation of knowledge and wisdom'. But the use of propositional revelation should not blind us to the presence of many other rhetorical forms. The rhetoric used depends on the nature of the truth being conveyed, and the style of its communication. We have just seen the variety of motivations used to entice God's people to follow the ways of wisdom. The spirituality of wisdom is discovered in the way in which it is offered, which in turn matches its content.

Wisdom calls people to receive the rich spirituality of God's words that are precious, valuable and true:

Take my instruction instead of silver,
and knowledge rather than choice gold:
for wisdom is better than jewels,
and all that you may desire cannot compare with her.
(8:10–11)

Not everyone will receive wisdom. One of the warnings of the book is of the alien words that are the folly of fools:

Whoever corrects a scoffer wins abuse;
whoever rebukes the wicked gets hurt.
A scoffer who is rebuked will only hate you:
the wise, when rebuked, will love you.

(9:7–8)

Fools speak folly:

As charcoal is to hot embers and wood to fire,
so is a quarrelsome person for kindling strife.

(26:21)

God speaks through Wisdom, but an alien voice is also heard, and is active in calling people to folly, wickedness and death.

Then a woman comes towards him,
decked out like a prostitute, wily of heart.
She is loud and wayward;
her feet do not stay at home;
now in the street, now in the squares,
and at every corner she lies in wait.

(7:10–12)

Those who learn the way of Wisdom can speak good words to others:

A word fitly spoken
is like apples of gold in a setting of silver.
Like a gold ring or an ornament of gold
is a wise rebuke to a listening ear.

(25:11)

Wisdom knows not only what to say, but also when not to speak:

Like vinegar on a wound
is one who sings songs to a heavy heart.

(25:20)

God speaks through Wisdom, often discerned through observation of reality, and often mediated through the word of a teacher. Because these wise words come from God, they are reliable:

> Every word of God proves true;
>   he is a shield to those who take refuge in him.
>
> (30:6)

Here in Proverbs we find some facets of the now familiar structure of a spirituality of hearing and speaking. God speaks through Wisdom, and his words are intended to establish and sustain relationship and blessing. The wise hear and obey these words of wisdom, and build their lives on them. They are careful that they do not listen to alien words of folly that would lead them away from God to death. They will then speak wisdom to others, and bring life and blessing to them. Fools who do not heed wisdom will speak only words of strife, gossip and trouble. God's words of wisdom create and sustain life and blessing. A spirituality of the Word is fundamental to life as God's people in God's universe, for 'Every word of God proves true' (30:5).

In the wider perspective of the Bible, Wisdom personified as the mediator of the words of the Lord points forward to Jesus Christ:

> [T]he reality of God's creative wisdom is eventually given personal expression in the New Testament. There the function of Christ in creation fulfils everything that is stated here of wisdom's role . . . Jesus Christ, being God, perfectly exemplifies the creating-redeeming wisdom of God. (Goldsworthy 1993: 80–81)

Wisdom is taught by God, and teaches the wisdom of God. Good life in the land points forward to eternal life in Christ Jesus.

Jeremiah: My words in your mouth

The prophet Jeremiah provides us with a richly personal and emotional insight into a spirituality of the Word, from the perspective of one whose life was tied up with his ministry as a prophet of God.

From the opening of the book the centrality of words is clear. The book begins with the phrase 'the words of Jeremiah' (1:1), and then describes him as one 'to whom the word of the LORD came' (1:2). Jeremiah's call is then vividly described as 'the word of the LORD came to me', and the message is 'I appointed you a prophet to the nations' (1:4–5). When Jeremiah complains, 'Truly I do not know how to speak' (1:6), the reply comes: 'you shall speak whatever I command you' (1:7).

Then to reassure Jeremiah, 'the LORD put out his hand and touched my mouth; and the LORD said to me, "Now I have put my words in your mouth"' (1:9). There could be no clearer depiction of the gift, call and enabling of the prophet, as God puts his words in his mouth: 'The divine hand had put the divine word within his mouth . . . From this moment the Word that will be spoken will be the Word of the Lord' (Thomson 1959: 9).

As words of the Lord are powerful, so they are powerful in the mouth of Jeremiah, as his commission is given:

> See, today I appoint you over nations and over kingdoms,
> to pluck up and to pull down,
> to destroy and to overthrow,
> to build and to plant.
>
> (1:10)

This is also the direct work of the Lord: 'And just as I have watched over them to pluck up and break down, to overthrow, destroy, and bring evil, so I will watch over them to build and to plant, says the LORD' (31:28). The words and the works of the Lord will be achieved through the words of the Lord from the mouth of the prophet. This is a graphic description of the work of God in conveying his words into and then from the mouth of the prophet to the people.

Jeremiah's words are also effective when written down by his scribe Baruch: 'Then Jeremiah called Baruch . . . and Baruch wrote on a scroll at Jeremiah's dictation all the words of the LORD that he had spoken to him' (36:4). The words Baruch has written down are those dictated by Jeremiah, literally 'from his mouth'. As long ago Aaron had served as Moses' mouth as Moses served as the mouth of the Lord (Exod. 4:15–16), so now Baruch passes on the words of the Lord from the mouth of Jeremiah. This is so that Baruch can read the words to the people and then to King Jehoiakim. The king rejects the words and burns the scroll, and so rejects the words of the Lord. As Thomson points out, 'They were rending (qara') God's Word, instead of rending (qara') their garments' (1959: 17).

What is it like to be the messenger of the Lord, to have the words of the Lord in your mouth? Jeremiah's experience shows that he is not removed from his message, a mere conduit for God's words. On the contrary, he is called to incarnate the experience of the Lord and of his people, yet without losing his own identity (McConville 1993: 76). He experiences within himself both the urgency of the message of

God's judgment, and the great reluctance of his people to receive that message. The divine drama of the Word is played out within the personal experience of the prophet:

> My anguish, my anguish! I writhe in pain!
>   Oh, the walls of my heart! . . .
>   I cannot keep silent;
> for I hear the sound of the trumpet,
>   the alarm of war.
>
> (4:19)

Jeremiah pleads with the Lord on behalf of the people, and pleads with the people on behalf of the Lord:

> Then I said, 'These are only the poor,
>   they have no sense.'
>
> (5:4)

When the people do not respond, the Lord's reply is to make his words in the mouth of the prophet the more devastatingly powerful:

> I am now making my words in your mouth a fire,
>   and this people wood, and the fire shall devour them.
>
> (5:14)

Jeremiah suffers on behalf of God: he feels God's frustration, both his anger and his compassion; and he suffers on behalf of his people: he suffers the effects of their refusal to receive God's words. This suffering is clearly expressed:

> O that my head were a spring of water,
>   and my eyes a fountain of tears,
> so that I might weep day and night
>   for the slain of my poor people!
>
> (9:1)

Jeremiah incarnates in himself the conflict between God and his people, as he feels with God's emotion, and also feels the strength of the people's rebellion. This is a faint foreshadowing of the sufferings of Christ, in which is focused both the compassion and forgiveness of God and also the rebellion and sin of the world.

Jeremiah spoke, and also conveyed his message by powerful symbolic actions. He did not marry, as a warning of the judgment that would fall on parents and children (16:1–4). He made a yoke, and put it on his own shoulders as a sign of the way in which many nations, including Judah, would submit to the yoke of the king of Babylon (27:1–15). He bought a field at Anathoth as a sign that his people would return after their exile (32:15). Jeremiah does these symbolic actions on instruction from the Lord. The actions by themselves were ambiguous; and Jeremiah's actions were always accompanied by words from the Lord that explain them. Thompson describes this as 'the symbolic action accompanied by a spoken word' (1980: 74). Both the actions and the words were the one communication from God. Later theology used the expression 'visible words', and Jeremiah's actions were visible words. Again, Jeremiah is in a way incarnating his message in his life and actions: 'The "word of God" is an expression of the divine mind, what God thinks and plans, says, does, purposes. Hence a spoken word plus a visible "word" could convey the divine mind very forcefully' (1980: 71).

These were also how the Lord's word was achieved: 'being Yahweh's word it initiated the event it portrayed' (Thompson 1980: 76). It is not that words are powerless, and that actions are used to replace them. Both words and visible words accomplish God's work.

It is not that visible words are used because the people are highly spiritual. The prophet Moses used visible words when Egypt was judged, and Ezekiel used them when God's people were judged. Visible words explained by spoken words are used when people are hard of heart.

What then of the response of the people to the words of the Lord through Jeremiah? They attacked him with the most serious slander, that his words were mere wind, that 'He who speaks is not in him' (5:13, Thomson's translation, 1959: 10). They turned 'deaf' or 'closed' or literally 'uncircumcised' ears to him:

> See their ears are uncircumcised [New Revised Standard Version fn.],
>   they cannot listen.
> The word of the LORD is to them an object of scorn;
>   they take no pleasure in it.
>
> (6:10)

This vivid expression shows both that their reaction was like that of those who were not the people of God, and also demonstrates that the significance of circumcision included the need for radically changed ears as well as hearts, for changed hearing that will result in changed living. In order to 'remove the foreskin of your hearts' (4:4), they will first need to circumcise their ears, their hearing of the words of the Lord. God's people need to have circumcised ears, that they may have circumcised hearts, that they may serve God. Hearing the word of God is not effortless, easy or painless.

If the people of God refuse to hear God's words, then they fill their hearing with alien words. If they will not hear true words through Jeremiah, they will hear false words through false prophets. The false prophets flourished in Jeremiah's day because demand produces supply, and there was a ready market for their words. How are these false prophets described? 'They speak visions of their own minds, not from the mouth of the LORD' (23:16), for:

> who has stood in the council of the LORD
>   so as to see and to hear his word?
>
> (23:18)

Their words originate in their own minds, not in the mind of the Lord. Yet they are active in ministry:

> I did not send the prophets,
>   yet they ran;
> I did not speak to them,
>   yet they prophesied.
>
> (23:21)

The result of their ministry of speaking words that do not come from God is not second-rate service of God, but that the name of the Lord is forgotten. 'They plan to make my people forget my name by their dreams that they tell one another, just as their ancestors forgot my name for Baal' (23:27). The result of the ministry of these false prophets is that

> all of them have become like Sodom to me,
>   and its inhabitants like Gomorrah.
>
> (23:14)

So God is opposed to the false prophets who seduce his people away from their obedience to him: 'See, I am against those who prophesy lying dreams, says the LORD, and who tell them, and who lead my people astray by their lies and their recklessness, when I did not send them or appoint them' (23:32).

There are few more powerful pictures in the Bible of the dramatic effect of words, and of the immense gulf between the words of the Lord spoken through his prophet, and the false and alien words that bring his people to ruin.

The words of Jeremiah are not only of disaster. Through him the Lord speaks of the return from exile in Babylon (29:10), of the new covenant in which God will put his law in them and write it on their hearts, and forgive their iniquity and remember their sin no more (31:31–34). In Jeremiah's last recorded words the destruction of Babylon is predicted, that destruction which will mean the return of the people of God from exile, and the next stage of the working out of God's plan of salvation. As the Lord has put his words in the mouth of Jeremiah, so he uses those words to achieve his saving plan in his world.

We miss the point of the prophecy and the book if we think that so much emphasis on hearing and obeying the words of God means that the people of God can maintain or repair their relationship with God by means of their measured obedience. The purpose of the words of the Lord is to call the people to return to the covenant love of God, to live in his love. What they have broken, God will restore, by maintaining his love, and ultimately by establishing a new covenant. While those who go into exile in Egypt do so because 'they did not obey the voice of the LORD' (43:7), God is determined to achieve his covenant purpose with those he loves:

> I have loved you with an everlasting love;
>   therefore I have continued my faithfulness to you.
> Again I will build you, and you shall be built,
>   O virgin Israel!
>
> (31:3–4)

And, 'The days are surely coming, says the LORD, when I will make a new covenant with the house of Israel and the house of Judah . . . they shall all know me, from the least of them to the greatest . . . for I will forgive their iniquity, and remember their sin no more' (31:31, 34). This is fulfilled in our great High Priest, who by his once-for-all sacrifice of himself, by the blood of the eternal covenant, has perfected for ever those who are sanctified (Heb. 8:8–13, 10:14).

So the message of the book of the prophet Jeremiah is that the Lord has put his words in the mouth of the prophet in order to warn the people of judgment and to call them to return to their God, whose covenant love never fails. If they disobey the words of the Lord, they will be judged. If they obey those words, they will again enjoy fellowship with their God:

> Is Ephraim my dear son?
>   Is he the child I delight in?
> As often as I speak against him,
>   I still remember him.
> Therefore I am deeply moved for him;
>   I will surely have mercy on him . . .
>
> (31:20)

Here is an effective spirituality of the Word. As we have studied the Old Testament books of Genesis, Deuteronomy, Job, Psalms, Proverbs and Jeremiah, we have seen the following features of biblical spirituality: its *content and focus* is God in Christ, its *practice* is hearing the word of God by faith, its *experience* is that of meeting God in his Spirit-given words, and its *result* is trust in Christ and our heavenly Father.

We have seen these elements of its structure within the biblical revelation: it is based on the God who speaks, and his words create and sustain life and blessing, and establish relationships. We are called to hear, believe and obey God, to receive that life and blessing, and are brought into relationship with God. If we do not hear God, but reject, neglect, disbelieve or disobey him, then those same words bring curse and death. We must receive the words of God, and must also reject alien words that will seduce us away from God. So we receive the Spirit-given words of God in Scripture, and are called to believe and obey them as part of our response to God. Jesus is both the Word of God, and also the one who hears, speaks and does God's words. Jesus' obedience to God's words leads him to death and resurrection, when he dies in our place because of our disobedience. We respond by trusting and obeying God as we believe his gospel word about his Son Jesus Christ. We praise God according to his words, and speak words to others that bring blessing, not cursing. We pray to God in response to the words of truth he has spoken to us. Finally, we look forward to the new heaven and earth promised by God's Word.

Chapter Three

The New Testament: The words that I have spoken are spirit and life

Luke: That you may know the truth

One of the most interesting test cases in the use of the Bible as a resource for spirituality is Luke 24. It is the climax of Luke's Gospel, and has been used to support a variety of spiritualities.

Luke conveniently summarizes the purpose of his Gospel in the first few verses, as he explains that he wants Theophilus to 'know the truth concerning the things about which you have been instructed' (1:4). So chapter 24 must be a fulfilment of this aim. Clearly there are three stories in chapter 24: the first at the tomb of Jesus, the second on the road to and in Emmaus, and the third back in Jerusalem.

There are three common uses of Luke 24 in Christian spirituality, which can be described as the proof of the empty tomb (based on history); the encounter with the risen Christ (based on experience); and meeting Christ in the breaking of bread (based on the Lord's Supper). Let me expand and critique them.

The proof of the empty tomb

This uses the first story. The women did not expect that the tomb would be empty, that Jesus would have risen from the dead. They visited the tomb to anoint the body of Jesus, but when they entered the tomb, they did not find his body (v. 3). Later Peter visited the tomb, and found lying by themselves the linen cloths in which Jesus' body had been bound (v. 12).

This evidence for the empty tomb gives us a sure ground for faith in Jesus Christ, not just that he rose from the dead, but that all that he said about himself was true, that he was indeed the Messiah and the Son of God. In answer to the question 'Who moved the stone?' we know that God moved the stone when he raised Jesus from the dead. This knowledge enables us to have certain faith in Jesus Christ.

This use of Luke 24 as the basis for spirituality presents some problems. The first is that although the women and Peter saw that the tomb did not contain the body of Jesus, they were unconvinced that Jesus was alive, according to Luke 24. The women 'were perplexed' (v. 4), and Peter was 'amazed' (v. 12). According to the theory, they of all people should have become firm believers in the risen Christ because they saw that the tomb was empty. But that sight did not convince them.

The second problem is that the theory makes no use of the rest of Luke 24, which in fact includes the process by which the women and Peter become confident in the resurrection of Christ. In taking the details of the empty tomb out of context in chapter 24 we lose the evidence that Luke thought necessary to produce a confident spirituality of the risen Christ.

I do believe that the tomb was empty, because Christ's physical body had been resurrected and transformed. The evidence is in the Bible, it is a traditional part of Christian doctrine, and it is a sign that God will not replace his creation but transform it. But the empty tomb is not the basis for the spirituality of Luke 24.

The encounter with the risen Christ

This use of Luke 24 offers an Emmaus road experience of the risen Christ. Of course it centres on the second story, and it invites people to share in the experience of those two disciples who talked with Jesus as he travelled with them. As they did not recognize him, though he was present with them (v. 16), so too we may not recognize the Christ who is present with us on our journey. All we have to do is to trust that he is present, and we too will find that our hearts burn within us as we walk with Jesus.

Whereas the first theory was based on history, this one is based on experience. It promises an experience of Jesus walking with us, our inner experience of his company. It may associate this experience with Bible study, because the disciples experienced their hearts burning within them 'while he was opening the Scriptures to us' (v. 32), or it may ignore this detail and offer a more wide-ranging experience of Christ, not linked to times of Bible study.

This theory has been popular among Evangelicals, and is now popular also among those promoting an existential experience of Christ without the distractions of the historical resurrection of Christ or the need to study the Bible.

Of course it uses only one story from Luke 24, and so misses out on the full picture Luke is painting. It is attractively simple, but fails to observe the important distinction Luke draws between those who were present when 'the Lord Jesus went in and out among us' (Acts 1:21) and later believers. It is only those who were present who were eyewitnesses and 'earwitnesses' of 'these things' (24:48). There is an important distinction between the presence of the risen Christ as described in Luke 24, and the kind of experience of Christ possible after the ascension referred to in Luke 24 and Acts 1. And we should point out that those who had the most vivid experience of the risen Christ appearing before them (as he does in the third story), speaking to them, showing them his wounds, and eating fish before them, were still not convinced (24:36–43)! In fact even they failed to distinguish between the risen Christ and a ghost – exactly the distinction that an experience-based spirituality fails to grasp. Again this theory misses out on what is in Luke 24.

I do believe that we can have an encounter with the risen and ascended Christ, but this is not what Luke is teaching us in this chapter.

Meeting Christ in the breaking of bread

This use is also based on the second story, and more particularly in Emmaus itself, when the two disciples have a meal with Christ: 'When he was at the table with them, he took bread, blessed and broke it, and gave it to them . . . [Later they tell] how he had been made known to them in the breaking of the bread' (Luke 24:30, 35).

There is a simple equivalence between the experience of the two disciples in knowing Jesus in the breaking of the bread and our own sacramental experience in the Lord's Supper. We are encouraged to recognize Jesus being made known to us as he was to those disciples. We too can know Jesus as they did in the breaking of the bread. This too is an attractive theory, not least because it also breaks down the distinction between those early disciples and ourselves, and promises us their experience.

There are, however, some difficulties with this use. It concentrates on the second of the three stories, and does not make use of the whole of Luke 24. A greater difficulty is the identification of the 'breaking of bread' in Luke 24 with the Lord's Supper. Is it an ordinary meal, or is it a sacramental meal? Let us look at the evidence:

- In Luke 22:19, at the last supper: 'Then he took a loaf of bread, and when he had given thanks (*eucharistēsas*), he broke it and gave it to them'.

- In Luke 24:30, at Emmaus: 'he took bread, blessed (*eulogēsen*) and broke it, and gave it to them'.
- In Acts 27, the account of Paul's shipwreck, we read that Paul wanted soldiers and sailors to eat some food after fourteen days of hard work trying to keep the ship afloat. We read in verse 35, 'he took bread; and [after] giving thanks to God (*eucharistēsen*) in the presence of all, he broke it and began to eat'.

This last meal was a desperate attempt to feed hungry sailors, not a sacramental meal! Note too that the word 'eucharist', often used today of the Lord's Supper, is *not* used in Luke 24, though it is in Luke 22 and Acts 27! The breaking of bread in Luke 24 does not indicate a sacramental occasion. It looks more like an ordinary meal, the kind of meal Jesus and his disciples had shared together many times. Of course in Luke 22 Jesus invited the disciples to receive bread and wine in remembrance of him, and as a way of participating in the benefits of the new covenant in his blood, but this is not what Luke is saying in Luke 24. To use Luke 24 in this way is to miss the basis for certainty that Luke is offering in his Gospel.

This use also makes the second story the heart of the chapter, whereas I hope to show that the third story is the climax of this chapter in Luke.

What then is the spirituality of Luke 24?[1] To find an answer to this question, we need to notice that the use of the sequence of three stories is common in Luke, and it is instructive to look at another example of this in chapter 15.

In this chapter are three parables, given in a sequence in order to respond to the accusation that Jesus 'welcomes sinners and eats with them' (Luke 15:2). The first two parables of the lost sheep and the lost coin both end with the invitation to 'Rejoice with me' for the lost has been found (vv. 6, 9). To both these parables are added the 'Just so' sayings, both about joy in heaven over a sinner who repents. These two short parables set the scene for the third longer parable. The older brother, like the Pharisees and the scribes of verses 1–2, will not join in the celebration when his brother returns home. The father tells the older brother that his brother 'was lost and has been found' (v. 32), a clear connection with the first two parables. But in a dramatic climax, we do not hear of the response of the older brother. Will he finally

[1] I have borrowed many of the following insights on Luke 24 from a sermon by R. C. Lucas.

join the celebration? Will he join in the joy in heaven over one sinner who repents? The challenge to the Pharisees and scribes remains hanging in the air. Note that here the third story depends on the build-up of the first two stories, and forms a natural climax to the chapter.

We find a similar climax in Luke 24, and the shape of the chapter and language used makes it clear that the uses of this chapter we have already looked at miss the point of the chapter. What are the verbal and theological links that tie the chapter together, and provide its natural and unmistakable climax in the third story? The turning point of each of the three stories comes with a reference to previous teaching:

- In the first story the women perplexed by the empty tomb are addressed with these words by two men in dazzling clothes: '*Remember how he told you* . . . that the Son of Man must be handed over . . . crucified . . . and on the third day rise again' (24:6–7).
- In the second story, Jesus speaks these words to the two disciples:

  > 'Oh, how foolish you are, and how slow of heart to believe *all that the prophets have declared*! Was it not necessary that the Messiah should suffer these things and then enter into his glory?' Then beginning with *Moses and all the prophets*, he interpreted to them the things about himself in all the scriptures. (24:25–26)

  (In the first story the two men remind the women of what *Jesus* has told them, and in this second story Jesus reminds the disciples of what *Moses and the prophets* have told them).
- In the third story the disciples are not brought to confident faith by the appearance of the risen Christ, even when he shows them his wounds, and eats some fish! How are they convinced? In this story the notion of *Jesus'* teaching, from the first story, and *Moses'* teaching, from the second story, are combined in these words:

  > These are *my words* that I spoke to you while I was still with you – that everything written about me in the *law of Moses, the prophets, and the psalms* must be fulfilled. (24:44)

  Then, in case anyone has missed the point, we have this summary of the content of *Jesus' and Moses'* teaching:

> Thus it is written, that the Messiah is to suffer and to rise from the dead on the third day, and that repentance and forgiveness of sins is to be proclaimed in his name to all nations, beginning from Jerusalem. (24:46–47)

So the teaching of the three stories reaches its climax in the third story, where the origin and content of the gospel is made clear. The gospel is foretold in the Old Testament and in Jesus' teaching, and its content is the suffering, death and resurrection of the Messiah/Son of Man, and the proclamation of repentance and forgiveness in his name to all nations. The point of the chapter is not just the resurrection of Christ, but the resurrection of Christ as part of the gospel. And the basis for faith is not the empty tomb, an experience of the risen Christ, or the breaking of bread, but the trustworthiness of both the Old Testament and Jesus' teaching. 'Each episode sets forth the witness of prophecy as the sufficient and only persuasive evidence for the resurrection' (Ellis 1966: 271).

This of course is good news to Theophilus, who was too late to see the empty tomb, and too late to meet the risen Christ. Yet Theophilus can have 'certain faith'. What is good news for Theophilus is good news for any who want certain faith, to know the truth of what they have been taught about the Lord Jesus Christ. For anyone can read or hear read the Old Testament and Jesus' teaching, and have both the Scriptures and their minds opened by God (24:32, 45). This is the true and certain spirituality of Luke 24.

Romans: Strengthened by gospel proclamation

John Goldingay has told us that Romans is 'the basic text for evangelical spirituality', used alike by J. I. Packer, Martyn Lloyd-Jones, John Stott and Watchman Nee (Goldingay 1992: 3). In fact for many, Romans 1 – 8 is the part of the letter they know best, and, in practice, *is* the letter. This is of course a trap, for chapters 9 – 16 describe the practical spirituality meant to flow from chapters 1 – 8. What happens when these two parts of Romans are separated? I think we can identify three applications of Romans 1 – 8 in current Evangelical spirituality, each of which has some truth in it, but each of which misses the point of the letter.

Romans as the key to the Christian life

This use of Romans focuses on chapters 5 – 8, and is concerned to articulate what is normal Christian life and experience. Of course Evangelicals differ in their interpretation of these chapters. Are we in fact free from sin? Does chapter 7 describe Christian living? What is life in the Spirit? The focus is on the life of the individual believer, and these chapters are read and then used as a key to normal Christian spirituality.

Romans as a doctrinal test

Here the focus is not on how we live, but on what we believe. It is the truth of the gospel that is the issue, and Romans 1 – 8 is read as defining that truth over against legalism, works-righteousness, and Christianity that does not focus absolute attention on Jesus Christ and his propitiatory death on the cross. I must believe this, and the church must believe this, for justification by faith is the doctrinal test of the church. As Luther told us, by this test the church either stands or falls.

Romans as an incentive for evangelism

Here the application of Romans is not 'How should I live the Christian life?' or 'What must I believe?', but rather, 'If this is the gospel, then I must ensure that others hear and believe in the Lord Jesus.' Because the gospel Paul proclaimed is the power of God for salvation for everyone who believes, then I must do my best to ensure that many others have an opportunity to hear and believe.

While living the Christian life, maintaining true doctrine and doing evangelism are all part of Christian obedience, the clarity and simplicity of these applications of Romans blind us to the use Paul himself makes of Romans 9 – 16. To make the most of Romans as a source of true spirituality, we need to pay close attention to chapters 9 – 16. When we do so, we find that the three uses of Romans 1 – 8 outlined above miss the mark, not least in their tendency to individualism. They state true Christian duties, but do not reflect Paul's intention in this book.

We can engage in a very simple exercise that will help us see at a glance the application Paul makes of Romans 1 – 8 by noting some of the imperatives of chapters 9 – 16.

- [You Gentiles] do not vaunt yourselves over the branches [the Jews]. (11:18)
- Do not become proud, but stand in awe. (11:20)
- Note then the kindness and the severity of God. (11:22)

The application of the final words of chapter 8, '[nothing] will be able to separate us from the love of God in Christ Jesus our Lord' (8:39), is the issue of the salvation of Jews and Gentiles. Paul wants his readers to trust in God's electing love, and to remember how God's gospel plan is being worked out. The application is that Gentiles should not think themselves superior to the Jews, nor take the covenant kindness of God for granted.

- Present your bodies as a living sacrifice . . . Do not be conformed to this world . . . [do not] think of yourself more highly than you ought to think . . . [for we] are one body in Christ. (12:1, 2, 3, 5)

The application is not how the individual Christian should offer himself or herself to God, but on how to do this as a member of the body. In chapters 9 – 11 the application is concerned with how we respond to God as members of our Jewish or Gentile community: here the application is how we respond to God as a member of the church, the body of Christ. In the imperatives that follow, Paul encourages believers to use their gifts in mutual service, in prophecy, ministry, teaching, exhortation, giving, leadership and compassion (12:6–8).

- Let every person be subject to the governing authorities . . . Pay to all what is due to them . . . taxes . . . revenue . . . respect . . . honour. (13:1, 7)

Here the message is about how we live in human society, respecting government, and all to whom honour is due under God. This spirituality of living as positive members of our society for God is not found in any of the three uses of Romans 1 – 8 outlined above!

- Put on the Lord Jesus Christ, and make no provision for the flesh, to gratify its desires. (13:14)

Yes, here there is an application that reflects one of the uses, that of how to live the Christian life. It is interesting to see how Paul applies some of the teaching of those earlier chapters.

- Welcome those who are weak in faith, but not for the purpose of quarrelling over opinions . . . Who are you to pass judgement on servants of another? (14:1, 4)

- Welcome one another, therefore, just as Christ has welcomed you, for the glory of God. (15:7)

The long section 14:1 to 15:13 is on the theme of welcoming others who have a different practice of the Christian life, and different beliefs that underlie that practice. We might have thought that the application of justification by faith would be 'Know that you are accepted': but here we find that it is 'Know that other believers who have a different practice of the Christian life are accepted, and accept them.' We might have thought that Paul would have instructed the strong in faith either to correct the weak in faith, or to cast them out of the pure church. Instead he tells them to welcome them, even if it involves personal discomfort, after the example of Christ (15:3)! The application of justification by faith is here not doctrinal rigour and practical uniformity, but knowing God's grace for others in the church who are different. Later we read a warning to beware of 'those who cause dissensions and offences, in opposition to the teaching that you have learned' (16:17). But this does not nullify Paul's previous teaching in chapters 14 and 15, and may reinforce it.

In other letters Paul does call for doctrinal clarity and discipline, and this is a duty of the church and its leaders. But Paul does not call for it in Romans, and we therefore should not use this letter for another agenda. The application of justification by faith in Romans is not that we should correct others, but that we should accept them!

- Greet Prisca and Aquilla . . . Greet also the church in their house . . . Greet my beloved Epaenetus . . . Greet Mary . . . Greet Andronicus and Junia . . . Greet Tryphaena and Tryphosa . . . Greet the beloved Persis . . . (16:3–12)

These are not Paul's greetings to these friends and fellow-workers, but Paul's instructions to the believers at Rome to greet those whom he names, those of their own fellowship. Perhaps Paul wants them to recognize those who are valuable to him, and who are working hard for God among them. In these chapters Paul does not make an explicit appeal to the Romans to do evangelism, though he does want the Romans to send him on his journey to Spain (15:24), he does explain his gospel strategy (chs. 9 – 11, 15), and he does want them to honour gospel workers. In this way he wants them to join in God's gospel strategy for the world, and to support it.

The spirituality of Romans is far richer than the reductions popular among us. All we need to do is to read the whole book as Paul wrote it, and we will soon understand, teach and practise the spirituality Paul intended.

In Romans Paul certainly has great expectations of words. By words the gospel is proclaimed, which is the power of God for salvation for everyone who has faith (1:16). This gospel is attested by the law and the prophets (3:21). Abraham's faith is responsive to the spoken promise of God (4:13, 17, 18, 20, 21). It is by words that the truth about the gospel is made clear, as Paul describes the wrath of God, the all-pervading sinfulness of humanity, and the great work of God in providing his Son to be the sacrifice of atonement by his blood to be received by faith. The gospel brings assurance of justification, freedom from the law, sin and death, the presence, work and witness of the Spirit, adoption as God's children, and the confidence that God will achieve his saving purpose in his saints, and that nothing can separate them from God's love in Christ Jesus. As Christ is proclaimed, both Jews and Gentiles come to faith in him, for 'faith comes from what is heard, and what is heard comes through the word of Christ' (10:17).

As the Romans receive Paul's words they will be strengthened by this proclamation of the gospel, and their spirituality will be marked by faith and obedience in every area of their lives. This is the fruit of Paul's gospel, the proclamation of Jesus Christ. May this fruit be found in our churches today.

Colossians: Let the word of Christ dwell in you richly

A helpful way of thinking about many New Testament documents is to see them as debates about the nature of true Christian spirituality. This approach is clearly useful in studying Colossians. We should not think of a 'Colossian heresy', as if it were the thought-out and articulated product of theologians. It was a way of living the Christian life that differed in some important ways from that taught by Paul. Those who practised it claimed that their way represented a full or complete spirituality, and perhaps they suggested that those who held on to Paul's model needed to gain a higher and fuller spirituality. Paul's reply is to present full Christian spirituality found in Christ, which is why he uses the language of 'fullness' and 'fulfilled'. He urges the Colossians not to move away from a spirituality based on full gospel truth of the fullness of God in Christ.

I believe that the spirituality found in Colossians is of great value and relevance today. Here is an outline of that spirituality. For the sake of convenience and clarity I have summarized this material in thirty lessons in true spirituality.

1. Paul writes 'to the saints and faithful brothers and sisters in Christ in Colossae' (1:2). This is not spirituality for an elite group, but common spirituality for the ordinary members of the church at Colossae. They are 'saints', made holy by God, and they are 'faithful brothers and sisters' as they respond to God in faith.
2. Paul writes that he has heard of 'your faith in Christ Jesus', the 'love that you have for all the saints' and their 'hope laid up for you in heaven' (1:4–5). Paul's famous triad of faith, love and hope is for him a sign of authentic Christianity.

   While we might focus on faith, or on love (in the West we are unlikely to focus on hope!), Paul looks for all three. These three mark the new loyalties of believers: their 'faith' is in Christ, they 'love' Christ's people, and their 'hope' is to share in Christ's future at his return. Nothing more and nothing less than faith, love and hope are marks of authentic Christian spirituality.
3. Paul notes that they are people of faith, love and hope because they are gospel people, because the gospel has born fruit in them (1:6). People do not have faith, love and hope because we urge them to do so. These are the fruit of the gospel, preached, heard and believed. This gospel Paul also describes as 'the word of the truth' and 'the grace of God' (1:5–6). It is a message, a 'word', spoken and heard. It is a true message, and it is the message of God's grace. Paul will fill out the content of this message later in this letter.
4. The Colossians learnt this message from 'Epaphras, our beloved fellow-servant' and 'a faithful minister of Christ' (1:7). The gospel is most often heard from a human messenger, and Paul wants the Colossians to value Epaphras and his ministry. Valuing the gospel messenger is a way of valuing the gospel.
5. Paul tells the Colossians that he has not ceased praying for them, that every time he prays for them he thanks God for them; and he also tells them what he is praying for them (1:3, 9). Unceasing intercessory prayer is fundamental to true spirituality. Thankfulness in prayer is an essential ingredient in intercession. Telling people what we pray for them is a way of doubling

the encouragement when God graciously grants what we pray. We are encouraged when our prayer is answered, and so are those for whom we pray. They receive what we pray, and they also know that God has answered our prayers for them.

6. Those who are people of faith in Christ, have love for the saints, and who have hope of heaven, still need to grow. It is 'For this reason' (1:9) that Paul continues to pray for them. What is the content of his prayer? It is that they will be 'filled with the knowledge of God's will', so that their lives are 'worthy of the Lord, fully pleasing to him', that they bear fruit in every good work, and that they endure and keep on giving thanks to God (1:9–12). Paul's prayer is optimistic, and his view of what kinds of lives can be lived by ordinary believers is very moving. It is a great model of prayer for genuine gospel spiritual growth in fellow-believers.
7. As Paul's thanksgiving for the Colossians is gospel-focused, so also he prays that they will be people who are thankful to God, and whose thankfulness is focused on the gospel. When Paul's prayer is answered, they will be 'joyfully giving thanks to the Father, who has enabled you to share in the inheritance of the saints in the light. He has rescued us from the power of darkness and transferred us into the kingdom of his beloved Son, in whom we have redemption, the forgiveness of sins' (1:11–14). Spiritual growth never goes beyond gospel thankfulness for forgiveness in Christ. Gospel thankfulness is the summit of Christian experience and spirituality on earth.
8. Paul next reminds the Colossians of the significance of Jesus Christ, God's Son (1:15–20). True spirituality is full of Christ, and looks to no other person, mediator or spiritual force. True spirituality is full of Christ, because 'in him all the fullness of God was pleased to dwell' (1:19).
9. Christ is also 'the image of the invisible God' (1:15). Biblical spirituality acknowledges the invisibility of God, the unique status of Christ as the revealer of the invisible God, and the marvel of Christ's work in us, removing the old self and renewing us to be what we were meant to be, so that we can live as images of our creator, with old distinctions broken down, as we recognize that Christ is in all believers (3:11).
10. Full spirituality is full of Christ's dignity, his supreme status and his work in creating and sustaining the universe. For 'in him all things in heaven and earth were created . . . all things have been created through him and for him . . . in him all things hold

together', as also all things are reconciled in him (1:16–17, 20). The supremacy of Christ in creation is fundamental to true Christian spirituality, because if his role and significance in creation is diminished, then fear of created beings, false reverence for them, or a destructive asceticism may well abound (2:8, 20–25). A 'Christless' universe soon becomes a universe opposed to fully Christ-based, Christ-sufficient and Christ-centred spirituality.

11. If true spirituality must know Christ's supremacy in creation, so too it must know of his supremacy in redemption. This is evident in four ways: Christ is the head of church, the firstborn from the dead, all the fullness of God dwells in him, and through him and his death on the cross God has reconciled all things to himself (1:18–20). Here we see Christ's humanity (head and firstborn), his divinity (all the fullness of God in him), and his saving work (reconciliation by his blood shed on the cross). Christian spirituality will focus on these central truths about Christ, and not on the details of his life, such as a particular miracle, way of relating to an individual, healing or teaching.
12. The striking measure of Christ's work of reconciliation on the cross is found in believers. It is not that we are people with a perfectly formed God-shaped blank, ready to be filled. Nor are we those with a deep and perfectly formed hunger, waiting to be filled. Paul says that we were estranged, estranged from God, hostile in mind: our thinking was opposed to God, and we were doing evil deeds – our actions were opposed to God (1:21).

    Christ's work of reconciliation is so radical, extensive, powerful and effective that those who were estranged, hostile and doing evil, will one day be presented 'holy and blameless and irreproachable before him' (1:22). How great is Christ's work on the cross, to take people who are so far from God, and bring them so close to God. True spirituality will marvel at God's grace and power in Christ, and the breathtaking change he achieves for us and in us.
13. One way in which God works to preserve us and keep us so that we will be presented 'holy and blameless and irreproachable before him' (1:22) is by urging us as Paul urges the Colossians to 'continue securely established and steadfast in the faith, without shifting from the hope promised by the gospel', that is, the gospel Paul serves (1:23). Orthodoxy serves gospel perseverance, not human pride. True spirituality is marked by standing firm in the universal gospel taught by Paul. Beware the 'journey' that leads

away from this gospel: it also leads away from being presented holy to God by Christ.

14. Paul is a 'servant of this gospel' (1:23), and also 'servant' of 'the church' (1:24–25). No room for introspective or self-centred spirituality here. No room for serving the gospel but refusing to serve the church. No room for serving the church but refusing to serve God's gospel plan for the world. Paul serves the gospel *by* serving the church, and serves the church *by* serving the gospel, and so should we.
15. 'I am now rejoicing in my sufferings for your sake' (1:24). How does Paul serve the gospel and the church? By receiving the sufferings inflicted on him in the course of doing his ministry. When Paul was converted and commissioned on the Damascus road, he was told how much he would suffer for the sake of Jesus' name (Acts 9:16). The idea that we might serve the gospel by suffering for it is unpopular today. Paul's spirituality included suffering for gospel ministry. This was suffering for the sake of others, not suffering for his own sake. Suffering, if somewhat muted today, is a familiar theme in traditional spirituality.
16. 'What is lacking in Christ's afflictions' (1:24) does not refer to Paul contributing to Christ's redemptive suffering on the cross, but to the suffering endured by the people of God as they wait for Christ's return. Whereas many spiritualities confuse the suffering of Christ's atoning sacrifice with the sufferings of God's people, Paul does not confuse them. The word he uses here for 'sufferings' he does not use of Christ's saving sufferings. Those in gospel ministry suffer in their ministry, but do not make atonement for their sins.
17. In Colossians 1:26–27 Paul writes of a 'mystery'. When many writers use this word today, they usually mean something mysterious or hidden. For Paul, a 'mystery' is a mystery that has been revealed, as here. The content of this mystery, long hidden but now revealed, is that God will not only bless the Gentiles, but that Christ will be found 'in' (or better 'among') them (1:27). Paul's preoccupation is God's gospel plan for all the nations, an idea often regarded as an optional extra by Christians today. What a pity if the search for spirituality distracts us from taking part in God's big gospel plan! This plan is at the centre of Paul's spirituality, as it should be at the centre of ours.
18. What part does being warned and taught play in your spirituality? For Paul, warning everyone and teaching everyone is the

necessary process in order to present everyone mature in Christ (1:28). I suspect that warning and teaching are unfamiliar themes in most versions of Christian spirituality, but that is their loss, and the loss of those who follow them. Notice too the word 'everyone', used three times in 1:28. Movements of Christian spirituality are often elitist, with time and energy spent on the promising few. Paul's aim is to 'present everyone mature in Christ' (1:28). Paul is more like a godly local church preacher and teacher working for the maturity of the body of Christ than a spiritual director who works with a few interested people.

19. There is no place for effortless ministry in Paul, no secret of 'letting go and letting God', no secret of instant success without hard work: 'For this I toil and struggle' (1:29), and 'For I want you to know how much I am struggling for you' (2:1). Paul's toil and struggle is not a sign that God is not working: on the contrary, Paul's continued hard work is the sign that God *is* at work: 'I toil and struggle with all the energy that he powerfully inspires within me' (1:29).

    Paul has not found the secret of struggle-free ministry. Nor does he hide his struggling from the Colossians; in fact he wants them to know it. How is Paul struggling to warn and teach the Colossians, whom he has not met? By writing to them. Paul finds writing this letter a struggle, as he works to proclaim Christ in a way that will bring change to the Colossians. Let us not listen to those siren voices offering superspiritual results without the hard work of preaching Christ, warning and teaching everyone with all wisdom (1:28–29).

20. In 2:6–7 we come to the heart of the Christ-centred spirituality Paul wants for the Colossians. It will be theirs if they (a) continue to live in Christ, rooted strongly in him; (b) remain established in the faith, the gospel they were taught; and (c) abound in thanksgiving.

    God's remedies against falling away from Christ are living in Christ, holding fast to the faith and abounding in thanksgiving. Are these the three remedies you use every day? Pious Christians use the first, orthodox Christians the second, and enthusiastic Christians the third. God through Paul tells us to use all three! Let us continue to live in Christ, remain established in the faith and abound in thanksgiving!

21. Paul gives the reason for continuing in Christ in 2:9–10. It is because the whole fullness of deity dwells bodily in Christ, and

so 'you have come to fullness in him' (2:10). When we already have the fullness of God in Christ, why would we want to look anywhere else?

This is the context for his warning in 2:4, 8, that the Colossians may be deceived by plausible arguments, or be taken captive through philosophy and empty deceit. Discernment is a virtue in spirituality: gullibility leaves us open to being deceived. It is not the case that all spiritual roads lead to Christ. Theological caution is a key ingredient in true Christian spirituality. Those who put their discerning minds in neutral are sure to be deceived. We are called to that spiritual chastity, that self-discipline and self-restraint that is a prerequisite for a pure devotion to Christ.

22. Asceticism, self-denial, self-punishment and moral severity have often been marks of Christian spirituality, especially when there has been deep awareness of personal sin. It appears that the Colossians were aware of their tendency to sin and self-indulgence, but were using wrong methods to find relief. The Colossian package seems to have included circumcision (2:11–15), laws about food, drink and religious festivals (2:16), the self-abasement before angels and visions (2:18), and strict regulations about what must not be handled, tasted or touched (2:22).

Paul has three objections to this spirituality:

- It takes people's attention away from Christ, his death, resurrection and forgiveness (2:12–13), his headship of his body the church (2:19), and his supremacy over all powers (2:10, 20).
- It makes people live in shadowland, that Old Testament period when God gave shadows that pointed forward to Christ. These shadows included circumcision, rules about food and drink, and religious festivals, including the sabbath.
- It is earth-bound, making people focus on objects, experiences, religious activities on the earth. But Christ is seated at the right hand of God, and we should raise our eyes of faith to him (3:1–4). To be heaven-focused, rather than earth-focused, is to turn to Christ by faith. We should look to Christ, who is at the place of greatest power and honour in the universe, at God's right hand.

23. The Colossians were right to look for moral change as a practical result of their spirituality. Their mistake was to confuse earth-bound symbols with heavenly realities. Because we died and were

raised and made alive with Christ (2:12–13), and because therefore our life is hidden with Christ in God (3:3), we can make moral changes in our daily lives by the power of his death and resurrection.

These moral changes will be first negative, then positive. First we will put to death fornication, greed, anger, slander and so on (3:5–9), and then we can put on compassion, kindness, humility and so on (3:12–15). True spiritual moral change will need to be both negative (putting things to death) and positive (putting on virtues). The order seems to be important in this spirituality of moral change. Is this part of your daily spirituality? Are you looking to Christ in heaven, and using the power of his death and resurrection to put to death whatever is earthly? Are you then looking to Christ for power to put on new habits of godly living?

24. 'The peace of Christ . . . to which indeed you were called in the one body' (3:15). For many, spiritual peace is individual or even solitary peace, and spirituality is a search for that peace. Indeed many people use God as a means to gain a feeling of peace. When that happens, it means we are really serving peace, not God. Here in Colossians 'the peace of Christ' is body-peace, Christ's peace ruling in his body, the church. What is corporate in the Bible we individualize to our loss. It would be an irony to cause division in the church, or to separate from the church, because we wanted to keep our own inner peace!
25. How does 'the word of Christ' dwell 'richly' in us (3:16)? Not by ever longer sermons from the minister, but when all the members of the church teach and admonish each other in all wisdom. Paul has his distinctive ministry of warning and teaching (1:28), but so here do the members of the church. Is mutual teaching and admonishing part of your church life? The corporate spirituality of the church is of first importance to Paul, and the focus of almost all of his letters. Individual spirituality flourishes best when corporate spirituality is in good condition, and this happens when 'the word of Christ' dwells richly among us.
26. Be thankful! Have you noticed how often Paul encourages the Colossians to thankfulness? Look at the following: 'joyfully giving thanks to the Father' (1:11–12), 'abounding in thanksgiving' (2:7), 'be thankful' (3:15), 'with gratitude . . . sing' (3:16), 'whatever you do . . . giving thanks' (3:17). He doesn't write, 'remember that you ought to be thankful', or 'feel thankful'; he writes, 'be thankful'.

Sustained thankfulness, expressed extravagantly and openly, personally and corporately, in word and in song, is a key to spiritual health, because it is the right way to respond to God's grace in Jesus Christ.

27. True spirituality involves recognizing our reciprocal responsibilities in our daily lives and relationships, for Christ's sake (note how often the Lord is referred to in 3:18 – 4:1). Our natural tendency is to read these verses to find out what others owe us! We should read them to find what we owe others!
28. Daily work, even the most humble, is a way in which we 'serve the Lord Christ' (3:24). Some spirituality can be so 'spiritual' that it despises daily work, the kind of work slaves did in Paul's day. True spirituality is expressed in daily work as well as in our praise and thanksgiving. Our paid and unpaid daily work is one way in which we serve and honour the living Lord Jesus Christ.
29. Devoted and alert prayer, with thanksgiving (4:2) is our duty and joy. There are some forms of spirituality that regard petition and intercession, praying for others and for ourselves, as the lowest form of prayer. They speak contemptuously of 'shopping-list prayers'. But Jesus himself gave us a 'shopping-list prayer' that included prayer for our 'daily bread'! And Paul gives specific prayer requests, namely an open door for the word (in prison), and that he may reveal it boldly (4:3). We may pray that people get out of prison: Paul prays for boldness in prison for gospel proclamation!
30. Epaphras is a model for strenuous prayer: 'He is always wrestling in his prayers on your behalf, so that you may stand mature and fully assured in everything that God wills' (4:12). So much for prayer as a relaxation exercise! Epaphras had to wrestle in prayer because his prayer was so ambitious, a rebuke to our sometimes limited and apathetic prayers. 'Big prayers for a big God' is a good motto, and strenuous prayer is the price.

    And how good to know that as Paul was 'wrestling' in his ministry (1:29; 2:1), Epaphras was 'wrestling' in his prayer for the same purpose: everyone mature in Christ. Ambitious and hard-working ministry needs the backing of ambitious and hard-working prayer!

    May the word of Christ dwell richly in our churches.

Hebrews: God has spoken

The God of the letter to the Hebrews is, from first to last, the God who speaks. The book begins, 'Long ago God spoke to our ancestors in many and various ways by the prophets, but in these last days he has spoken to us by a Son' (1:1–2). And we read in chapter 12, 'See that you do not refuse the one who is speaking' (12:25).

The natural model for God's revelation is that of speaking, that powerful metaphor of communication of truth and the establishing of relationship. God is fundamentally a speaking God, and these verses convey the variety of God's communication, its movement from the diversity of the Old Testament to the unity of the New, and to the focus of God's revelation in his Son. The revelation of God in the Son is the theme of Hebrews, this revelation promised in the Old Testament and fulfilled in the New. Christ is shown to be our great High Priest and once-for-all sacrifice, who makes 'purification for sins' (1:3). God has spoken through his Son, who declared the great salvation he came to bring; this message was attested to by those who heard him, and passed on to the writer and his friends (2:3). Because God has spoken through his Son, 'we must pay greater attention to what we have heard, so that we do not drift away from it' (2:1), and make sure that we do not refuse the one who speaks.

We should not think that the words God has spoken to us by a Son imply that God's action through his Son is merely explanatory, as if all that were needed for New Covenant life were more information or encouragement. God's words not only explain; they also achieve. Or better, they both achieve and explain what they have achieved. They are performative speech-acts, not just information. God's speaking through his Son achieves the work of perfecting his people through Jesus' work as priest and sacrifice in his atoning death. God's speaking through many and various ways in the Old Testament, and through the words of Hebrews, encourage us to trust in and look to Jesus, the pioneer and perfecter of faith (12:2). 'God's self-disclosure is therefore primarily understood as given in audible, as over against visual, terms' (Hughes 1979: 6).

In Hebrews 1:1–3 it is clear that God's Old Testament 'speaking' involves more than words. It was 'in many and various ways'; and to say that 'he has spoken to us by a Son' is to use the metaphor of language to indicate the importance and effectiveness of God's revelation through the Lord Jesus. This metaphorical use is also found in John 1, where the Son is described as the 'Word' (John 1:1, 14). Words and speaking must be powerful if this metaphor of language is used to describe the incarnation and its effects.

'Speaking' is a powerful metaphor because words are so characteristic of effective communication. The way in which God communicates the significance of his Son, his person and work is through words, of which Hebrews itself is such a powerful example. And while the language of 1:1–2 implies a contrast between God's speaking in the Old and New Covenants, there is also continuity, as the Old Testament is such a rich source for us to understand the meaning of the Son.

The words of God are the means that God uses to establish, build, maintain or restore relationship with his people. In a primary sense the Old Testament is that word of God, not just for the people of the Old Covenant, but also for the people of the New. God is the one who speaks through the Old Testament. This is made clear as the words of the Old Testament are attributed to the Father, the Son and the Spirit: in chapters 1, 2 and 3:

- In 1:5 the words of the psalm and 2 Samuel are attributed to God the Father as addressing his Son: 'You are my Son: / today I have begotten you' and, 'I will be his Father, / and he will be my Son.'
- In 2:13 the words of Isaiah are attributed to the Son, Jesus: 'I will put my trust in him,' and, 'Here am I and the children whom God has given me.'
- In 3:7–8 the words of Psalm 95 are attributed to the Holy Spirit: 'As the Holy Spirit says, / "Today, if you hear his voice, / do not harden your hearts as in the rebellion"'.

The writer clearly accepts that God is the author of the Old Testament. Since the God who speaks in the Old Testament is the one later revealed as Father, Son and Holy Spirit, it is perfectly reasonable to attribute those words to the Father or the Son or the Spirit.

At the same time, the writer of Hebrews does not take words from the Old Testament out of their historical context, but notes the significance of that context, and of their human authors. So, while in 3:7 we read, 'Therefore, as the Holy Spirit says, / "Today, if you hear his voice"', in 4:7 the same quotation is introduced with these words: 'saying through David much later, in the words already quoted, "Today . . . if you hear his voice"'. Indeed the argument of chapter 4 about the 'rest' available to the people of God depends on taking each Old Testament quotation in its context. Here both the human author and his setting in Old Testament history are crucial to the argument of Hebrews. Hughes comments, 'the greatest part of his exegetical work is built around the eminently sound principle of hearing what the scriptures have to say about themselves' (1979: 56).

For the author of Hebrews, the Old Testament is the contemporary word of God. For it is, 'as the Holy Spirit says' (introducing the words of Ps. 95), and in 10:15, 'the Holy Spirit also testifies to us' (introducing the words of Jer. 31). We should not think that the Old Testament is obsolete: God speaks now through its words, and reveals his Son to us, and calls us to respond in faith and obedience to him. The Word of God is not dead, powerless or ineffective: 'Indeed, the word of God is living and active, sharper than any two-edged sword, piercing until it divides soul from spirit, joints from marrow; it is able to judge the thoughts and intentions of the heart' (4:12).

What then are the alien words that might seduce the readers away to a false spirituality? Quite simply, they are the words of the Old Testament read without Jesus Christ, or 'Christless' Old Testament spirituality. It is to hold to the shadow, and miss the substance. Calvin pointed out so clearly how instructive it is to see that the relationship between the Old and New Testaments is that of both continuity and contrast. He first claims the continuity: 'They had and knew Christ as Mediator, through whom they were joined to God and were to share in his promises' (*Institutes* 2.10.2). He then asserts the contrast: in the Old Testament the heavenly heritage of the people of God is displayed under earthly benefits, whereas under the New 'the Lord leads our minds to meditate upon it directly' (*Institutes* 2.11.1).

It is especially instructive to reflect on the contrasts between the spirituality described in the Old and that of the New. We can see three such contrasts in Hebrews.

The first is that of Old Testament 'shadow' and Christ's 'substantial' ministry. The 'shadow' is Old Testament earthly ministry. So he describes the earthly ministry of the priests in these terms: 'They offer worship in a sanctuary that is a sketch and shadow of the heavenly one' (Heb. 8:5). Here the contrast is between the shadow on earth and the reality in heaven, that heavenly sanctuary which is the place of Christ's ministry: 'we have such a high priest who is seated at the right hand of the throne of the Majesty in the heavens, a minister in the sanctuary and the true tent that the Lord, and not any mortal, has set up' (8:1–2). So therefore 'Jesus has now obtained a more excellent ministry . . . which has been enacted through better promises' (8:6).

The contrast is that of time as well as place: 'Since the law has only a shadow of the good things to come and not the true form of these realities, it can never, by the same sacrifices that are continually offered year after year, make perfect those who approach' (10:1).

Here:

> [T]he language may be Platonic, but the idea is strictly temporal in accordance with Jewish and Christian eschatology . . . for the Platonic model earthly phenomena are the forms which correspond with the eternal ideas, whereas for Hebrews they are partial and temporary manifestations of God's intentions. (Lindars 1991: 51)

The role of the shadow, and its connection with what Paul in Colossians calls the substance (Col. 2:17), is an important one for spirituality. The writer of Hebrews explains that the earthly sanctuary built by Moses was made according to the pattern that he was shown on the mountain, a sketch and shadow of the heavenly one (8:5), as we have seen. So the physical sanctuary, the objects it contained, and the ministry offered in it have only a temporary role, that of pointing *forward* to the coming of Christ, and *upward* to his heavenly ministry. Holy places, objects and people on earth are part of the God-provided shadow, which is fulfilled in Christ. So true Christian spirituality, what Hebrews calls 'perfection' (10:14), or the 'better' (8:6), is not found in earthly places, objects or people; it is found by faith in our great High Priest, his once-for-all sacrifice, and his intercession for us at the right hand of God. The writer of Hebrews has his strongest warnings for those who would retreat from 'perfection', from the 'better'. For, turning away from Christ and his atonement invites God's judgment. This leads us to the next contrast.

The second contrast is that of earth and heaven. This contrast comes out of the shadow–substance contrast we have already seen, but goes beyond it. A superficial reading of Hebrews 11 might lead to the idea that the people of God in the Old Testament were given the land, whereas the people of God in the New Testament are promised a heavenly inheritance. In fact the contrast is more subtle than this, and provides continuity as well as contrast: 'By faith Abraham obeyed when he was called to set out for a place that he was to receive as an inheritance . . . By faith he stayed for a long time in the land he had been promised, as in a foreign land, living in tents . . .' (Heb. 11:8–9). Then the substance of Abraham's faith is revealed: 'For he looked forward to the city which has foundations, whose architect and builder is God' (11:10). The point is made clearer when all the people of Abraham are described: 'All of these died in faith without having received the promises, but from a distance they saw and greeted them . . . they desire a better country, that is, a heavenly one . . .' (11:13, 16).

So those Old Testament saints saw the same inheritance that is ours, a city whose architect and builder is God, a heavenly country. When they looked at the land, they saw beyond it to what it represented, their heavenly inheritance. As Calvin wrote, 'in the earthly possession they enjoyed, they looked, as in a mirror, upon the future inheritance they believed to have been prepared for them in heaven' (*Institutes* 2.11.1). This explains the ending of that great chapter 11 of Hebrews: 'Yet all these, though they were commended for their faith, did not receive what was promised, since God had prepared something better so that they would not, without us, be made perfect' (11:39–40).

The contrast between earth and heaven is most clearly seen in chapter 12, between Mount Sinai, representing the Old Covenant, and the heavenly Mount Zion, representing the New. The point of the contrast is that Mount Sinai was the place of the people's deliverance, and the making of the Old Covenant, but Mount Zion (or Jerusalem) was their heavenly destination as the people of God. Mount Sinai represents something that may be touched, and a frightening voice whose hearers begged that not another word be spoken to them, where even Moses was trembling with fear. Mount Zion is the city of the living God, the heavenly Jerusalem, the assembly of the firstborn, and where we meet Jesus the mediator of a new covenant, and his sprinkled blood. So, for all true believers in both Old Testament and New, their true home is in heaven, with Jesus, and their true hope is in his sprinkled blood.

The point is that even those who had what we might regard as an 'earthly spirituality', namely land and prosperity, looked beyond that to their heavenly reward, to Jesus and his atonement. This leads to the next contrast.

The third contrast is between lesser and greater privilege. The contrast is put most graphically in these words: 'See that you do not refuse the one who is speaking; for if they did not escape when they refused the one who warned them on earth, how much less will we escape if we reject the one who warns from heaven!' (12:25).

This contrast builds on the general idea that greater blessing brings greater responsibility, and greater responsibility brings with it the danger of greater judgment. Whereas we might have expected that the Old–New contrast would have been between judgment and mercy, here the point is that the New represents greater blessing, so greater responsibility, so greater judgment. So also:

> Anyone who has violated the law of Moses dies without mercy 'on the testimony of two of three witnesses.' How much worse punishment do you think will be deserved by those who have spurned the Son of God, profaned the blood of the covenant by which they were sanctified, and outraged the Spirit of grace? (10:28–29)

So in chapter 12 the contrast is between God's voice shaking the earth at Mount Sinai and his warning from heaven that 'Yet once more I will shake not only the earth but also the heaven' (12:26), for 'our God is a consuming fire' (12:29). True spirituality takes these warnings seriously. As we look to a heavenly inheritance and a heavenly salvation in our great High Priest, so we hear the one who warns us from heaven, and do not refuse the God who speaks.

As the writer of Hebrews wants his readers to respond to his words, and the word of God, so he also makes clear the result of the failure to heed God's words. Those who will be impossible to restore to repentance are those who have 'tasted the goodness of the word of God' and 'then have fallen away' (6:5–6). His readers have become 'dull in understanding', literally 'dull in hearing' (5:11). He writes so that 'you may not become sluggish [literally 'dull' in hearing], but imitators of those who through faith and patience inherit the promises' (6:12).

Notice what kind of spirituality the writer of Hebrews wants. They will come to God through Christ and his atoning death as priest and sacrifice. They will offer God acceptable worship with reverence and awe (12:28), as they continue in mutual love, keep their lives free from the love of money, remember their leaders, are not carried away by all kinds of strange teachings, do good and share what they have, obey their leaders, and pray for the writer and his friends (13:1, 5, 7, 9, 16, 17, 18).

It is also evident that he expects those who are taught to be teachers of others. We learnt from 5:11–14 that the readers have these four characteristics: they are dull in hearing, unable to teach others, unskilled in the word of righteousness and like children. The writer wants them to be quick to learn, able to teach others, trained to distinguish good from evil and mature. The contrast between infants and those who are mature could not be clearer. So too God's remedy for the deceitfulness of sin is that they should 'exhort one another every day' (3:13), and they are also told to engage in 'encouraging one another, and all the more as you see the Day approaching' (10:25).

We should not think that the message of the book is mere moralism: 'Keep on doing what God tells you to do.' For the purpose of the book is to draw the readers to Christ, their great High Priest, and to the forgiveness of their sins, the benefit of the New Covenant. The application of the message is:

> [S]ince we have confidence to enter the sanctuary by the blood of Jesus, by the new and living way that he opened for us through the curtain (that is, through his flesh), and since we have a great priest over the house of God, let us approach with a true heart in full assurance of faith . . . (10:19–22)

If the warning in chapter 12 is 'See that you do not refuse the one who is speaking' (12:25), the encouragement is 'let us give thanks, by which we offer to God an acceptable worship with reverence and awe' (12:28). The words of God through the Old Testament and through the writer of Hebrews are intended to bring back his people to faith in Christ, and so to fellowship 'with a true heart in full assurance of faith', to the very presence of God (10:22). Do not refuse the God who speaks!

1 Peter: The living and enduring word of God

What is the spirituality of the Word in 1 Peter? We can summarize it by looking at the five chapters

1 Peter 1: Born again through the word

Peter is the preacher of the new birth:

- The original cause of the new birth is the 'great mercy' of the 'God and Father of our Lord Jesus Christ' (3).
- The historical origin and power for the new birth is 'the resurrection of Jesus Christ from the dead' (3).
- The immediate cause is 'You have been born anew, not of perishable but of imperishable seed, through the living and abiding word of God' (23), that is, 'the good news that was announced to you' (25). The immediate cause of new birth is the word of the gospel.

- The human response to the new birth is 'you have purified your souls by your obedience to the truth' (22).

Peter underlines the dramatic and great change that has taken place. Before their new birth his readers were 'conformed to the desires that you formerly had in ignorance' (14), caught up in 'the futile ways inherited from your ancestors' (18). Now they must 'be holy yourselves in all your conduct; for it is written, "You shall be holy, for I am holy"' (16).

1 Peter 2: Declaring the mighty acts of God

Peter teaches his readers the great dignity that is theirs in Christ: 'But you are a chosen race, a royal priesthood, a holy nation, God's own people' (9).

He then explains the wonderful result of this work of God in making them his own: 'in order that you may proclaim the mighty acts of him who called you out of darkness into his marvellous light' (9). To declare God's mighty acts will mean doing so in many contexts. They will do this when they address their praise to God; when they speak to each other of God's goodness to them; and when they speak of God to those who do not yet know him. Because God has acted and spoken, they too can speak of God's mighty acts in Christ.

1 Peter 3: Won without a word

Here Peter tackles the difficult situation of mixed marriages, where wives who are Christians have husbands who are not. Peter describes the non-Christian husbands as those who 'do not obey the word' (1), meaning, of course, the word of the good news, the gospel of Christ. He advises the wives to try to win over their husbands 'without a word' (1), that is, without aggressive verbal evangelism. Instead the husbands will be won over when they see 'the purity and reverence of your lives' (2). So although Peter has described that new birth happens by the word, and that Christians are to declare God's mighty acts, he wants wives to avoid using words in their struggle to bring their husbands to faith in Christ. This could not mean that the husbands will be won without anyone declaring the word to them. Someone else must do this, but wives should not, lest they seem to be not respecting their husbands (1, 5).

It is encouraging to read that Peter is optimistic about the conversion of these men; the hope of their wives is that they may be won for Christ and come to obey the word of the gospel. Later Peter shows how this principle is worked out in a different context, that of persecution: 'Always be ready to make your defence to anyone who demands from you an account for the hope that is in you; yet do it with gentleness and reverence' (15–16). Here again Peter reminds them of the kind of life and the model of ministry required, marked by gentleness and reverence.

1 Peter 4: Speaking the very words of God

Here Peter writes of the responsibilities all Christians have in serving each other and loving each other. He tells them to maintain constant love for each other (8), and then explains how this will be expressed in mutual service. He writes of two kinds of gifts, speaking and serving, by which he means speaking and practical actions of service:

> Like good stewards of the manifold grace of God, serve one another with whatever gift each of you has received. Whoever speaks must do so as one speaking the very words of God; whoever serves must do so with the strength that God supplies, so that God may be glorified in all things through Jesus Christ. (10–11)

Speaking is mentioned first, for Peter wants to build up the expectation that God will work among his people as they use their gifts, and that God will be glorified through their mutual service. There is an important parallel between speaking 'the very words of God' and serving 'with the strength that God supplies' (11). God is the source of both the words and the strength. Those who speak must make sure that what they speak is in accord with the word of God, the gospel (1:25); as those who serve must ensure that God is empowering them, so that they serve according to the instruction of God, and so by his power. Peter expects that the true words of God and the power of God will be shown in the mutual ministry of ordinary Christians.

1 Peter 5: Stand in the true grace of God

Here is a summary of the purpose of Peter's ministry of the Word: 'I have written this short letter to encourage you, and to testify that this is the true grace of God. Stand fast in it' (12).

Encouragement is a common and characteristic word to describe the purpose of the spoken or written ministry of the Word in the New Testament. It is used of the sermon that the officials of the synagogue in Pisidian Antioch requested of Paul (Acts 13:15), and as a description of the letter to the Hebrews (Heb. 13:22). Peter has the expectation that this letter will encourage, and that it will do so by its witness to the true grace of God (5:12). The connection between true grace and encouragement is important. It is not that Peter is concerned about heresy, but he is concerned that Christians know what is the right response to God's grace, how to live as Christians. This instruction will encourage them, strengthen them and urge them to stand fast in God's true grace. May we also stand in God's true grace.

1 John: The word of God abides in you

It has often been noted that the spirituality of 1 John has three features: freedom from sin, love of fellow-believers and commitment to the truth. How does 1 John hope to bring this about? The introduction is where John explains his methodology.

The origin of this spirituality is the 'word of life' (1:1). This word of life must refer to Jesus Christ, because John tells us that this is what we have heard, have seen with our eyes, and have looked at and touched with our hands (1:1). He then tells us 'this life was revealed' (1:2). Jesus is described as the 'word of life': he is 'word' because 'word' is such a powerful way to describe effective communication, and he is word 'of life' because eternal life is the result of believing in him. John and his colleagues have been in a position of great privilege, which has not been the situation of his readers. John writes on behalf of those who have heard, seen, looked at and touched the word of life, to whom this life has been revealed. The primary and historic revelation has been to John and his colleagues, and this revelation was aural (they heard it), visual (they saw it and looked at it) and tactile (they felt it with their hands).

The revelation of the Word of life is passed on to John's readers by words: 'this life was revealed, and we have seen it and testify to it, and declare to you the eternal life that was with the Father and was revealed to us' (1:2). The primary revelation was verbal, visual and tangible: it is passed on to John's readers by declaration (1:2–3), and this is achieved by his writing (1:4) and by their reading or hearing.

This distinction is very important. The result of the incarnation is not that the people to whom John is ministering can themselves hear, see and touch the word of life: only John and his contemporaries have been able to do that, as they have received that primary revelation. What others, including us, can do, is to receive the written testimony and declaration of John.

When they do read and receive this declaration, the result is fellowship. John and his colleagues have fellowship with the Father and with his Son, as they have seen the Word of life; if John's readers receive his written declaration they will have fellowship with John and his colleagues, and thus be in fellowship with the Father and the Son (1:3). John is writing so that this fellowship may happen, and so that then 'our joy may be complete' (1:4). This will happen as John passes on to his readers what he has heard: 'This is the message we have heard from him and proclaim to you' (1:5). The distinction between the original eyewitnesses/earwitnesses and subsequent believers who come to faith through their witness is also expressed in John 17. Here we read of the distinction Jesus made between his immediate disciples, 'They were yours, and you gave them to me, and they have kept your word' (John 17:6), and subsequent believers, 'those who will believe in me through their word' (John 17:20).

In 1 John we find a spirituality of the Word. For John describes believers with the following phrases: 'whoever obeys his word' (2:5); 'the word of God abides in you' (2:14); 'Let what you heard from the beginning abide in you' (2:24); 'we obey his commandments' (3:22); and 'Those who believe in the Son of God have the testimony in their hearts' (5:10).

There is a clear contrast between those who do and those who do not accept these words: 'If we say that we have not sinned, we make him a liar, and his word is not in us' (1:10); 'Whoever . . . does not obey his commandments, is a liar, and in such a person the truth does not exist' (2:4); and, 'Those who do not believe in God have made him a liar by not believing in the testimony that God has given concerning his Son' (5:10). If we do not receive God's words, we treat him as a liar. We should not think that the Christian life is just a matter of education, of believing the declaration of John and his colleagues. Christians are those who are born of God, and God's seed (his word) abides in them (3:9). They have received the Spirit (4:13); they have received 'the anointing' (2:27). There is no disjunction between their believing John's declaration and the work of God in them, for 'the Spirit is the truth' (5:6), and the anointing is so that they will know the truth (2:27). They are made his children by his procreative word, and have received the Spirit, his anointing, and have his witness in their hearts (5:10).

They must refuse false teaching, and will do so by listening to John and his teaching, which comes from God (4:6). They will also keep themselves from idols (5:21). John summarizes his declaration with these words: 'And we know that the Son of God has come and has given us understanding so that we may know him who is true; and we are in him who is true, in his Son Jesus Christ. He is the true God and eternal life' (5:20).

Words, witness, declaration and truth are fundamental to the spirituality of 1 John. The readers receive John's words as the witness to the Word of life. They have been born of God, by the procreative word of God. They have received the Spirit, God's anointing. God has put his witness in their hearts. As John assures the believers, 'the word of God abides in you' (2:14).

Revelation: Listen to what the Spirit is saying to the churches

While for many the book of the Revelation is frightening and hard to understand, on another level its basic message is straightforward. While some of the details may be difficult, its main message is another expression of the overall gospel message of the Bible. While it may appear to have little to do with spirituality, in fact it is a call and an effective challenge to spiritual discernment and spiritual obedience.

What is this book?

I hope to show again that the basic structure of biblical spirituality is expressed in this marvellous book. We begin with the questions of content and form. There are certain key words that together explain both the content and form of this book. These words are found in the introduction to the book, which explain what it is, and in its final exhortations, which explain how to use it. It is a 'revelation', and its content is explained by the following phrases in 1:1–2: 'revelation' = 'Jesus Christ' = 'what must soon take place' = 'the word of God' = 'the testimony of Jesus Christ'. It is important to note the parallels:

- We know from the beginning of the book what it is – a 'revelation'.
- The subject of the 'revelation' is Jesus Christ.
- The context of that revelation is 'what must soon take place'.
- The form and origin of the revelation is 'the word of God'.
- The revelation has been carried out through 'the testimony of Jesus Christ'.

We should expect to meet Jesus Christ in this book, the same Jesus we have met all through the Bible. It is a Christ-centred book, expecting a Christ-centred response, and breathing a Christ-centred spirituality. This Christ-centred spirituality is emphasized in the words of praise with which John begins his letter, firstly in its trinitarian context. Note that the first description of Jesus Christ is that he is 'the faithful witness': 'Grace to you and peace from him who is and was and is to come, and from the seven spirits who are before his throne, and from Jesus Christ, the faithful witness, the firstborn of the dead, and the ruler of the kings of the earth' (1:4–5). And then we praise Christ and his saving work: 'To him who loves us and freed us from our sins by his blood, and made us to be a kingdom, priests serving his God and Father, to him be glory and dominion for ever and ever. Amen' (1:5–6). The subject of the revelation, Jesus Christ, is named and praised.

And what of the form of the book? In what form does the revelation come? The short answer is 'words', and these words are at the same time a revelation, a prophecy (1:3) and a letter (1:4).[2] The way in which the revelation/prophecy/letter is received is by being read, heard and kept: 'Blessed is the one who reads aloud the words of the prophecy, and blessed are those who hear and who keep what is written in it' (1:3). To be 'kept' is to be preserved, not discarded, and to be heeded, not ignored.

The verbal nature of the book is important to remember. Though John has visions, no-one else has them. What the readers and hearers have is the words that describe, accompany and explain the visions. And these words are sufficient to bring the blessing promised in 1:3: 'Blessed is the one who reads . . . and blessed are those who hear and who keep'. The revelation was given for the benefit of the servants of Jesus Christ (1:1), and comes to them in the sufficient and best form possible, that of words. The chain of giving is clear: God, Jesus Christ, angel, John, reader, hearers. At the point where the revelation moves on from John, it is in the form of words, and as such it has remained available not only to the seven churches, but also to Christians all down the ages, offering the same blessing today to those who read, hear and keep.

The same points about the nature of this book are found in its explanatory opening and reiterated in the concluding exhortations:

- These words are trustworthy and true. (22:6)
- Blessed is the one who keeps the words of the prophecy of this book. (22:7)

[2] My thanks to Allan Chapple for this insight.

- When John fell down to worship the angel, he replied, 'I am a fellow-servant with you and your comrades the prophets, and with all those who keep the words of this book' (22:9).
- The book is then referred to as Jesus' 'testimony for the churches' (22:16).
- And the solemn warning is given to respect the God-given words:

> I warn everyone who hears the words of the prophecy of this book: if anyone adds to them, God will add to that person the plagues described in this book; if anyone takes away from the words of the book of this prophecy, God will take away that person's share in the tree of life and in the holy city, which are described in this book. (22:18–19)

What matters is the response to *the words*; adding to or taking from the words is the opposite of *keeping* the words (1:3; 22:7); and the judgments are severe and are about the eternal destiny of the hearers. Nothing is more important than exact hearing and keeping! This is essential spirituality of the Word.

People often associate this book with judgment and punishment and miss the good news in it, so we should remember that the book begins and ends with the promise of happiness: 'Blessed is the one who reads . . . and blessed are those who hear and who keep . . .' (1:3). 'Blessed is the one who keeps the words of the prophecy of this book' (22:7).

We should also notice that the repeated call 'Let anyone who has an ear listen to what the Spirit is saying to the churches' at the end of each of the messages to the seven churches (chs. 2, 3) is a summons to right hearing, and identifies the words of Revelation with what the Spirit is saying. True spirituality is open to those who hear these words.

What of the visions?

What then should we make of the use of those powerful visions that fill the book and haunt our imagination? Visions may be an attractive medium for those hoping for a more open style of communication, where there is more room for observers to be creative in their interpretation, or where the impact is perceived to function 'deeper' than through mere words. We need to remember the following.

We do not have the visions; we have not seen them: what we do have is John's account of the visions in words, words that are the substance of the revelation we have received.

The pattern of visions in the biblical tradition is of vision and interpretation, where words are also given to explain the meaning of the vision. The importance of the words of interpretation is increased in significance because it is often delayed until God gives not only the vision but also its interpretation. So Pharaoh's dreams of seven sleek cows and seven ugly and thin cows, and of seven plump ears of grain and seven thin and blighted ears of grain must wait for interpretation until Joseph comes not only with the interpretation, but also with the appropriate response (Gen. 41). Similarly until Daniel is summoned the dreams of Nebuchadnezzar and the vision of Belshazzar remain unexplained (Dan. 4, 5). The biblical pattern is of interpreted visions. This pattern is continued in Revelation, where there is a subtle and important range of connections between the visions and the words. The words convey the visions; the words explain the visions; and the words provide complementary truths about the visions.

The meaning of the visions is explained by the words: the dragon in 12:3 is also called 'that ancient serpent, who is called the Devil and Satan, the deceiver of the whole world' in 12:9. Sometimes the explanation is delayed for dramatic effect, but through a careful reading of the whole book most visions can be understood. Where they remain unclear, the explanation is often found elsewhere in Scripture, as the cumulative revelation of the Bible reaches its climax. So the words that describe the vision may bring interpretation with them from their previous biblical context.

There is also a subtle revelatory relationship between what is seen and what is heard, between the vision and the words that accompany it. So in 5:5 John *hears* that 'the Lion of the tribe of Judah, the Root of David, has conquered, so that he can open the scroll and its seven seals'. But what he *sees* in 5:6 is 'a Lamb standing as if it had been slaughtered'. What John hears and what he sees are complementary truths about Jesus Christ. 'Christ as a Lion overcame by being slaughtered as a Lamb' (Beale 1999: 352). For the readers and hearers, both vision and words come in words, but the drama of the revelation is heightened by John both seeing and hearing. The same subtle connection between what John hears and what he sees is found in 7:4–17. John *hears* 'the number of those who were sealed, one hundred and forty-four thousand' (7:4), and then John *sees* 'a great multitude that no one could count' (7:9). This is the same group described in two different ways (Beale 1999: 425), and we notice the subtle relationship between what John hears and what he sees.

We might have thought that visions are a superior form of revelation, because they are visual and more spiritual; also that visions are superior to the duller categories of law (Leviticus), history (2 Chronicles) or argument (Romans). Beale argues that there is a more sinister reason for the use of visions. He links the use of visions to the use of parables, and points out that parables and visions are used in the Old Testament when the people have become slow to hear and rebellious against God's words (1999: 176–177, 236–239). He says of Israel in Isaiah's day, 'They had become spiritually hardened to rational, historical and homiletical warnings. As a consequence, the prophets began to take up different forms of warning. They started to employ symbolic action and parable in order to get attention' (1999: 237).

Some might claim that visions are preferable to words, because their meaning is less precise, because they do not achieve propositional revelation and because they are more open in meaning, leaving more to the imagination and preferences of the reader.

This shows a misunderstanding of the function of words and the visions they describe in the book of Revelation. Visions, like words, can be precise or imprecise according to their purpose. In fact the visions in Revelation are often precise in meaning; the vision in 5:1–7 makes it clear that there is only one who can take and open the scroll, and this is made more clear by the vision. The message of the vision can be and often is explained by words, as 5:1–7 is clearly expressed by the words

> You are worthy to take the scroll
> and to open its seals,
> for you were slaughtered and by your blood you ransomed for God
> saints from every tribe and language and people and nation.
>
> (5:9)

The word 'proposition' would not be appropriate to describe these words, because they perform another function, but they do have definite and clear meaning. It is the same meaning as the vision of which they are a part.

Some visions are intentionally more open-ended, so that readers in different circumstances can identify aspects of the work of the dragon or the beasts in their own day, and realize the cosmic significance of idolatry. But here as well, visions have meaning. Jesus can be identified with a Lion or Lamb, but not with a dragon or serpent;

Babylon is no Jerusalem. The visions are conveyed and explained by words, and make more striking the message of the words of this prophecy. The spirituality of Revelation is a spirituality of reading, hearing and keeping the words of this revelation, prophecy and letter.

What spirituality will result from this book?

A helpful way to understand Revelation is to realize that the application of the message of the book comes not towards the end, as is more usual in letters in the New Testament, but at the beginning, in the messages to the seven churches in chapters 2 and 3. The visions are then added to bring home to the people of those churches how great is their God, how wonderful and powerful is the Lord Jesus, and how dangerous is compromise with evil and idolatry. The visions are meant to shock the churches into realizing the eternal consequences of their daily actions, in which they either identify with God and the Lamb, or with the dragon and the beasts. The vivid language is to wake them up to their situation. In the letters to the seven churches each letter is also is addressed to all the churches: 'Let anyone who has an ear listen to what the Spirit is saying to the churches' (2:7 etc.)

Let us take as an example the letter to the angel of the church at Pergamum (2:12–17). What spirituality have we here?

- It will be a spirituality that knows that it is addressed by the Glorious One who walks among the churches to protect, care for, and admonish and correct them (1:12–16).
- It will be a spirituality that is corporate, consciously aware that its spiritual tone is set by all the members of the congregation, who together are responsible to listen to what Christ and the Spirit are saying 'to the angel of the church' (2:12).
- It will recognize the urgency of submitting to the sharp two-edged sword that comes from the mouth of Christ, that is, the words he speaks (2:12).
- It will know that Christ understands the particular pressures of its context: 'I know where you are living' (2:13), and take account of the world in which it is set: 'where Satan's throne is', 'where Satan lives' (2:13). The Christians of Pergamum need to recognize the deeper significance of the temple dedicated to Caesar worship, and the other pagan cults of Asclepius, Zeus, Athene and Dionysus (Beale 1999: 246). They are under great spiritual pressure, and this pressure will be both political and religious.
- They should be encouraged that Christ knows and values their

faithfulness to him in holding fast to his name, and not compromising their commitment to their Lord, by submitting to the worship of other gods (2:13).

- Yet their corporate spirituality is compromised because they allow some of their number to engage in eating food offered to idols and in fornication, that is, letting themselves be seduced away from the spiritual chastity required of Christians in practice and in teaching (2:14–15). There are two problems: one is that some are engaging in these practices; the other is that the church as a whole is letting this happen. In corporate spirituality the actions of some affect the state of all, and the state of all makes some more liable to sin.
- They need to learn a spirituality of repentance, and put away from them this false spirituality, or Christ says that he will come and fight against them, and 'make war against them with the sword of my mouth' (2:16).
- With the warning comes an encouragement to persevere, an application of the vision of the New Jerusalem in chapters 22 and 23. It is the promise of the 'hidden manna' and 'white stone' with the 'new name' to those who conquer (2:17). Manna refers to the true food and sustenance Christ gives those who do not take part in idolatry. The manna, the white stone and the new name all encourage them to endure to the end, to look forward and wait for the coming of Christ (Beale 1999: 252–258; and see Rev. 22:20). Their spirituality needs to be forward-looking, enduring victoriously as they wait for Christ's return.

In summary it is a spirituality that recognizes the presence of Christ among his churches, and submits to the words that come from his mouth. It is spiritually discerning and discriminating, holding fast to Christ alone, and not seduced by compromise with other spiritualities through idolatry or false teaching. It is well prepared for the dangers of its context, and the evil that surrounds it, but is not overwhelmed by the power of that evil, as it recognizes the almighty power of Christ. It is a spirituality that knows how to repent at the words of Christ. It is a spirituality of endurance, able to live with the hiddenness of Christ's provision, and prepared to wait for his return, and the glories that will bring. It is a spirituality responsive to the words of Christ and the Spirit in the revelation and prophecy of John. It is sustained by the blessing promised to all those who receive these words.

The rest of the book reinforces the point that this response is not a luxury but a dire necessity. The visions show the enormity of evil, the power of the dragon, Satan, and the political and religious pressures of his servants, the two beasts. The language of 'plagues' comes from God's judgment on the gods of Egypt, now his judgment on the whole world. The name Babylon points to the greatness of the opposition to the people of God. At the same time God rules from his throne, Christ the Lamb has died and risen and will conquer, and God's people are kept safe by God's power, Babylon will be destroyed, and the new heaven and the new earth, the new Jerusalem will be prepared as a bride for her husband.

It is Christ-centred spirituality, communicated from Christ and the Spirit in the words of a prophetic letter, and resulting in praise to God and the Lamb, and the certain expectation of Christ's return.

Let us listen to what the Spirit is saying to the churches!

Chapter Four

Calvin's theology of revelation: Faith hearing the word of Christ

If 'faith comes by hearing, and hearing by the word of Christ' (Romans 10:17), how can we think of the whole Bible, including the Old Testament, as the word of Christ, that is, both the word that originates from Christ, and the word that has Christ as its subject? To answer these questions I want to give an outline of Calvin's theology of revelation under these four headings: Theological foundations, Christ's one covenant, One people of God, and One Word of God.[1]

Theological foundations

By revelation we can know God the Creator and the Redeemer. We are called to a knowledge of God, 'not that knowledge which . . . merely flits in the brain, but that which will be sound and fruitful if we duly perceive it, and if it takes root in the heart' (*Institutes* 1.5.9). God reveals both 'himself and his everlasting Kingdom in the mirror of his works with very great clarity' (*Institutes* 1.5.11). God's revelation is intended to enable us to know him.

We cannot know God directly. It is beyond our ability for us to know him. This is in part because God is infinite and we are finite; it is also because we are sinners and he is holy. So Calvin writes, 'when the heaven of heavens cannot contain Him, how can our minds comprehend Him?' (Wallace 1953: 1 = *Commentary on Ezekiel* 1:8), and 'since there is a perpetual and irreconcilable disagreement between righteousness and unrighteousness, so long as we remain sinners he cannot receive us completely' (*Institutes* 2.16.3).

So God accommodates to our capacity: 'in descending among us by the exercise of His power and grace, He appears as near as is needful and as our limited capacity will bear' (Wallace 1953: 3 =

[1] In this section I am deeply indebted to Wallace 1953 and to Wilcox 1993.

Commentary on Psalms 78:60). This revelation appears first of all in signs and symbols, and then in Christ. God also accommodates to our capacity in the Bible. Indeed, as I have shown elsewhere, Calvin's theology of preaching includes the accommodation of God to his people in Scripture, in the secret work of the Spirit, and in providing preachers and teachers of his Word (Adam 1996: 137–145).

All knowledge of God is mediated through Christ, the one mediator: 'all divinely uttered revelations are correctly designated by the term "word of God", so this substantial Word is properly placed at the highest level, as the wellspring of all oracles' (*Institutes* 1.13.7). The knowledge of God the Redeemer is first revealed in what we call the Old Testament, and then in the New. But all God's self-revelation comes to us through Christ. Calvin quotes Irenaeus: 'the Father, himself infinite, becomes finite in the Son, for he has accommodated himself to our little measure lest our minds be overwhelmed by the immensity of his glory', and adds, 'God is comprehended in Christ alone' (*Institutes* 2.6.4). Even the saints of the Old Testament 'participated in the same inheritance and hoped for a common salvation with us by the grace of the same Mediator' (*Institutes* 2.10.1). For there is only one God and one mediator, so therefore the Old Testament believers 'had Christ as the pledge of their covenant, and put in him all trust of future blessedness' (*Institutes* 2.10.23). All this is argued at length in *Institutes* 2.9.10.

True knowledge about God is given in Scripture: 'so Scripture, gathering up the otherwise confused knowledge of God in our minds, having dispersed our dullness, clearly shows us the true God' (*Institutes* 1.6.1). And God also works in our hearts, by the secret work of the spirit, so that Scripture is self-authenticated by God: 'those whom the Spirit has inwardly taught truly rest upon Scripture' (*Institutes* 1.8.5).

This knowledge of God is mediated in one covenant, in two modes of dispensation. Calvin develops the similarities and differences between the Old and the New Covenants in the *Institutes*, Book 2, chapters 9–11. For all people 'adopted by God into the company of his people since the beginning of the world were covenanted to him by the same law and by the bond of the same doctrine as obtains among us' (*Institutes* 2.10.11). He wants to argue this because there is only one mediator, Jesus Christ, and therefore all people relate to God in the same way, through Christ.

There is one big message of the Bible about Jesus Christ, revealed in promise in the Old Testament and in fulfilment in the New. Calvin's insight is that this does not mean the Christ is absent from the Old Testament, but is revealed there in types and shadows. It is still Christ who is revealed, and the revelation is effective, and those who respond in faith put their trust in the Christ who is to come. Calvin's doctrine of the Trinity saves him from the error of thinking that Christ is a late arrival in the history of salvation.

Christ's one covenant

Calvin develops his theme of one covenant, and how it differs in mode of dispensation: 'The covenant made with all the patriarchs is so much like ours in substance and reality that the two are actually one and the same. Yet they differ in the mode of dispensation' (*Institutes* 2.10.2).

He first demonstrates that there is really one covenant by indicating that the Old Testament saints enjoyed what we might have regarded as distinctly New Covenant blessings of salvation. He shows that the saints from earliest days looked to God in faith, and hoped for an inheritance that was not merely earthly, but would be fulfilled in the resurrection. For saints from the earliest days knew that fellowship with God which is eternal life. He quotes the writer of Hebrews when he says that Abraham, Isaac and Jacob 'looked forward to a well-founded city, whose builder and maker is God', and later writes 'they desire a better country, that is a heavenly one. Therefore God is not ashamed to be called their God, for he has prepared for them a city' (*Institutes* 2.10.13).

He claims, as we have seen, that the Old Testament saints had Christ as the pledge of their covenant, and put in him all hopes of future blessedness. He then concludes, 'the Old Testament or Covenant that the Lord made with the Israelites had not been limited to earthly things, but contained a promise of spiritual and eternal life' (*Institutes* 2.10.23). For they, like us, trusted in God's mercy, since 'with them was made the covenant of the gospel, the sole foundation of which is Christ' (*Institutes* 2.10.4). So then, 'they had and knew Christ as Mediator, through whom they were joined to God and were to share in his promises' (*Institutes* 2.10.2).

Two modes

Of course Calvin also notes the differences between the two modes of dispensation, and he develops these in chapter 11, where he outlines five major differences.

Whereas in the Old Testament earthly benefits displayed heavenly benefits, in the New Testament we meditate directly on them in the ascended Christ (paragraphs 1–3). Next he explains that truth in the Old Testament was conveyed by images and ceremonies, which are a kind of shadow, the substance of which, in the New Testament, is Christ (paragraphs 4–6). Another major difference is that Old Testament religion was literal rather than spiritual, and few had their hearts changed, whereas in the New the work of the Spirit is to change and cleanse the heart (paragraphs 7–8). He then points out that even strong believers under the Old Covenant had to keep the ceremonies of that covenant, even though they had faith in Christ to whom those ceremonies pointed. He uses the image of childhood and maturity to characterize the difference between the two eras (paragraphs 9–10). His final piece of evidence is that in the Old Testament the covenant of grace is largely confined to one nation, whereas in the New, people from all nations are called to faith in Christ (paragraphs 11–12).

The better mode

Ronald Wallace has gathered together from other writings of Calvin some more ways in which the New Covenant or new mode of dispensation differs from the Old (1953: 32–39). He demonstrates with quotations from Calvin's commentaries the following points about revelation under the New Covenant:

- *It is more rich and full.* The Holy Spirit was 'more abundantly given' under the gospel than under the law, when God gave his redemptive gifts 'not so freely and extensively as now' (33 = *Commentary on Joel* 2:28).
- *It is more vivid and distinct.* Christ was formerly beheld at a distance by the prophets, but now has made himself familiarly and completely visible (34 = *Commentary on John* 8:56). 'Under the law was shadowed forth only in rude and imperfect lines that which is under the Gospel set forth in living colours and graphically distinct' (34 = *Commentary on Hebrews* 10:1). He also uses the contrast of sketch drawing and full portrait:

> As painters do not in the first draught bring out the likeness in vivid colours and expressively but in the first instance draw rude and obscure lines, so the representation of Christ under the law was unpolished – a first sketch, but in our

sacrament it is seen drawn out to the life. (34 = *Commentary on Colossians* 2:18)[2]

- *It is more satisfying*. Calvin gives the example of Simeon welcoming the young Christ to the temple, who 'after seeing Christ, prepared himself calmly and with a satisfied mind for death', thus showing that 'he was before unsatisfied and anxious' (35 = *Commentary on 1 Peter* 1:10).
- *It is more familiar and loving*. The dispensation of the law is full of terror 'but the Gospel contains nothing but love, provided it be received by faith' (36 = *Commentary on Hebrews* 12:19). Or again, 'in the precepts of the law, God is seen as the rewarder of perfect righteousness . . . but in Christ His countenance beams forth full of grace and gentleness towards poor unworthy sinners' (36 = *Institutes* 2.7.8).
- *It is more substantial*. 'Grace was in a manner suspended until the advent of Christ – not that the fathers were excluded from it, but they had not a present manifestation of it' (37 = *Commentary on Colossians* 2:14). But in the New Covenant Christ has 'in a manner opened heaven to us so that we might have a near view of those spiritual riches which before were under types exhibited at a distance' (37 = *Commentary on 1 Peter* 1:12).
- *It is more simple*. This simplicity is reflected in the context of patterns of worship, for in the Old Covenant God accommodated himself to the 'weaker and unripe apprehensions of the fathers by the rudiments of ceremony, while He has extended a simple form of worship to us sharers in the New Covenant who attained a mature age' (38 = *Commentary on Psalms* 50:14).

Christ in the Old Testament

Yet despite the evident superiority of revelation in the New Covenant or mode, it is clear that Christ is revealed under the Old Covenant or mode; for how else could Christ say of the Old Testament Scriptures, they 'testify on my behalf' (John 5:39). What is the sketch of Christ in the Old Testament that is to become his vivid portrait in the New? What is the Old Testament shadow of the New Testament substance? Old Testament believers hoped in Christ. So Calvin asserts that 'God willed that the Jews should be so instructed by these prophecies that

[2] See also Parker 1986: 56–62 for an explanation of the sketch–portrait imagery.

they might turn their eyes directly to Christ in order to seek deliverance' (*Institutes* 2.6.4). For the way to grasp hold of Christ is by faith: 'We enjoy Christ only as we embrace Christ clad in his own promises . . . only we must notice a difference in the nature or quality of the promises: the gospel points out with the finger what the law foreshadowed under types' (*Institutes* 2.9.3).

Again, Wallace has gathered together evidence from Calvin's commentaries to show the many ways in which Christ is revealed in the Old Testament (1953: 40–60). Wallace comments:

> All the differing forms of the old revelation shadow forth the outward form that revelation is to take in Jesus Christ and under the New Covenant . . . moreover it is through these Old Testament forms that we are given the categories through which we can understand and proclaim the true significance of Jesus Christ. (41)

How then is Christ revealed in the Old Testament?

- *Christ is foreshadowed in Israel.* So Calvin comments on the exodus:

  > Christ cannot be separated from His Church . . . what happened in the Church [Israel], ought at length to be fulfilled in the Head . . . God, when He formerly redeemed his people from Egypt, only showed by a certain prelude the redemption which he deferred till the coming of Christ. (44 = *Commentary on Hosea* 11:1)

- *He is foreshadowed in the return from the exile*: 'The deliverance from Babylon was but a prelude to the restoration of the Church, and was intended to last, not for a few years only, but till Christ should come and bring true salvation, not only to their bodies, but likewise to their souls' (44–45 = *Commentary on Isaiah* 9:2). So Christ, Head and body [Israel] is present in the Old Testament, as he is present in the New. Israel prefigures Christ and the church, not in an arbitrary connection, but in reality.
- *Christ is foreshadowed in individuals*: 'in Joseph was adumbrated [foreshadowed] what was afterwards more fully exhibited in Christ, in order that each member may form itself to the imitation of his example' (47 = *Commentary on Genesis* 37:18–19).

But the clearest type of Christ is *David*:

- 'The heavenly Father intended that in the person of his Son these things should be visibly accomplished which were shadowed forth in David' (48 = *Commentary on Psalms* 22:18).
- *Christ is foreshadowed in political institutions*. The kingdom God set up under David is a type of the kingdom of Christ: 'God then gave a living representation of His Christ when He erected a Kingdom in the person of David' (49 = *Commentary on Habakkuk* 3:13). So too Hezekiah is a 'figure of Christ' and his kingdom is a 'type of the Kingdom of Christ whose image Hezekiah bore' (49 = *Commentary on Isaiah* 33:17).
- *In the glory David's kingdom showed there is a foreshadowing of the glory and universality of the kingdom of Christ*: 'the homage which foreign nations rendered to the people of God as only the beginning of that homage which various nations rendered to the Church of God, after Christ had been revealed to the world' (50 = *Commentary on Isaiah* 45:14).
- *Christ is foreshadowed in the ritual of tabernacle and temple*. 'In the whole legal priesthood, in the sacrifices, in the form of the sanctuary, we ought to seek Christ' (51 = *Commentary on Hosea* 1:11). The tabernacle was 'a sort of visible image of God' (53 = *Commentary on Hebrews* 9:19), and pointed to the coming Christ. So too was Aaron 'an image of God's only begotten Son and our true Mediator' (53 = *Commentary on Numbers* 12:9). As well 'the sacrifices were types of Christ' (54 = *Commentary on Leviticus* 1:1), and the freedom from blemish required in sacrifices shows 'the celestial perfection and purity of Christ' (55 = *Commentary on Exodus* 12:5).
- *Christ is foreshadowed in signs and visions*. So, for example, Jacob's ladder is a sign of Christ:

  > [T]here is nothing in this vision intricate or ambiguous . . . It is Christ alone therefore who connects heaven and earth; He is the only Mediator who reaches from heaven down to earth; He is the medium through which the fullness of all celestial blessings flows to us, and through which we, in turn, ascend to God. (56 = *Commentary on Genesis* 28:12)

- *The material foreshadows the eternal*. Why did God choose this gradual method of revelation?

> It was requisite for a people inexperienced and feeble to be trained gradually, by means of temporal benefits to entertain a better hope . . . The Lord did not formerly set the hope of the future inheritance plainly before the eyes of the fathers (as He now calls us and raises us directly towards heaven), but he led them by a circuitous course. Thus He appointed the land of Canaan as a mirror and pledge to them of the celestial inheritance . . . that being aided by such helps, according to the time in which they lived they might by degrees rise towards heaven . . . All the promises of God were involved, and in a sense clothed in these symbols. (58 = *Commentary on Psalms* 112:2; *Commentary on Genesis* 27:28)

For we have to understand that the God who is described and revealed in the Old Testament is the God who is later more fully revealed as the Father, the Son and the Spirit. (What other God is there?) So it cannot be inappropriate to recognize the signs of the Son's presence in the Old Testament. God the Son is certainly present, and, as Christ is the mediator of all of God's revelation, all the actions and words of God are mediated through the Son.

So then:

- *Christ speaks through all the prophets.* Calvin argues this in his preface to his commentary on Isaiah. He applies the promise of God in Deuteronomy 18:15 to the raising up of Christ as the great prophet, because 'he is the head of the Prophets, and all of them depend on him for their doctrine, and with one consent point to him' (1981, 20: xxvii). Calvin describes the ministry of Old Testament prophets as follows. They derive their doctrine immediately from the law, and interpret it in their own day. The law consists of three parts, according to Calvin: doctrine of life, threatenings and promises, and the covenant of grace, with its special promises. So the prophets explain in more detail the doctrine of life, and what it means to obey God; they apply the threatenings and promises to their own day; and they 'express more clearly what Moses says more obscurely about Christ and his grace, and bring forward more copious and more abundant proofs of the free covenant' (1981, 20: xxvi).
- *Christ rules through all the kings and leaders.* Calvin comments:

> For though God is said to sit in the midst of the gods, because by him kings rule, we yet know that the throne of David was

> more eminent than any other; for it was a priestly kingdom and a type of that celestial kingdom which was afterwards fully revealed in Christ. (1981, 20: 76)

For if kings are empowered by God to rule, then this power is of course mediated through Christ. So their rule is both a demonstration of Christ's power, and also a prefiguring of the power of Christ to come.

- *Christ forgives through Old Testament sacrifices and priests*. Calvin says, 'If anyone asks whether the sins of the fathers were remitted under the Law . . . they were remitted, but remitted by the mercy of Christ' (1959–71, 12: 122).

For what power to forgive could God use other than that of Christ's atonement? For if Old Testament sacrifices did not use the power of Christ, they were merely visual aids. So Calvin writes, 'the ceremonies would have provided the people of the Old Covenant with an empty show if the power of Christ's death and resurrection had not been displayed therein' (*Institutes* 2.7.16). So we can see that Calvin's idea of 'types' of Christ is that they not only point forward to and reveal something of their future 'antitypes', but also share in the power of the Christ to come. In them the power of Christ is displayed, and the covenant promises are preached again to the people of God. If we are part of the people of God, whether we live in Old or New Testament times, we trust in the same one mediator, one covenant and one gospel.

From our perspective it may seem that Calvin finds too much of Christ in the Old Testament. It is good to remember that in his day he was accused of interpreting the Old Testament in a Jewish rather than Christian way. This was because he did not follow many of the traditional Christian interpretations of the Old Testament, which found many direct references to Christ and the Trinity.[3]

One people of God

If Calvin's view of the revelation of Christ in the Old Testament is of central importance to his exegesis of that Old Testament, so too is his

[3] See the chapter 'The Jewish Appearance of Calvin's Exegesis', in Puckett 1995: 52–81.

theology of the one people of God. Indeed there are two striking features of Calvin's doctrine of the people of God. One is the identity of God's people under both covenants, and the other is the identity of Christ with his people, as head of his body, under those same two covenants.

The people of God are one in every age, because God is one, because there is one head of the body and because God's people are all saved by the death and resurrection of Christ. Calvin develops these ideas in terms of his image of childhood and adulthood:

> Therefore the same inheritance was appointed for them and for us [for Old Testament saints and New Testament believers], but they were not yet old enough to be able to enter upon it and manage it. The same church existed among them, but as yet in its childhood. (*Institutes* 2.11.2)

The people of God under the Old Covenant were also saved by Christ, 'the Old Testament was established upon the free mercy of God, and was confirmed by Christ's intercession' (*Institutes* 2.10.4). The people of God are one, because God chose one people for himself through Christ. For 'since among all the offspring of Adam, the Heavenly Father found nothing worthy of his election, he turned his eyes upon his Anointed, to choose from that body as members those whom he was to take into the fellowship of life' (*Institutes* 3.22.1). So the covenant people of God are one body, even though they appear under two dispensations. Christ is the head of his body in both the Old and New Testaments. For example, when Calvin comments on God's words in Isaiah 49:3 'You are my Servant', he makes the following observation:

> This passage must not be limited to the person of Christ, and ought not to be limited to Israel alone . . . When the whole body of the Church is spoken of, Christ is brought forward conspicuously so as to include all the children of God . . . In like manner, under the name Israel, by which he means Christ, Isaiah includes the whole body of the people, as Members under the Head. (1981, 20: 11)

So Christ and his people are one, in both Old and New Testaments. Because the people of God are one, they can have the same hope in the same God:

> [F]or those to whom he is Father the church may also be Mother. And this was so not only under the law but also after Christ's coming . . . the church could neither totter nor fall. First, it stands by God's election, and cannot waver or fail any more than his eternal providence can. Secondly, it has in a way been joined to the steadfastness of Christ, who will no more allow his believers to be estranged from him than that his own members be rent and torn asunder. Besides, we are certain that, while we remain within the bosom of the church, the truth will always abide with us. Finally, we feel that these promises apply to us: 'There will be salvation in Zion', 'God will be in the midst of Jerusalem forever, that it may never be moved.' (*Institutes* 4.1.1, 3)

Notice the strength of Calvin's last comment, that 'we feel that these promises apply to us'. We may do so because we are part of the same people of God to whom these words were addressed; we hope in the same God and Christ. For us to feel the application of these words is not to take to ourselves words that really belong to others, but words that belong both to them and us, as we are joined in one body.

This unity of the people of God, allowing for their different dispensations, is also reflected in the similarities of the pattern of their life under God. This is seen in both their models of ministry and their sacraments. For Calvin identifies a common theme in both Old and New Testaments, that of the preaching and teaching of the Word of God.

He begins with a description of the ministry of the Word in the Old Testament:

> What the patriarchs had received they handed on to their descendants . . . But where it pleased God to raise up a more visible form of the church, he willed to have his Word set down and sealed in writing, that his priests might seek from it what to teach the people, and that every doctrine to be taught should conform to that rule . . . there followed the prophets, through whom God published new oracles which were added to the law. (*Institutes* 4.8.5, 6)

He then continues with a description of the ministry of the Word in the New:

> God has so fulfilled all functions of teaching in his Son that we must regard this as the final and eternal testimony from him . . . No other word is to be held as the Word of God, and be given place as such in the church, than what is contained first in the Law and the Prophets, then in the writings of the apostles; and the only authorized way of teaching in the church is by the prescription and standard of his Word. (*Institutes* 4.8.7–8)

If this is the case, then we would expect to find a number of similarities between the Old and New Testament ministries of the Word, and Wallace (1953) gives some examples. When Calvin comments on Daniel asking one who stood by him the truth, he adds, 'let us fly to Christ Himself, who in these days reaches us familiarly by means of pastors and ministers of the Gospel' (116 = *Commentary on Daniel* 7:15.). In writing on one of Moses' sermons in Deuteronomy, Calvin comments, 'None will ever be a good minister of the word of God unless he is first of all a scholar' (120 = *Commentary on Deuteronomy* 5:23). And like Joseph's task in explaining the meaning of the dream of Pharaoh's baker, the ministry might be unpleasant, but it must not be shirked. 'That freedom must be maintained by prophets, and teachers, that they may not hesitate by their teaching to inflict a wound upon those whom God has sentenced to death' (121 = *Commentary on Genesis* 40:16). So the preacher today can share the confidence of the prophet Micah, if the same Word is heard: 'I go not forth as a private individual, nor have I presumptuously intruded into this office, but I am armed with God's command; nay, God himself speaks through my mouth' (122 = *Commentary on Micah* 6:9).

Within this general framework of understanding the similarities in the ministries of the Word in the Old and New Testaments, we can make good use of these quotations from Calvin, gathered by Graham Miller. In them Calvin is exegeting the Old Testament, but applying his teaching to ministers of the Word of the New Covenant (see Miller 1992: 252–260):

- No one ought to be deemed a sound teacher, but he who speaks from God's mouth. (253 = *Commentary on Jeremiah* 23:16)
- To assert the truth is only one half of preaching . . . except all the fallacies of the devil be also dissipated. (252 = *Commentary on Jeremiah* 29:8)

- God's servants ought to speak from the inmost affection of their heart. (252 = *Commentary on Ezekiel* 3:3)
- Though the Law was written, yet God would ever have the living voice to resound in His Church, just as now-a-days preaching is inseparably united with Holy Scripture. (253 = *Commentary on The Four Last Books of Moses*, Book 2: 235)
- We ought to imitate the Prophets, who conveyed the doctrine of the Law in such a manner to draw from it advices, reproofs, threatenings and consolations, which they applied to the present condition of the people. (253–254 = *Commentary on Isaiah*, Preface)
- When the minister executes his commission faithfully, by speaking only what God puts into his mouth, the inward power of the Holy Spirit is joined with his outward voice. (255 = *Commentary on Psalms* 105:31)
- God governs his Church by the external preaching of the word. (257 = *Commentary on The Four Last Books of Moses*, Book 1: 335)
- Whoever rejects the faithful teachers of the word, shows that he is a despiser of God himself. (260 = *Commentary on Jeremiah* 29:18–19)

If the ministry of the Word is common to the Old and New Testaments, so too are sacraments. Indeed Calvin goes so far as to say, 'the apostle [Paul] makes the Israelites equal to us not only in the grace of the covenant but also in the signification of the sacraments' (*Institutes* 2.10.5). He also links covenants, signs and sacraments in the following words: 'the Lord calls his promises "covenants" and his sacraments "tokens" of the covenants', and points out that in the Old Testament 'whenever God gave a sign to the holy patriarchs it was inseparably linked to doctrine, without which our senses would have been stunned in looking at the bare sign' (*Institutes* 4.14.6, 4).

The sacraments of the Old Testament performed the same function as those in the New, that of pointing to Christ. 'Yet those ancient sacraments looked to the same purpose to which ours tend: to direct and almost lead men by the hand to Christ, or rather, as images, to represent him and show him forth to be known' (*Institutes* 4.14.20). Also:

> [N]o promise has ever been offered to man except in Christ. Consequently, to teach us about any promise of God, they must show forth Christ . . . the former [Old Testament]

> foreshadowed Christ when he was as yet awaited; the latter [New Testament] attest him as already given and revealed. (*Institutes* 4.14.20)

Calvin disagrees with the idea found in Roman Catholic teachers that the Old Testament sacraments only foreshadowed God's grace, while New Testament sacraments give it as a present reality:

> Therefore, whatever is shown us today in the sacraments, the Jews of old received in their own – that is, Christ with his spiritual riches. They felt the same power in their sacraments as we do in ours; these were seals of divine good toward them, looking to eternal salvation. (*Institutes* 2.14.22)

The central point is that of the common experience of God's people under both Old and New Testaments, the experience of the grace of Christ. God's people are one!

As we have seen, Calvin draws attention not to the earthly fulfilment of the promises to the patriarchs of the land, but to their spiritual and heavenly fulfilment in Christ. It is quite wrong to criticize this as 'mere spiritualizing'. For Calvin, as we have seen, substantial fulfilment is found in Christ, and the land was only a foreshadowing of that substantial inheritance promised to all who hope in Christ. So to look for a fulfilment of the promises on earth is to look in the wrong place, because we should raise our eyes to heaven, to see the glory and power of the ascended Christ.[4] But for him the Old Testament promises are prophetic of the New. We all hope in the one mediator, in the one covenant of grace, in the one gospel. Calvin does not look for an earthly fulfilment of the promises of God to the Jews, because he believes that all who hope in Christ have the same reward and covenant hope.

One Word of God

Having looked at the theological foundations of Calvin's biblical theology, we have outlined that theology in terms of one mediator, one covenant, one gospel and then one people of God. We now turn

[4] Calvin was criticized in his day for being too sympathetic to the historical fulfilment of Old Testament promises for the Jews, and was nicknamed *Calvinus Judaizans*, Calvin the Judaizer (Calvin 1981, 12: 417–425; and see also Puckett 1995: 4–7).

to the final subject of this section, one Word of God. What can we learn about the Bible from Calvin's writings?

The Bible is about Christ

So we find that

> [T]he knowledge of Christ must be sought from the Scriptures. Those who imagine what they like about Christ will ultimately have nothing but a shadowy ghost in His place . . . we must hold that Christ cannot be properly known from anywhere but the Scriptures . . . it follows that the Scriptures should be read with the aim of finding Christ in them. (Calvin 1959–71, 4: 139).

By the Scriptures here is meant the Old Testament, but if Christ is the subject of the Old, he is certainly also the subject of the New. So the gospel refers to the proclamation of the grace manifested in Christ, and knowledge of the person and work of Christ comes from a close study of the New Testament evidence (e.g. *Institutes* 2.17). For we have in the Bible the covenant promises of God, so 'We enjoy Christ only as we embrace Christ clad in his own promises' (*Institutes* 2.9.3).

All the Bible is about Christ

It is worth repeating this theme, because a casual reading of Calvin may lead some to think that he distinguishes between 'law' and 'gospel' in such a way that only part of the Bible points to Christ. This is not the case, for 'it was especially committed to Moses and all the prophets to teach the way of reconciliation between God and men, whence also Paul calls "Christ the end of the law"' (*Institutes* 1.6.2).

So the Word of God is not divided; it is not one Word to people of the Old Testament and another Word to the people of the New, but one Word about Christ to the one people of God. The Word increases in clarity from shadow to substance, but its subject remains the same.

The Bible is God's cumulative revelation

As we have seen, Calvin gives a marvellous summary of the way in which God kept adding to his words until the time of Christ:

> Among the patriarchs God used secret revelations, but at the same time to confirm these he added such signs that they could have no doubt that it was God who was speaking to them.

> What the patriarchs had received they handed on to their descendants . . . But when it pleased God to raise up a more visible form of the church, he willed to have his Word set down and sealed in writing, that his priests might seek from it and teach the people, and that every doctrine to be taught should conform to that rule . . . There then followed the prophets, through whom God published new oracles that were added to the law. [God] commanded that the prophecies also be committed to writing, and be accounted part of his Word. At the same time, histories were added to these, also under the labour of the prophets, but composed under the Holy Spirit's dictation. I include the psalms with the prophecies, since what we attribute to the prophecies is common to them. Therefore, that whole body of teaching, put together out of law, prophecies, psalms, and histories, was the Lord's Word for the ancient people . . . [finally] God will not speak as he did before . . . nor will add prophecies to prophecies, or revelations to revelations. Rather, he has so fulfilled all functions of teaching in his Son that we must regard this as the final and eternal testimony from him . . . content with the perfection of Christ's teaching, we may learn not to fashion anything new for ourselves beyond this or to admit anything contrived by others. (*Institutes* 4.8.5–7)

The Bible is the Spirit's Word

For Calvin 'Scripture is the school of the Holy Spirit' (*Institutes* 3.21.3). Moses, for example, 'wrote his five books, not only under the guidance of the Spirit of God, but as if God Himself had suggested them speaking out of His own mouth' (1981, 20: 328). The words of Scripture do not come from the pleasure of men 'but are dictated by the Holy Spirit' (Calvin 1959–71, 10: 330). Amos 'possessed the discernment of the Holy Spirit' (1981, 20: 323), and Ezekiel 'spoke only from the mouth of God, as the organ of the Spirit' (Calvin 1981, 20: 213).

The Spirit brings his words home to our hearts

God not only caused the Scriptures to be written originally, but also sends the Spirit to bring those same words deep into the hearts of believers. 'For as God alone is a fit witness of himself in his Word, so also the Word will not find acceptance in men's hearts before it is sealed by the inward testimony of the Spirit' (*Institutes* 1.7.4). By this means God provides both external verification and internal conviction in believers:

> For by a kind of mutual bond the Lord has joined together the certainty of his Word and of his Spirit so that the perfect religion of the Word may abide in our minds when the Spirit, who causes us to contemplate God's face, shines; and that we in turn may embrace the Spirit with no fear of being deceived when we recognize him in his own image, namely, in the Word. (*Institutes* 1.9.3)

Here Calvin is asserting both the original inspiration by the Spirit and the present work of God in sealing the inspired words in our hearts and lives. He does not fall into the modern trap of replacing the doctrine of original inspiration by the doctrine of present illumination. Nor does he fall into the other modern trap of implying that God has worked in the past to provide the Scriptures and is now inactive. For Calvin, 'the power of the word of God is perpetual, and it is so efficacious that it exerts its power, so long as there is a people that fears and worships him' (Calvin 1981, 20: 336). So Calvin recognizes that the Bible comes from the Spirit of God, and that the two are inseparable:

> The 'Spirit' is joined with the word, because, without the efficacy of the Spirit . . . the preaching of the gospel would avail nothing, but would remain unfruitful. In like manner, 'the word' must not be separated from 'the Spirit', as fanatics imagine, who, despising the word, glory in the name of the Spirit, and swell with vain confidence in their own imaginations. (1981, 20: 271)

The Bible is the final and complete Word of God

This cumulative Word of God, gathered over so many years, is also the final Word of God:

> Let this be a firm principle: No other word is to be held as the Word of God, and given place as such in the church, than what is contained first in the Law and the Prophets, then in the writing of the apostles; and the only authorized way of teaching in the church is by the prescription and standard of his Word. (*Institutes* 4.8.8)

So Calvin warns against the claims of the 'enthusiasts' of his day:

> What say these fanatics, swollen with pride, carelessly forsaking and bidding farewell to God's Word, they, no less confidently than boldly, seize upon whatever they may have conceived while snoring? [but] . . . the children of God . . . are not unaware that the Word is the instrument by which the Lord dispenses the illumination of His Spirit to believers. (*Institutes* 1.9.3)

In the Bible we hear the living words of God

Though Calvin asserts that God's revelation is rooted in history, and that it is the product of the accumulation of God's words over many past generations, yet he also asserts that as we hear the Bible read we hear God speaking to us in the present:

> Now daily oracles are not sent from heaven, for it pleased the Lord to hallow his truth to everlasting remembrance in the Scriptures alone. Hence the Scriptures obtain full authority among believers only when men regard them as having sprung from heaven, as if there the living words of God were heard. (*Institutes* 1.7.1)

When we hear the Bible read, we hear 'the public oracles of the Holy Spirit' (*Institutes* 2.10.19). For we must see 'manifest signs of God speaking in Scripture', but this can happen, because 'God is a fit witness of himself in his word', so, 'the same Spirit . . . who has spoken through the mouth of the prophets must penetrate into our hearts to persuade us that they faithfully proclaimed what had been divinely commanded' (*Institutes* 1.7.4). Or again, 'Scripture is from God . . . we feel that the undoubted power of his divine majesty lives and breathes there. By this power we are drawn and inflamed, knowingly and willingly, to obey him' (*Institutes* 1.8.5). And when God does so work in his Word and in our hearts, 'we affirm with utter certainty (just as if we were gazing upon the majesty of God himself) that it has flowed to us from the very mouth of God by the ministry of men' (*Institutes* 1.7.5). So God is active in the ministry of the Word. It is powerful because God has made it powerful. This is the effect on the hearer: 'It is certain that if we come to church we will hear not only a mortal man speaking but we shall feel (even by his secret power) that God is speaking to our souls, that he is the teacher' (Calvin, *Sermons on 1 and 2 Timothy*, quoted in Parker 1992: 42). So in the Bible, whether it is read or preached, we hear the living words of God.

We should respond to the Bible with faith

Of course the final object of faith is Christ. But we will have true knowledge of Christ, if we receive him as he is offered by the Father: namely, clothed with his gospel. For just as he has been appointed as the goal of our faith, so we cannot take the right road to him unless the gospel goes before us (*Institutes* 3.2.6). For Word and faith stand or fall together:

> Therefore if faith turns away even in the slightest degree from this goal toward which it should aim, it does not keep its own nature, but becomes uncertain credulity and vague error of mind. The same Word is the basis by which faith is supported and sustained; if it turns away from the Word, it falls. Therefore, take away the Word and no faith will remain. (*Institutes* 3.2.6)

To respond to the Bible with faith is to have faith in God who addresses us in the words of the Bible, and in his Son, the Lord Jesus Christ, who is revealed in the Bible, clothed in his promises, clothed in his gospel.

The Bible is the sufficient Word of God

> No other word is to be held in as the Word of God, than what is contained first in the Law and the Prophets, then in the writings of the apostles . . . the only thing granted to the apostles was that which the prophets had had of old. They were to expound the ancient Scripture and to show that what is taught there has been fulfilled in Christ. (*Institutes* 4.8.8)

And what should happen after the apostles? He claims that

> this . . . is the difference between the apostles and their successors: the former were sure and genuine scribes of the Holy Spirit, and their writings are therefore to be considered oracles of God; but the sole office of others is to teach what is provided and sealed in the Holy Scriptures. (*Institutes* 4.8.9)

So Christians in general, and ministers in particular, are to exercise self-discipline in confining their certain knowledge about God to that revealed in the Word, 'A strict adherence to the Word constitutes spiritual chastity', and claims that 'to try to establish contact with God without the Scriptures is like trying to "behold His face by shutting our eyes"' (Wallace 1953: 99, 98 = *Commentary on Psalm* 106:39; and *Corpus Reformatorum* 8: 427).

Summary

So, as we have seen, for Calvin, the Bible is the one Word of God, and Christ is the subject of both Old and New Testaments. It is constituted by a cumulative revelation, and is the final and complete message of God for humankind. It is the Spirit's Word, and its words are brought home to our hearts and lives by the same Holy Spirit. It is at the same time the living Word of God, and also the words of human beings. It calls for a response of faith and obedience, and it is the complete and sufficient Word of God for the world. We end this study of Calvin's theology of the one Word of God with his description of the effect of that Word on human lives:

> Just as old or bleary-eyed men and those with weak vision, if you thrust before them a most beautiful volume, even if they recognize it to be some sort of writing, can scarcely construe two words, but with the aid of spectacles will begin to read distinctly; so Scripture, gathering up the otherwise confused knowledge of God in our minds, having dispersed our dullness, clearly shows us the true God. This, therefore, is a special gift, where God, to instruct the church, not merely uses mute teachers, but also opens his most hallowed lips. (*Institutes* 1.6.1)

The Bible is God speaking his one Word to all. So faith comes by hearing, and hearing through the word of Christ.

In this chapter we have seen the theological basis for the spirituality of the Word as found in the Reformed tradition of John Calvin.

Again we have seen that the content and focus of the spirituality of the Word are God in Christ, its practice is hearing the word of God by faith, its experience is that of meeting God in his words, and it results in trust in Christ and our heavenly Father.

Chapter Five

Issues in spirituality: Sanctify them in the truth; your word is truth

Words and images, faith and sight

The humiliation of the word?

Any defence of the use of the Bible as a resource for spirituality must take note of what Jacques Ellul calls 'the humiliation of the word' in our culture (Ellul 1985). James Daane writes of the common view of words today, 'Words are puffs of air, mere sounds that die on the wind, lacking inherent power . . . mere symbols, meaning whatever their user wants them to mean' (1980: 17).

Os Guinness writes of this phenomenon as follows:

> We are part of the generation in which the image has triumphed over the word, when the visual is dominant over the verbal and where entertainment drowns out exposition. We may go so far as to claim that we live in an age of the image which is also the age of the anti-word and which potentially is the age of the lie. (1995: 157)

He points out that there are three main maxims that underlie advertising, which itself expresses the trends in communication in our society. They are to simplify thought, intensify emotions and magnify symbols (1995: 159).

While there are simple thoughts, intense emotions and important symbols in the Bible, the prevalence of this mode of communication makes it difficult for modern people to grapple with the whole message of the Bible. While the Bible contains many lives, actions, images, visions and events, the form in which it comes to us is words. We do not have an authentic *Jesus* video, nor have we seen the visions of John recorded in Revelation. We have the words of the Bible. This written record may at first appear to be a fragile and ineffective means of communication, and yet in the hand of God it has sustained Christian faith, spirituality and practice for 2,000 years.

In fact words are powerful, especially if those words are God's words. For God's creation and forming of the world is achieved by his speaking. When he said, 'Let there be light,' there was light. Jesus is called the Word of God because he is the full and effective revelation of God. The Bible encourages us to be hopeful about the power of words.

Guinness points to some very interesting differences between sight and sound, seeing and hearing, which he summarizes from Jacques Ellul:

- Sight is intentional while sound is largely involuntary . . . in seeing, we are the subject, the ones in control, those at the centre of our universe . . . Sound comes to us and we receive it immediately . . . We are the ones *addressed* whether we like it or not . . .
- Sight is largely effortless, whereas sounds are often demanding . . .
- Sights and images are more to do with appearances while sound and words take us into meaning. (1995: 160–161)

For:

> Reality is elusive. The paradox is that sight which we think is so certain is far less certain than we realize, whereas words with all their mystery, irony, and ambiguity, appearing to be fragile and fleeting, are the primary means whereby we can deal with things that are true and sure. (1995: 162)

The move away from listening to words to looking at signs explains much of the religious appetites of our generation. So there are people who look to the East in order to get away from wordy preaching to find something to see and contemplate. Pictures and icons, signs and wonders are the flavour of the times. 'We are not in a day of the Word, but a day of the eye' (Guinness 1995: 166–167).

I hope to show that the Bible is a great resource for true spirituality, and also provides the means by which we may test all spiritualities. In the haunting words of Alexander Jones:

> Now what if God should choose to take the word into his service? Supposing God were to use the tongue of man – what then? If, therefore, through the medium of written sentences

> God elects to reveal himself to man in one favoured millennium of history; and if – since God is a wise God – that revelation is tuned to the reception of its hearers; and if – because God is a God of truth – that revelation can never contradict itself as it increases in volume but must now cry aloud the selfsame thing that it once whispered, then the thousand years of revelation is a period to be considered in its entirety, to be savoured fully only when it is complete. (1961: 2)

If biblical spirituality is not to be lost, then we need to recover our trust in the power of words, especially the words of the Bible.

For consider: is a picture worth a thousand words? How many pictures would you need to convey that idea? Or think how easy it is to give an impression of deep suffering in a dramatic presentation, a crucifix or picture of the crucifixion, but how difficult it is to convey the meaning of the atoning death of Christ by this means. Here is Susan Sontag, writing on photography: 'Photographs, which cannot themselves explain anything, are inexhaustible invitations to deduction, speculation, and fantasy. Only that which narrates can make us understand' (1979: 23).

D. H. Lawrence attempted to pour scorn on Christian faith and practice by writing of 'poor little wordy Christianity'. While in fact many religions involve the use of words, Christianity as a religion of a book (like Judaism and Islam) places particular emphasis on words. Words are not only used by believers, but have also been used by God in the process of revelation. The first revelation of God in Genesis 1 is of the God who speaks. It is this speaking God who makes men and women as his speaking images. If words have no power, then God has no power, and 'the gagging of God' is effectively achieved (Carson 1996).

While from one perspective words are being humiliated, from another the power of words is being rediscovered. One of the results of modern linguistic research is the growing understanding of what words can achieve. Words create a world of meaning for a community: 'our language results in social attitude, behaviour, roles, and structures . . . to use language is to create, or recreate, a world' (Ronald J. Allen, in Van Seters 1988: 167). According to Anthony Thiselton, words, and in particular biblical texts, can produce transforming effects, as well as transmit disclosures about the nature of reality (1992: 17). That is, words can effect change in the world, as well as reveal the nature of the world. He gives the examples of a legal will and a love letter; in both cases words are used as the instruments of change. They are speech-acts, which make a creative impact on readers (1992: 32). He points out that this does not require a 'magical' view of language, distinctive to a primitive world view, but that language functions in the same way today (1992: 292). The power of words is especially evident in the context of a theology of covenant promise (1992: 193). The story of creation is not only intended to give information; it is also intended to address us about our status as created beings, and our responsibilities within this created world (Thiselton 1992: 274).

When Kevin Vanhoozer writes about 'God's mighty speech-acts' (1994: 143–181), he is using modern speech-act theory to explain a doctrine of Scripture. He uses J. L. Austin's example of making a covenant as a speech-act, and claims that the 'canon is a collection of diverse speech-acts that together "render" the covenantal God' (1994: 176). He demonstrates that these speech-acts are polygeneric, and includes warning, greeting, statement and question: the Bible contains a greater variety of speech-acts than the propositional, and God does many things with human language other than asserting truths (1994: 173, 175). He shows that this view of God speaking breaks down the false distinction between personal and propositional truth, and quotes Paul Helm: 'There is no antithesis between believing a proposition and believing a person if the proposition is taken to be the assertion of some person' (1994: 178). So the Bible contains the varied speech-acts of the personal God. This idea corresponds to Calvin's comment on the words of God:

> [Paul] calls God true, not only because he is ready to stand faithfully by his promises, but also because whatsoever he says in words he fulfills in deeds; for he so speaks that his command immediately becomes his act. (From *Commentary on Romans* 3:4, quoted in Richard 1974: 157)

Of course the Bible contains many more forms of speech than quotations of God's direct speech. God speaks directly in only some parts of Scripture. Yet in a wider sense we can assert that all of the Bible is God's word in that those who spoke or wrote did so as his representatives, and that the words written down have the authority of God. This view needs to take into account the varied forms of language in the Bible. The words 'There is no God' in Psalm 14:1 are the words of fools, and do not represent truth revealed by God, as is clear in the context.

The Bible as the word or speech-act of God includes not only God's direct speech, but also many other forms of direct and indirect communication. Wayne Grudem lists over twenty-two New Testament texts in which words spoken or written by others in the Old Testament are attributed to God (Carson and Woodbridge 1983: 37–40). So, for example, in Mark 7, what Jesus called 'the commandment of God' in verse 9, he also cites as Moses' words in verse 10, and as 'the word of God in verse 13. In Acts 1:16 Peter attributes the words of David in Psalms 69 and 109 to 'the Holy Spirit through David'. In 1 Corinthians 9:9–10 Paul equates what 'is written in the law of Moses' with what God is now speaking. In Hebrews 1:6–7, quotations from Deuteronomy 32 and Psalm 104 which are not in those texts described as words of God are both described by the writer of Hebrews as what God says. It is not just the words described as coming from God that are the words of God, but the whole of the Old Testament. Jesus' own words have the status of Scripture in 1 Timothy 5:18.

So modern understanding of the power of words in human communication help us to understand a little more of how the words of the speaking God effect what they promise, of the power of God's words. The most powerful example of the power of God's words is seen in the way in which the Lord Jesus himself submitted to, fulfilled and carried out the words of God from the Old Testament. His life was formed by the desire to act according to those words: 'everything written about me in the law of Moses, the prophets, and the psalms must be fulfilled' (Luke 24:44). In the words of Walter Brueggemann, 'Because we live so close to the biblical text, we often fail to notice its generative power to summon and evoke new life. The poetic speech of text and of sermon is a prophetic construal of a world beyond the one taken for granted' (1989: 4).

Pictures, statues and videos

What then about the issue of representations of Christ, of the *Jesus* video, of pictures of Jesus in children's' Bibles? Should we have a manger crib at Christmas? It is one of the odd features of Protestantism that those strongly opposed to statues and representations of God in church buildings provide children with Bibles that include pictures of Jesus, and may support the use of the *Jesus* video in evangelism. The Westminster Larger Catechism tells us:

> What are the sins forbidden in the second commandment? The sins forbidden in the second commandment, are all devising,

> counselling, commanding, using and any wise approving, any religious worship not instituted by God himself; tolerating a false religion; the making any representation of God, or all or any of the three persons, either inwardly in our mind, or outwardly in any kind of image or likeness of any creature whatever; all worshipping of it, or God in it or by it . . . all superstitious devices, corrupting the worship of God, adding to it, of taking from it, whether invented and taken up of ourselves, or received by tradition from others . . . (Westminster Confession 1958: 193–195)

Historically, one reason that statues and pictures of Jesus began to be used was because it was felt that illiterate lay people could not rightly understand the Bible, and so these aids became 'books for the illiterate' (Pelikan 1974: 94). The Reformers wanted to open the Bible to lay people, to train them to read and understand it, and to put aside statues and pictures because they were not the God-given means to know God. In the words of the Heidelberg Catechism:

> But should we allow pictures instead of books in churches, for the benefit of the unlearned?
>
> No. For we should not presume to be wiser than God, who does not want Christendom to be taught by means of dumb idols, but through the living preaching of his Word. (McGrath 1999: 112)

Lying behind this objection is the Old Testament warning about making representations of God. Any such representation is a lie, because it cannot convey the important facts about God. For God is all-powerful, invisible, fills the universe with his presence and is able to speak, see and hear. No representation of God conveys these truths: in fact, any representation of God contradicts these truths.

Some have argued that the incarnation of Christ has changed the situation, that because God became incarnate, therefore we should visualize God (McGrath 1999: 113–114). This matter was an issue in the early church at the time of the great debate about the use of icons. It is important to note, in the words of Lossky, that icons are more than visual aids:

> The cult of the holy images which express things in themselves invisible, and render them really present, visible, and active. An

> icon or a cross does not exist simply to direct our imagination during our prayers. It is a material centre in which there reposes an energy, a divine force, which unites itself to human art. (1957: 189)

Pelikan summarizes the arguments in favour of the use of icons in the great debate in the Eastern Orthodox Church in the eighth and ninth centuries:

- That illiterate people needed them because they could not understand the Bible.
- That people were originally 'made in the image of God', and therefore could visually represent God.
- That Jesus was the express image of the invisible God, and therefore it was possible for a visual object to represent God.
- That it was common practice to know the distinction between an original and its image, and yet to treat the image with the respect due to the original.
- That it was common practice to treasure the clothing of someone who had died.
- That it was an appropriate concession to those pagans who were used to images of their gods.
- That sight was a spiritual gift, and that icons lead us through the use of matter to the spiritual reality behind the matter.
- That the use of icons was a way of dispelling the use of idols.
- That icons had been effective in doing miracles.
- That the use of bread and wine to convey the presence of Christ in the eucharist was evidence that other material objects could also convey his presence. (Pelikan 1974: 93–134)

Here are the arguments against the use of icons:

- That illiterate people might well misuse and misunderstand the point of icons.
- That it is impossible for icons to portray or convey divinity.
- That 'image of the invisible God' is only to be ascribed to Christ, and not to representations of him.
- That this use of icons was an invention.
- That the use of icons is not commanded in the Bible.
- The use of representations of God is forbidden in the Ten Commandments.

- Only the bread and wine of the eucharist were the God-given signs and representations of Christ.
- The worship of icons is a form of idolatry.
- Icons of Christ either pretend to convey his divinity, which they cannot do, or only portray his humanity, which is then not a true representation of Christ.
- That Christ was visible and tangible only in his earthly life on earth, and is now not on earth, but in heaven. (Pelikan 1974: 93–134)

For a variety of reasons, those who promoted the use of icons won the day, and they are still part of the spirituality of the Eastern Orthodox tradition. The Reformed tradition has agreed that representations of God are deceptive, and are forbidden by Scripture. This was not a decision about the use of art, but a theological decision about how God has made himself known to us, and a fear of any idolatry that might distract us from knowing God. It was also a decision that ordinary believers should have access to the Bible, and be trained to read it. Neil McGregor has shown what a great impact there was when statues and wall paintings were removed and replaced by words in the form of the Ten Commandments, the Creed, the Lord's Prayer on the east wall in English churches at the time of the Reformation (McGregor 2000). Diarmaid MacCulloch writes of the experience of the impact of a Reformed Church of England church building in 1553: 'The greatest visual impact came from words: words in painted plaster, boards, or printed posters . . . turning the church interior into the pages of a giant scrapbook of scripture' (2002: 159).

To use depictions of Christ for children and enquirers must be regarded as an oddity, when they are those who are least equipped to understand the special rules that must be applied to avoid errors in apprehension. Another objection to the use of statues and images is that we look at pictures of people when they are absent, but not when they are present. If Christ is present where two or three are gathered in his name, then there is no need for aids to our memories. Using those aids seems to suggest that he is absent.[1] For Paul it was by preaching that 'before your eyes . . . Jesus Christ was publicly exhibited as crucified' (Gal. 3:1).

We should also think of this issue in the light of the Bible's distinction between living by faith now, and the vision of God we will have

[1] See also the discussion of icons in Ellul 1985: 102–106.

after the return of Christ. Paul shows us the helpful distinction between the partial knowledge we have now and the full knowledge we will have when Christ returns: 'For now we see in a mirror, dimly, but then we will see face to face. Now I know only in part; then I will know fully, even as I have been fully known' (1 Cor. 13:12). He makes it clear that there is a divine order in this, 'when the complete comes, the partial will come to an end' (1 Cor. 13:10). Knowledge now is certain but partial; knowledge then will be complete and personal, face to face. Similarly Paul can characterize our existence as 'away from the Lord' (2 Cor. 5:6), and then explain that this is why 'we walk by faith, not by sight' (2 Cor. 5:7).

Yet those who walk by faith also have the Holy Spirit: we are marked with the seal of the Holy Spirit, 'the pledge of our inheritance' as we wait for our 'redemption as God's own people' (Eph. 1:13–14). The Holy Spirit within reminds us that we are God's children, and prompts us to call on God our Father (Rom. 8:15–16). The presence of the Spirit comforts us and also makes us long for the future that is ours in Christ. The sign of the presence of the Spirit is the fruit of love, joy, peace, patience, kindness, generosity, faithfulness, gentleness and self-control (Gal. 5:22–23). As our churches are temples of God's Holy Spirit (1 Cor. 3:16), so also our bodies are temples of God's Spirit: 'do you not know that your body is a temple of the Holy Spirit within you?' (1 Cor. 6:19). Christian spirituality gives us comfort and reassurance that we are God's children, makes us long for the return of Christ, and is lived out in our human bodies in all the godly fruit of the Spirit.

This view of faith now and sight then provides the vital context for our research into the spirituality of the Word. It explains that 'faith' is the characteristic of this age, as 'sight' is the characteristic of the age to come. It explains why the word has priority now, whereas vision will have the priority when Christ returns. This is why spirituality which tries to replace sound by sight, word by vision, is misleading; it is misleading because it is mistimed. It is yet another attempt to live now as we cannot live: of trying to live now as if Christ has already returned in glory.

There are of course many examples of this mistake in contemporary spirituality. The claims of perfect healing, spiritual perfection, a perfect church or of complete knowledge, are all attempts to live now as if Christ has already returned, as if the general resurrection had already occurred. So too is the replacement of a spirituality of hearing the audible by that of seeing the visible. We need to hear again the words of Jesus 'Blessed are those who have not seen, and yet have come to believe' (John 20:29). We walk by faith and therefore not by sight. We can see the beauty of the Lord by hearing about him in his word, and reflecting on and rejoicing in his character. We will not see the beauty of the Lord until he returns.

Polman, writing on the theology of Augustine, comments:

> There comes a time when Scripture as the Word of God has fulfilled its task. After all, the Bible was meant to kindle and support our longing for the fatherland, in which the Scriptures are fulfilled. According to St. Augustine, there are, 'two states of life, preached and commended to the Church from heaven, whereof the one is in faith, the other in sight; one in the temporal sojourn in a foreign land, the other in the eternity of the (heavenly) abode'. (1961: 231, quoting from Augustine's *Tractatus in Joannis Evangelium* 124, 5)

When Augustine is writing of the Mount of Transfiguration, when Peter wanted to build a dwelling for Christ, he takes this as Peter's desire to live in contemplation before the time is right: 'Come down, Peter, you who love to rest on the mountains, come down and preach the Word' (Polman 1961: 236, from Augustine on 2 Timothy 4:2). Now is the time for the Word; then will be the time for contemplation of God in Christ.

Sacred times, places, objects and actions

This is an important issue for Christian spirituality. For many traditions within Christianity, sacred times, places, objects and actions lie at the centre of their spirituality. They think that Christianity without these aids is impoverished if not fundamentally deficient. But the Reformed tradition has been opposed to at least some of these practices, and has regarded them as futile or destructive of true Christian faith and practice. While Reformed and Evangelical Christians place great emphasis on the 'means of grace' provided by God and clearly ordained in the Bible, they have been opposed to other practices not found in the Bible, and also opposed to the use of some practices in the Old Testament, but which are fulfilled in Christ. As Rice points out:

> One reason for this high role for scripture is the concern for Reformed Christians about the dangers of idolatry. The

> Heidelberg Catechism describes idolatry: 'It is to imagine or possess something in which to put one's trust in place of or beside the one true God who has revealed himself in his Word.' (1991: 95)

Notice the subtlety of idolatry. It may be a false God, or it may be a God-given practice that is too highly valued, or it may be a physical object or a mental construct that we use though it is not commanded by God. Holmes is wrong when he claims that 'Calvin was a rationalist who rejected pilgrimages, fasting, almsgiving, and other ascetical practices' (Holmes 2002: 126). Calvin does commend self-denial (*Institutes* 3.7.8). His opposition to pilgrimages is not because he is a rationalist, but he is opposed to any form of justification by good religious works, and because pilgrimages are not commanded by God, and will distract us from the means of grace that God has provided.

A contemporary example is the practice of lighting a candle as a method of offering a prayer to God. It looks effective, because it is visible, attractive and 'spiritual'. But there is no promise in the Bible that tells us that God regards a candle as an equivalent to a prayer, and a moment's reflection will show us that it is a remarkably thin replacement for an expression of personal relationship between the believer and his or her God.

So positively, Evangelical and Reformed Christians want to make the most of the 'means of grace' provided by God and explained in the Bible. Negatively, they do not want to be distracted, confused or misled by other religious practices that are not God-given. They are convinced by Paul's powerful imagery: 'I feel a divine jealousy for you, for I promised you in marriage to one husband, to present you as a chaste virgin to Christ. But I am afraid that as the serpent deceived Eve by its cunning, your thoughts will be led astray from a sincere and pure devotion to Christ' (2 Cor. 11:2–3).[2] And they are warned by the ease with which New Testament churches abandoned the faith of Jesus Christ.

These are complicated issues, but a biblical theology of spirituality will help us to begin to make sense of these matters.

Old Testament

Sacred times, places, objects and actions are certainly part of religion in the Old Testament.

[2] See Ortlund 1996.

We find the first reference to sacred time in Genesis 2. Here we read, 'God blessed the seventh day and hallowed it, because on it God rested from all the work that he had done in creation' (Gen. 2:3). This one day a week also becomes a day of holiness for the people of God. It is a participation in God's day of rest, and also a participation in redemption (Exod. 20 and Deut. 5).

This principle of the sabbath is later extended to include sabbaths of years, and the jubilee year is the seventh year. Other annual festivals include the Passover, the Feast of Weeks, the Feast of Booths and the Day of Atonement. These sacred times are of such importance that the religious activities of the people of God can later be summarized as 'New moon and sabbath . . . new moons and your appointed festivals' (Is. 1:13–14).

Sacred places include the land promised to Abram (Gen. 12:1), later called 'the holy land' (Zech. 2:12). So too are places of revelation for the early believers, like Jacob who called one such place Bethel, house of God (Gen. 28:19), another, God's camp (Gen. 32:2), and another, Peniel, face of God (32:30). So too Mount Sinai became a holy place when God descended to speak with and dwell with his people (Exod. 19 – 25). If the Holy Land had within it special places, later there would be one place, chosen by God, where he could be found: 'you shall seek the place that the LORD your God will choose' (Deut. 12:5). At the centre of Jerusalem was the temple, the 'exalted house', where God's name was to be found (1 Kgs. 8:13, 29). It is not that God is confined or limited to these holy places. The whole world is his, and heaven and the highest heaven cannot contain him, as Solomon's prayer makes clear (1 Kgs. 8:27). Nevertheless God has promised to be found in the place he has chosen, by the revelation (the name) he has given (1 Kgs. 8:29). His name is present, and it is towards this name that his people will pray for forgiveness; and because God's eyes are open day and night towards this place, he will hear and forgive.

Sacred places are also where sacred objects are found. While there was no representation of God, no picture or image of the mighty God (unusual in the Middle East at that time), there were still the sacred objects that pointed to the presence of God.

It is striking that the first two commandments are concerned with sacred objects, and both are negative commands. The first describes God as the Lord who brought you out of the land of Egypt, out of the house of slavery, and then includes the instruction 'you shall have no other gods before me' (Exod. 20:3). The second forbids the making of an idol: 'whether in the form of anything that is in heaven above, or that is on the earth beneath, or that is in the water under the earth' (Exod. 20:4). Not only are other gods forbidden, but any representation of the Lord is also forbidden. The point is reinforced with the first major and dramatic sin of Aaron and the people in making the image of a golden calf, and saying, 'These are your gods, O Israel, who brought you up out of the land of Egypt' (Exod. 32:4). The sin of worshipping other gods, and the sin of making a representation of God, are so great that the punishment is the ending of the covenant that God has made with his people. The first painful lesson of the covenant people of God after Mount Sinai is to remember the first two commandments, and not to make mistakes with sacred objects.

God gave to Moses at Mount Sinai the words he had spoken (Exod. 24:4, 12), and the responsibility of building a portable sanctuary 'so that I may dwell among them' (Exod. 25:8). The sanctuary was a tent, designed to be set up in the desert, and carried through it on the way to the land. In the most holy place were the ark or box, designed to carry the covenant, the words of God. The top of the ark had a cover of gold, the mercy seat. At either end of the mercy seat were the two cherubs, with their wings overshadowing the mercy seat (Exod. 25:10–22). This mercy seat was the throne of God on earth, where God would meet with his Moses, and deliver to him all his instructions for the Israelites (Ps. 80:1 and Exod. 25:22). God is not portrayed, but the signs of his presence are his words, his throne and his forgiveness, found within and on the ark.

This leads us to the sacred people of the Old Testament. While the whole nation of Israel is 'a priestly kingdom and holy nation' (Exod. 19:6), there are also some people called to particular responsibilities, who are set apart, made holy, for these tasks.

With sacred places, people and objects come sacred actions. These are always associated with the preservation of the covenant relationship between the Lord and his people, and deal with the need for sin to be dealt with and the relationship with God to be maintained. Circumcision is the sign of the covenant given to Abraham and his descendants (Gen. 17), and is a sign of the radical repentance and change needed to continue as God's people (Deut. 30:6). The daily, occasional and annual sacrifices are established so that sin can be atoned and fellowship with God maintained (Lev. 1 – 4).

It is important to notice that the purpose of the tabernacle, the priesthood and the sacrifices was to enable the holy God to dwell among his people without destroying them for their sin. We often think of this from a human perspective with the question 'How can a sinful people approach a Holy God?' and view the tabernacle as an answer to this question. This however is not the first question. The primary issue is 'How can a Holy God live among this people without destroying them?', and the tabernacle, priesthood and sacrifices are God's provision to enable this to happen.

It is certainly the case that in the Old Testament, sacred times, places, objects and actions are inextricably part of the revelation, and foundational to life with God. It is important to remember that these times places, objects, people and actions express the covenant relationship between the Lord and his people. They are expressions of covenant holiness: they are sacred because they are aspects of the covenant.

The moral dimension of sacredness in the Old Testament means that when God's people turn away from him, the sacred things have no positive value and indeed become a snare. The danger is to turn away from God, but to continue to trust in the sacred times, places, objects, people or actions when these things not longer express covenant relationship with God. In Isaiah's time the people continue to observe sabbaths, offer sacrifices and trample the courts of the temple, though they have 'despised the Holy One of Israel', and are 'utterly estranged' from him (Is. 1:4). In Jeremiah's time, 'This is the temple of the LORD' become deceptive words, as they have made God's house a 'den of robbers' (Jer. 7:4, 11).

There are two major sins in the Old Testament, both of which have to do with the use of sacred objects, places, times and people. One sin is to follow other gods, to trust their prophets, to engage in their worship, to worship their idols and to trust in them and serve them. The other sin is to use the sacred objects, places, times and people given by God, but to turn away from God, whose covenant they represent. The first sin is that of idolatry, and the second that of false security, holding the form but not the power of godliness.

Sacredness in the Old Testament serves God's covenant purposes: it is a gift, not intrinsic to the place, time, object or person. It is an aspect of the relationship between the holy God and the people he has made holy so that he may live with them.

Sacred times, places, objects, people and actions in Christian spirituality?

Many forms of spirituality make use of such sacred things, and many forms of Christian spirituality also focus on them as spiritual aids.

Marion Hatchett, drawing on the work of Mircea Eliade, describes the sanctification of life, time and space as the key to understanding rituals in human life and in Christian practice (1976: 5–11). Examples of sanctifying life include baptism, marriage, ordination and burial. Sanctifying time includes the pattern of the liturgical day, week and year. Sanctifying space includes the consecration of church buildings, the use of colours, and religious objects. For some, objects and actions used by the church are material signs of the presence of the spiritual world.

Lossky uses the insights of St Maximus about the liturgy:

> The ascent of the presiding Bishop to the altar and to his throne is an image of the Ascension. The entry of the assistant ministers symbolizes the entrance of the Gentiles into the Church . . . The reading of the Gospel, the descent of the presiding Bishop from his throne, the expulsion of the catechumens and penitents, and the closing of the doors of the church, symbolize the events of the Last Judgement, the second coming of the Lord, the separation of the elect from the damned, and the passing away of the visible world. Then the entry with the holy gifts represents the revelation of eternity; the kiss of peace – the union of all souls with God finally being accomplished. (1957: 189–190)

Lossky claims that there is a deep bond between theology and mysticism, between doctrine and spirituality (1957: 236). This bond is expressed in the liturgy, as we have seen, when every action has a deeper symbolic meaning, a revelation of God. A similar view is expressed by the architect Ninian Comper, writing about church buildings:

> What is a church? – It is a building which enshrines the altar of Him who dwelleth not in temples made with hands and yet has made there His Covenanted Presence on earth. It is the centre of Worship in every community of men who recognise Christ as the Pantokrator, the Almighty, the Ruler and Creator of all things; at its altar is pleaded the daily sacrifice . . . There is then no such thing as a Protestant church. A church is of its very nature Catholic . . . To enter therefore a Christian church is to enter none other than the House of God and the Gate of Heaven. (Comper in Wilson 1992: 38–39)

Comper's view is that a church is the House of God and Gate of Heaven because Christ is present there in the sacrament, when his sacrifice is pleaded daily at the altar. A church is a shrine for the sacramental presence of Christ.

Alister McGrath reflects on sacred spaces as places of pilgrimage within the history of Christianity (1999: 131–132). He lists five places of world significance: Jerusalem, Rome, Canterbury, Santiago de Compostela and Lourdes, and points out that the benefits of pilgrimages are the need for commitment, the opportunity to reflect on the qualities of the person associated with the site, the reminder that life itself is a pilgrimage, and the possibility that the places are endued with some spiritual quality (1999: 132–133). While Protestants have traditionally been suspicious of pilgrimages, some now take the opportunity to visit the Holy Land, or the sites of the seven churches of Asia.[3]

New Testament

We now look at the New Testament to see the use of sacred times, places, objects and actions in the church of that time. In terms of the New Testament, the issue that we are studying provides a fascinating perspective, because religions in the first century, including Judaism, focused on sacred times, places, objects and people, and therefore the conversion of both Jews and Gentiles to Christianity raised many issues about these aspects of spirituality. Should Gentiles adopt Jewish holy places, be circumcised and follow the food laws? Should they continue to use their own holy places and rituals? What should they do?

John

In John's Gospel one important theme is Jesus' visits to Jerusalem and the temple, culminating in his final visit at the time of his crucifixion and resurrection. His going up to Jerusalem is the fulfilment of 'He came to what was his own' (1:11). Granted this geographical focus on Jerusalem and the temple, what is their significance for Christian faith and spirituality?

When the Passover of the Jews was near, Jesus went up to Jerusalem, and began to clear the people selling cattle, sheep and doves and the moneychangers out of the temple (2:13–16). His reference to 'my

[3] Indeed Thomas Cook began his travel agency to help Protestant Christians to visit the Holy Land!

Father's house' asserts his identity and authority over the temple (2:16). When the Jews ask for a sign of his authority, Jesus' reply is 'Destroy this temple, and in three days I will raise it up' (2:19). By these words we learn that Jesus' own body has replaced the temple, that all that was true of the temple is now true in Jesus – here is the presence of God on earth, the place of atonement and forgiveness, the place of fellowship with God, the way in which God dwells among his people. Because Jesus is now the temple, true worship will soon not be in Jerusalem. For 'the hour is coming when you will worship the Father neither on this mountain [Mount Gerizim, where the Samaritans worship] nor in Jerusalem' (4:21). It is not that Jesus has dismissed Judaism and its religion, as 'salvation is from the Jews' (4:22). But this is the time of change, and, 'the hour is coming, and is now here, when the true worshippers will worship the Father in spirit and truth' (4:23). This is a theological statement, and is based on the fact that he is the true temple. It would be difficult to argue for continued pilgrimage to Jerusalem and the temple in the light of this teaching from John's Gospel.

Acts

Similarly in Acts there is a strong theme of Jerusalem and the temple. The day of Pentecost is celebrated amid many pilgrims who have come to Jerusalem (2:1, 5). The early church met in the temple, and Peter preached there (2:46; 3:11). The headquarters of the early church was in Jerusalem (8: 14), and there important decisions are made for the whole church (15:1–29). The Ethiopian eunuch is returning from pilgrimage to Jerusalem when he is converted to Christ by Philip (8:27–40).

Yet it would be difficult to argue for a Christian commitment to holy places from Acts. When Stephen is accused of teaching that 'Jesus of Nazareth will destroy this place and will change the customs that Moses handed on to us' (Acts 6:14), his reply is an argument that God is not bound to place, that 'the Most High does not dwell in houses made by human hands' (7:48). Similarly when Paul is preaching in Athens to a Gentile audience, he proclaims, 'The God who made the world . . . does not live in shrines made by human hands' (17:24). There is no commitment to the sacred places of Judaism or of the Gentile world. The climax of Acts does not lie in Paul constructing a building, shrine or pilgrimage centre in Rome; it lies in his daily teaching of the Bible, welcoming all who came to him (28:30–31).

Hebrews

Hebrews also provides important insights into the Christian interpretation of the sacred place of the land promised to Abraham, such a central theme in the Old Testament.

Faith is 'the assurance of things hoped for, the conviction of things not seen' (11:1), and then rightly points to Abraham as an example of such faith. The writer of Hebrews tells of Abraham setting out 'for a place that he was to receive as an inheritance' (11:8). In fact he lived in the Promised Land 'as in a foreign land', in tents, as did Isaac and Jacob (11:9). So although in one sense he received the land, it was not his permanent dwelling place. The writer of Hebrews explains how Abraham did this, by faith: 'For he looked forward to the city that has foundations, whose architect and builder is God' (11:10). We might have expected the author to claim that Abraham believed that one day his descendants would take over the land, as did happen. But this is not what he writes. Abraham's faith is that he sees that the Promised Land is only a temporary resting place at best, and that there was a God-built city to look forward to, a permanent place to live with God. In fact:

> All of these died in faith without having received the promises, but from a distance they saw and greeted them. They confessed that they were strangers and foreigners on the earth . . . they desire a better country, that is, a heavenly one . . . [God] has prepared a city for them. (11:13, 16)

The writer is not saying that *they* received a land but *we* receive a heavenly city, as we might expect. He is saying that they and we both look for heavenly country and city, built by God. So, to go on a pilgrimage to the earthly Jerusalem would be to visit a place that even Old Testament saints knew was not the fullness of God's promise! It is hard to imagine that the author of Hebrews would encourage either Jews or Gentiles on a pilgrimage to the Holy Land, Jerusalem or the temple. He wants to raise their faith to heaven, to Christ their great High Priest, to his once-for-all sacrifice, and their access through him to God. He wants to encourage them, 'you have come to Mount Zion . . . the city of the living God, the heavenly Jerusalem . . . and to Jesus' (12:22, 24). He does not want them to draw back, or to focus on possible earthly rewards. He is a travel agent, but not for an earthly destination!

It is an irony that the incarnation of Christ is often used as a reason in Catholic spirituality to have visible and tangible spirituality. In Hebrews the incarnation of Christ brings an end to the visible and tangible practices of Old Testament religion, because they point forward to the coming of Christ. They are 'shadow', not 'substance'.[4]

Eusebius of Caeserea taught that the spirituality of the New Testament was not concerned with the physical land such as the land of Israel or the city of Jerusalem, but that these were physical symbols of spiritual reality. Cyril of Jerusalem taught that Jerusalem was indeed 'a holy city' (McGrath 1999: 132). On the evidence we have seen from John, Hebrews and 1 Peter, it looks as if Eusebius was right!

1 Corinthians

We see similar ideas in 1 Corinthians. If in the Old Testament there is great interest in the building of the temple, so too there is in 1 Corinthians. Here the temple of the living God is not a building of wood and stone, but is the church at Corinth: '[You are] God's building . . . you are God's temple, and . . . God's Spirit dwells in you' (1 Cor. 3:9, 16). Everyone should build up the church (3:10). Two good mottos for their meetings are 'love builds up' (8:1) and 'Let all things be done for building up' (14:26).

It is important that we do not miss the extraordinary statement Paul is making about the church. There was one holy temple in the Old Testament, one throne of God on earth, one place where God dwelt among his people. Now the church of God at Corinth, sanctified in Christ Jesus (1:2), as elsewhere, is God's holy temple. Why would you visit the temple in Jerusalem, when you are that temple in Corinth? Paul expands this teaching even further when he tells the Corinthians that for each one of them 'your body is a temple of the Holy Spirit within you' (6:19). There were plenty of temples of the Holy Spirit in Corinth! Here is the natural extension of the principle of the incarnation, that the God who was previously found in a building in the Old Testament is now found in people in the New.

One of the features of decadent spirituality is that it places too much emphasis on objects, and not enough on people. It is interesting to note that in 1 Corinthians Paul uses the term 'body of Christ' to describe both the church and the bread in the Lord's Supper. He tells the Corinthians, 'Now you are the body of Christ and individually members of it' (12:27). And he writes of the Lord's Supper, 'The

[4] Rice 1991: chs. 4–7 expands on the means of grace.

bread that we break, is it not a sharing in the body of Christ?' (10:16). He also explains the link between the two: 'Because there is one bread, we who are many are one body, for we all partake of the one bread' (10:17).

It is of course remarkable that Paul uses these two ideas and links them so closely; the church is 'the body of Christ', and the Lord's Supper is a sharing in the body and blood of Christ (10:16). I take both as more than metaphors: both are statements of ways in which we participate, share in and have fellowship with Christ. Given this balance and link in 1 Corinthians, it is a remarkable feature of some churches that so much reverence is given to the bread as the body of Christ, and comparatively little to the people as the body of Christ! Liturgical practice that reflected the balance in 1 Corinthians would give both equal respect. Furthermore after the church has received the Lord's Supper, the body of Christ has received the body of Christ, all reverence should be given to the people. It is worth remembering that the fault at Corinth was too little respect for the church as the body of Christ, and that the church that does this received the Lord's Supper to its condemnation (11:29–30). I occasionally challenge my friends who give great reverence to the sacrament to give more reverence to the congregation in their liturgical practice, but without any success!

Why then are some who are generally opposed to special days so committed to the sabbath? Why is the instruction about the sabbath taken very seriously? The answer is that the law about the sabbath is seen as part of the moral law, while laws about the festivals are seen as part of the ceremonial law, which is fulfilled in the atoning death of Christ.[5]

Sacred times, places, objects and actions today?

Many assume that real spirituality is found in the use of sacred times, places, objects and actions, and that any spirituality which does not have them must be seriously deficient. These things gain credibility because they are found in different forms in many religions of the world, and seem to be the universal language of spirituality. The priority placed on them leads many people to assume that any form of

[5] There are a variety of opinions within the Reformed and Evangelical traditions about the continuing relevance for Christians of the sabbath law, as also about the continuing relevance of the Old Testament moral law.

Christianity that does not use them must be seriously lacking in spirituality, and that Reformed and Evangelical faith must therefore be seriously deficient.

What then are we to make of these ideas? Should church buildings be shrines of God's presence, sacred space where God is to found? Should Protestants call buildings Bethel, house of God? Should Catholics have a detailed liturgical year? Should Protestants regard Sunday as our version of sacred time? Should we honour sacred objects, like the Turin Shroud or Charles Simeon's teapot or C. S. Lewis's wardrobe? Should we be pilgrims to the Holy Land or Rome or Geneva or Wittenberg? Should Christians celebrate the Passover meal at Easter? Should we call our church building 'sanctuary' or 'tabernacle'?

Melito of Sardis (130–90), in his sermon on the Passover, used the idea of an architect or sculptor making a model of wax, wood or clay to make clear what was to be constructed, and then destroying the model once the structure had been built (Old 1998a: 286). If God has discarded the models, should we still use them, or use our equivalents of them?

Here are five guidelines that come from the Bible passages we have noted.

1. We should expect specific instructions from God in the Bible to make use of any of these. In the case of Old Testament times, places, objects and actions, we should note that all of these were the subject of specific instruction by God. The land was the gift of God, the tabernacle and temple were built with the detailed instructions provided by God, and sacred times like the sabbath and the festivals were set apart by God. God wants his will on these matters to be clear. There are no parallel instructions in the New Testament.
2. All these Old Testament features are shadows of the Christ who is to come. We should not return to the shadows when we have the substantial reality in Christ. The Promised Land pointed forward to the heavenly city and country, Jerusalem points forward to the heavenly city, and the tabernacle and temple foreshadow Christ and his people, as do the priesthood and the sacrifices. Circumcision points to the death and resurrection of Christ, and the sabbath points to the rest that is salvation in Christ. Christ is the key to interpret the Bible, and all the Old Testament types are fulfilled in him and the salvation he brought.

We must respect the shape of salvation history, and as we do not have crusades for Christian possession of the Holy Land, so we should not reduplicate other features of the Old Covenant provisions and promises.

3. When the people of God do make other objects, such as the golden calf in Exodus 32, they fall subject to the judgment of God. When they adopt the spiritual practices of the nations around them, they are condemned, in both Old and New Testaments. They are to 'flee from the worship of idols' (1 Cor. 10:14).
4. What about a liturgical pattern and sacred space that reflects the reality of heaven? It is often claimed that a church building with its sanctuary, altar and sacrament house reflects heavenly reality. In fact we do know what an earthly representation of heaven is like, and it is found in the tabernacle and temple of the Old Testament. There the focus was not on the altar of sacrifice, which was in the courtyard, but on the holy of holies. The ark of the covenant was the throne of God, the place of atonement, and held the documents of the covenant, that is, words written on the tablets of stone. The centrality of the words of God in the tabernacle and temple is still reflected today in synagogues around the world, where the Scriptures are kept in an 'ark' at the front of the building. We too should focus on the Word of God.
5. May we add to the activities given us by God, to fill them out with more spiritual meaning? A common example of this is giving a lighted candle to the newly baptized, as a symbol of their enlightenment and their duty to shine as a light in the world. This is hardly damaging in itself, and yet it does actually change the meaning of the baptism. Whereas baptism means death and resurrection, a candle means enlightenment. Death and resurrection is a far more dramatic and violent image than enlightenment, and yet as the water dries off or subsides, the enduring image has subtly changed to the more moderate image of candlelight. Salvation has been replaced by knowledge, and identification with Christ's death and resurrection by increased understanding.

There was considerable debate at the time of the Reformation about right liturgical activities. Some held that any activity was appropriate as long as it did not obscure gospel truth, while others held that only those activities ordered in the New Testament would be acceptable. Both these views are also held today. The position taken by the Church of England in 1662 was that other activities were acceptable as long as they served the gospel and did not obscure it, but that baptism and the Lord's Supper must be celebrated according to New Testament instruction, with no added activities such as reservation or adoration of the sacrament. The stricter Reformed position is that we should do only what we are instructed to do by God, and that anything beyond that is sin.

The fact that there are no detailed instructions about new covenant liturgy is important. Those who enjoy complex liturgy should remember that this is an optional extra, and cannot lie at the heart of Christianity. Those who like simplicity should remember that the lack of detailed instruction means that we are free to develop as we wish, as long as the gospel is reflected in our actions, and the necessities of Word, prayer and gospel sacraments are not obscured or lost.

A complex issue

We need to recognize the subtlety of what the New Testament teaches about the continued use of Old Testament practices. In Galatians the idea that Gentiles must be circumcised is absolutely opposed by Paul, but in Acts 16 he has Timothy circumcised so that he can take part in the mission to the Jews. This is because in Galatia the Judaizers are demanding that Gentiles be circumcised, and Paul knows that this action would compromise the sufficiency of Christ. In Colossians 2 Paul warns the people not to be forced into observing food or drink regulations, or festivals, new moons or sabbaths (Col. 2:16). In Romans 14 however he will not allow those who are weak in faith to be despised, even though they have regulations about food and drink and special days (Rom. 14:1–6). What should we make of these instructions?

- There are situations when the continued use of Old Testament practices is destructive, and also situations when they may be permitted for those who are 'weak in faith', or for evangelism.
- Jewish believers in Christ may not require Gentiles to submit to Jewish practices that were given to point forward to Christ. Now that the substance has come, they should not require the shadow.
- Those who continue Jewish practices must not require others to do the same. Those who continue to practise them should not regard themselves as superior: in fact they are 'weak in faith'.
- These matters are of secondary importance, and do not justify requiring people to leave the church: those who practise them innocently should be welcomed.

- Those who add them as a requirement for salvation must be corrected, as in Galatians. Those who teach that these or other practices are necessary should be refuted, lest they compromise the sufficiency of Christ.
- We should recognize that though there are detailed directions in the Old Testament about the rituals of true spirituality (tabernacle and temple, priesthood and sacrifice), there is a significant change in the New Testament. The activities of the church are directed, but the details of the rituals are not. We should teach the Bible, pray, baptize and share in the Lord's Supper. But few detailed instructions are given. Therefore the details of the rituals must be of secondary importance. For 'Christ's Gospel is not a Ceremonial Law (as much of Moses' law was), but it is Religion to serve God, not in bondage of figure or shadow but in the freedom of the Spirit'.[6]

The power of words

Words, mind and heart

One of the most powerful assumptions in our world is the polarity of mind and heart. It is evident in the way we separate our lives into two areas, one to be governed by the mind (what we think), and the other to be governed by the heart (what we feel). We assume that matters of the mind cannot be emotional, and matters of the heart cannot be intellectual, that the mind must always be dispassionate, and the heart irrational.

Of course modern psychology has questioned this division, and attempted to show that even when we think we are being rational, we are actually governed by deep emotions. But even this notion still perpetuates the polarity, by assuming that if we are really governed by our hearts, we are self-deluded to imagine that our minds have any influence. The issue is an important one for spirituality. If we ask the question 'Is spirituality fundamentally of the heart or the mind?', then the answer will have a profound effect on our spirituality. If we answer that spirituality is fundamentally of the heart, we will then assume that intellect and rationality are deeply unspiritual, and damaging to spirituality. If we answer that spirituality is fundamentally of the mind, then we will avoid emotion, and regard the safest spirituality as the most rational and controlled.

[6] Book of Common Prayer, from the preface, 'Of Ceremonies'.

This polarity in approaching spirituality has deeply affected us: the almost universal assumption has been that spirituality is of the heart, not the mind. Here are some of the results:

- Spirituality has tended to be consciously untheological.
- Spirituality has valued the intuitive, and avoided the rational.
- Christian traditions which have valued theology (e.g. the Reformed tradition) have been assumed to have no spirituality.
- Spirituality has been associated with less rational sources, such as objects, places, buildings and music.
- Spirituality has been dissociated from words, for fear that they will import an unhelpful rationality.

It is unnecessary to perpetuate the heart–mind polarity, because there is no reason why truth should not be passionate, and no reason why emotion should not be intellectual. The Bible is both an intellectual document (it contains ideas), and an emotional document (those ideas are expressed emotionally). There is no reason why we cannot be passionate about the truth, and no reason why truth cannot have emotional power. Jesus, quoting from the Old Testament the commandment about loving God with all your heart, soul and strength, added the words 'and with all your mind' (Mark 12:30).

Because spirituality has been associated with the heart rather than the mind, it has tended to neglect the value of theological insight and rational debate. If it has not been wary of words, then it has been drawn to a particular use of words, evocative, creative and poetic, rather than content-full, cognitive and clarifying. So there is a recognizable trend in spirituality to favour a particular kind of verbal communication, and to avoid language that includes clear content, information, evaluation or argument.

This tradition in spirituality has been expressed in the Romantic movement, in the poetry of Wordsworth, for example, and in the Gothic revival movement in the architecture of church buildings. So Wordsworth wrote:

> One impulse from a vernal wood
> May teach you more of man,
> Of moral evil and of good
> Than all the sages can.
>
> (Wordsworth, 'Prelude', quoted in Roston 1965: 180)

We will see below that the notion that spontaneous prayer is the most authentic prayer also reflects a Romantic view of reality.

As a generalization, Evangelicals have tended to favour a spirituality of the heart (invite Jesus into your heart), and the Reformed tradition has tended to favour a spirituality of the mind (gaining a biblical word view). Biblical spirituality is at the same time warm-hearted and clear-minded, omitting neither the emotions nor the mind. So Paul writes to Timothy that he should preserve the truth of the gospel: 'Hold to the standard of sound teaching that you have heard from me, in the faith and love that are in Christ Jesus' (2 Tim. 1:13). He writes to the Christians at Colossae about the need to stand firm in Christ, with intellectual clarity and passionate emotion: 'As you therefore have received Christ Jesus the Lord, continue to live your lives in him . . . established in the faith, just as you were taught, abounding in thanksgiving' (Col. 2:6–7). Here there are two safeguards against falling away. One is 'the faith', as they have been taught it; the other is enthusiastic and continuing thanksgiving.

There has been a significant change in outlook since the 1950s. After the Second World War, Evangelicals used to be ridiculed for being too emotional, and not intellectually rigorous. Now they are more likely to be rejected because they are too rational, too caught up in theological distinctions, too worried about the truth. The religious world has made a significant move away from the results of a scientific and rational study of the Bible to using it as one source for inspiration, as an example of theological reflection that should inspire us to do the same reflection, or as providing symbols and images that we can use in our own way, and fill with our own content.

It is sometimes claimed that because God is mystery, no words can do justice to him. This is to misunderstand the transcendence of God: it does not reduce his power to become immanent by means of human words, words that convey the truth that God intends.

The final move in following this Romantic ideal is to value creativity and freedom more than the Bible, and to transfer to other and varied sources. In the words of Murray Roston, 'For the romantic poet, the biblical ethos had been partly secularized. God had been largely replaced by the Spirit of Nature, the brotherhood of man by the pantisocratic society, and the Messiah by the dawn of the New World' (1965: 195). The issue is of great practical importance, and is expressed in the decisions ordinary Christians make about spirituality every day. This has been reinforced by the great impact of the charismatic movement, which has tended to promote the emotional rather than the theological side of Christian spirituality.

However, words are not merely cerebral or intellectual in content, but have emotional impact. A robust understanding of the power of words should mean that the heart–mind polarity is rejected as perpetuating a false dichotomy, that the full impact of words on the whole person is recognized. If this is true of usual human communication, it will also be true of God's words, which come with divine power. Spirituality for a postmodern age will engage both mind and heart, in a living relationship with God (Grenz 1996: 169–170).

It is instructive to note the advice of Jonathan Edwards, who wrote in the context of the New England Revival, and tried to make sense of religious experience from the perspective of Reformed theology. He warns against the idea that because a verse from the Bible has come spontaneously into the mind that it is a sign of God's favour, and of religious blessing. Spontaneity is no guarantee of godliness, and Edwards reminds us that as Satan used verses from the Bible in his debate with Jesus in the wilderness he could certainly use them and impress them in our minds, especially a misinterpretation of them. He also points out that those in the parable of the soils who had stony hearts first heard the word with joy, before it withered away through lack of depth (1986: 93). The test of any spirituality, whether emotional or rational, is whether or not it results in changed lives in those who practise it.

We know that those who have a purely intellectual assent to Christianity have a long way to go before they have learnt the cost of discipleship. This is also true of those who have a purely emotional response to Christianity. What is needed is the response of the whole person, to love God with heart, mind, soul and strength.

Rice quotes the Heidelberg Catechism to show that the Reformed tradition expects an equal response of heart and mind: 'It is not only a certain knowledge by which I accept as true all that God has revealed to us in his Word, but also a whole-hearted trust which the Holy Spirit created in me through the gospel' (1991: 57).

True spirituality need not and should not perpetuate the false distinction between heart and mind; and that true spirituality will find the whole person addressed by God's powerful words. Such spirituality will be 'true' because it represents God-given reality, and it will be 'true' because it works. So it will meet both modern and postmodern criteria (Grenz 1996: 172–174).

Prayer, mystic and prophetic

Friedrich Heiler gives us a useful summary of the distinction between mystic prayer and prophetic prayer. This distinction is useful to us because it will help us to see the difference between the use of prayer in, on the one hand, Catholic and some charismatic traditions, and, on the other hand, the practice of the Evangelical and Reformed movement.

Prayer and mysticism

The goal to which mysticism aspires is the isolation and the unification of the inner life by detachment from the world and union with God. Asceticism conduces the renunciation of the world of sense: 'Mystical prayer is a golden ladder which touches the sky and on which one climbs up to God. In union with God there is no room left for prayer, for the soul which has become one with God ceases to pray' (Heiler 1958: 174).

So prayer is just the first step in the process of becoming one with God. In that union there can be no prayer, because the act of prayer implies a distinction between the one who prays and the one to whom the prayer is offered:

> The mystic's prayer is frequently free unrestricted speech with God. The choice of words is that you work for the moment. When prayer is consciously and intentionally employed as a means to recollection and contemplation the utterance of a definite formula of prayer is customary. Mysticism shuts man off from the outer world and forces him back on the world within. The mystics express the high value of silent prayer by contrasting inner or contemplative with oral or outer prayer. Wordless prayer or silence is true prayer. Wordless prayer is a wordless breathing of love in the immediate presence of God. (Heiler 1958:176–178)

What then is the nature and content of mystical prayer? Prayer is the ascent of the mind to God. The praying mystic turns away from all external realities, suppresses by force of will all ideas and emotions directed towards it and focuses his whole attention on the highest spiritual reality, that is, on God. There are three modes or ways of prayer:

- The *purgative way* means detachment from the world, detachment from the feelings and desires of the self and implies the spirit and sorrow of repentance.

- The *illuminative way* implies rest and peace in God, identification of one's own will with God's will, exclusive turning to the highest good, fervent love of God.
- The *unitive way* is expressed in the consciousness of the presence and vision of God, ecstatic union with God and eternal vision of God, and union with Him in the world beyond (Heiler 1958: 180–184).

After contemplation comes ecstasy. The highest and holiest prayer of the mystic is ecstatic prayer, which is no longer prayer in the ordinary sense. All distinctions are abolished. The praying soul and the being prayed to are mingled in unity. In this, requests for external things are irreconcilable with the fundamental strand of mysticism. When they do occur, they play a secondary role, independent of mystical prayer (Heiler 1958: 190–193).

Prophetic prayer

This includes Evangelical and Reformed patterns of prayer:

> Usually, as with primitive man, it is the concrete need of the moment which gives occasion for the prayer. Crises, temptations and needs are the chief but not the only occasions for prayer. The experiences that form motives for prayer are emotions of great intensity. This is what the Old Testament calls the outpouring of the heart, and what John Bunyan calls, 'the opening of the heart, an affectionate pouring out of the soul, the unbosoming of a man's self'. (Heiler 1958: 228–235)

The content of prayer includes the following:

- *Complaint and question.* Calvin writes, 'from the depths of the abyss and from the jaws of death, the servants of God send up a cry to the Lord'. Jeremiah cries, 'why hast thou smitten us and there is no healing for us'.
- *Petition.* For Zwingli, prayer is 'a begging for the necessaries of life, calling on God for help'. The kernel of prophetic prayer is a simple request for deliverance from evil or the granting of gifts and favour. The content of the prayer includes ethical and social values for oneself and for others.
- *The means of persuasion.* Petition is reinforced by persuasion. A petitioner not only presents his desire to God, but 'he bolsters it

well with particulars', as Luther puts it. He gives motives and reasons; he seeks by every indication argument to move God to fulfil his wish.

- *Expressions of weakness and dependence, confession of sinfulness.* In Isaiah we read, 'we are the clay and thou our potter and we are all the work of thy hand'.
- *Expression of trust.* Prophetic prayer begins with the expression of need, but rises to a height where want and desire are forgotten and trust, joy and surrender prevail. Jacob's wrestling with God in the Genesis narrative is the prototype of the prophetic prayer of conflict. This prayer is not easy. Luther says prayer is 'the hardest work of all, a labour above all labours, since he who prays must wager mighty warfare against the doubt and murmuring excited by the faint heartedness and unworthiness we feel within us'. John Bunyan writes, 'Right prayer is accompanied with a continual labour after that which is prayed for.'
- *Expression of resignation.* This is found in Jesus' prayer in the Garden of Gethsemane. The prayer of Jesus 'Not as I will, but as you will' is the prototype of prophetic submission to the will and plan of God.
- *Thanksgiving.* Zwingli writes, 'prayer is first praise and glorifying and then a trustful appeal for aid in our necessities'. The giving of thanks is the joyful acknowledgment that God has granted his grace or benefit.
- *Praise.* Praise is the appropriate response to God the Saviour who has heard and answered the prayer.
- *Belief in the presence of God.* To pray is for Calvin 'A conversation with God', for Luther 'To come into God's presence and to speak with him.' John Bunyan writes, 'Prayer is our most direct and immediate personal approach to the presence of God' (Heiler 1958: 240–276).

Heiler's analysis provides a useful overview. There is one important issue for Reformed and Evangelical patterns of prayer. For Heiler, the Prophetic tradition is strongly influenced by the Romantic ideal of emotion-driven reality. The priority of emotion-driven prayer is an issue that relates to the relationship between mind and heart outlined above. Evangelical Christians have often valued 'heart-prayer', and have assumed that spontaneity is the ultimate expression of the heart. This is why they have often resisted the use of prepared or written prayers. The Reformed tradition has favoured what we might call 'mind-prayer', and has been less concerned that prayers are emotion-driven.

The priority of heart-driven spontaneous prayers is found within Protestantism in the Quaker movement, as we shall see. It nicely equates with the Romantic view that only the spontaneous is inspired. Apparently Samuel Taylor Coleridge put a great deal of effort into promoting the idea that his poem 'Kubla Khan' was the result of an opium-induced trance. While some such experience lay behind it, it bears all the marks of assiduous formation (Lefebure 1975: 252–258). In the world of Romantic ideas the spontaneous is the authentic.

The same idea is often found in Evangelical piety. Unfortunately it expresses an unnecessary and unhelpful limitation. It is not only the spontaneous that is inspired. The careful crafting of many parts of the Bible does not mean that they are not inspired. Luke has done careful research to produce his Gospel and Acts (Luke 1:1–4). Psalm 119 is an acrostic, in which each section begins with the next letter of the Hebrew alphabet; the same form is found in Lamentations. These represent painstaking attention to detailed preparation, and they are certainly inspired. If Beethoven composed because the music within him had to be expressed, then Bach sometimes composed because he needed more money to feed his twenty-two children! The use of prepared prayers is of course expressed every time we use the words of a psalm or other prayers from the Bible in our own praying. There is no reason to believe that the Holy Spirit cannot work ahead of time, that he works only at the last moment!

In general terms Evangelicals will tend to value spontaneity, while Reformed believers are more likely to allow planning and preparation. Similarly for Evangelicals 'guidance' by God is an experience, while for Reformed believers 'guidance' is what God does in his sovereign rule of the universe and care for us, even if it is not 'experienced' by us. Evangelicals are more open to the Romantic movement than are members of the Reformed tradition.

While it may seem an impossible task to change Evangelical practice, there is no theological or biblical reason to believe that only spontaneous prayer is authentic prayer. Our prayers are enriched if we are able to use both spontaneous and prepared prayers. We are called to know and serve God with mind and heart.

Receiving or avoiding God's words

As God's words come to us in the Bible, God's intention is always that they impact upon us. They will always have an intended result, whether to inform, encourage, rebuke, correct, train, equip, transform, change, invigorate or bring hope. There are many ways in which we can try to avoid the impact God's words will have on us, whether as churches or as individuals.

In the parable of the soils Jesus explained how this process happens. Jesus came 'proclaiming the good news of God' (Mark 1:14), and this interpreted parable explains the varied responses to his ministry of the Word.

Significantly, the seed is the Word: 'The sower sows the word' (Mark 4:14).

- Some seed falls on the path and is eaten by the birds. So Satan comes to take away the Word (4:15).
- Some seed falls on rocky ground, springs up quickly, and then dies away because it has no depth of soil. So if people have no root, they endure for a while, but then fall away when trouble or persecution arises because of the Word (4:16–17).
- Some seed falls among thorns. So some people hear the Word, but it is choked by the cares of the world, the lure of wealth and the desire for other things, so that it yields nothing (4:18–19).
- Some seed falls on good soil. These people hear the Word and accept it and bear fruit, thirty, sixty and a hundredfold (4:20).

With these words Jesus has made it clear how important good hearing is, that is, fruitful hearing, productive hearing, hearing that changes lives. No wonder he ended the parable with the words 'Let anyone with ears to hear listen!' (4:9).

How then should we hear the Word and accept it, so that it bears fruit in our lives?

- We should read and study the Bible, and pray that God will help us discern its meaning. We should use all the study guides available, and read it with the desire to meet God in his words: with intelligence, emotional engagement and the will to believe and obey what God tells us.
- We should hear the Bible read and explained when we meet with other Christians as the body of Christ.
- We should prepare ourselves in prayer to hear the Word of God preached Sunday by Sunday.
- We should learn parts of the Bible, and meditate on it 'day and night'.

- We should make sure that our families read and study the Bible together.
- We should use the Bible in daily conversations, so that the words of God are often in our mouths.
- We should allocate special time each week to study the Scriptures, so that we are trained to teach others.
- We should pray for those who are involved in the ministry of the Word in our churches.
- We should pray for those who preach and teach the Word of Christ to unbelievers.
- We should pray for churches around the world, that they might be mature in Christ.[7]

We also learn from the parable what hinders the Word.

Satan plucks the Word away; troubles or persecutions arise because of the Word, and those who have no depth fall away; some hear the Word, but it is choked by cares, desire for wealth and for other things. These obstacles to hearing remain relevant now as then, in every sort of human culture. What devices do we use to hear God's Word today and yet avoid its intended impact?

We can best answer this in terms of different types of personality.

- *Emotional people* can easily deflect the Word by turning the hearing of it into an emotional experience. This means that they can test the reality of the coming of the Word by means of testing its emotional impact, and then focus their response on that emotional experience. But once the emotion has passed, so has the Word.
- *Cerebral people* can easily deflect the Word by turning the hearing of it into an intellectual exercise. They substitute understanding it for responding to it, fitting it into their theological grid so that it does not impact their lives.
- *Ministry people* can easily deflect the Word by receiving it as a message to be passed on to others. They can always see the application to others, but not to themselves.
- *Practical people* can easily deflect the impact of the Word of God by reducing it to something easy to understand and to do. They will have no time for anything not immediately relevant. They will

[7] See Burroughs 1990, sermons 8–10, on how to prepare to receive the ministry of the Word each Sunday.

reduce the Bible to a set of instructions for daily living, and develop a legalism that blunts the power of God's Word.
- *Superficial people* will pay as much attention to the words of the Bible as to anything, and so will never be able to receive the words that can change them.
- *Reactionary people* are those who always want to contradict what anyone has asserted about anything. They too will find that their habit of life makes it very difficult for them to receive the Word of God and let it bear fruit in their lives.

People use a God-given strength, but for the wrong purpose. It is good to be emotional, cerebral, ministry-minded and practical. It can even be useful to know how to avoid being overwhelmed by ideas, or how to critique what we hear. But these strengths can be used to avoid the impact of God's words, and then they become great weaknesses.

It must also be the case that, in Western society, the massive increase in busyness must have a deleterious effect on our having time to hear God's words; and the increase in the sheer quantity of words we hear every day must make it more difficult to focus on the Word of God.

In every age it has taken self-discipline to be able to hear what God is saying: though the particular pressures have varied, the central task remains the same. The Word of God addresses every part of us: mind, emotions, heart, intellect will, desires, fears, hopes, intentions, relationships and actions. No wonder hearing and obeying God's Word is so demanding!

Summary

We have seen the distinctive features of Reformed and Evangelical spirituality, which corresponds to revelation, both in content and form. Christ is the mediator of the revelation of God, so this spirituality is Christ-centred, responding with faith in Jesus Christ, and especially to his saving death and resurrection. Christ has revealed the Father, so this spirituality is that of trust in God our Father, his love and kindness in Christ, and his sovereign and providential rule over everything. Christ has sent the Spirit, so believers are sealed or anointed with the Spirit, the Spirit witnesses within them that they are children of God, and they use the gifts of God in the service of their Father.

The response of trusting Christ and obeying him, of loving God with heart, mind, soul and strength is common to all believers; so spirituality is not just an option for the advanced, but is required of all the saints. It is a spirituality common to all the people of God. It is a spirituality of normal humanity, of daily life and duties, of work and play, of family and society.

God's grace and acceptance of us in Christ means that we do not have to search for God, find, ascend or journey towards him. God has come to us in his Son, Jesus, spoken to us in the gospel and welcomed us into his presence through Christ our High Priest. We now stand in God's grace, are now at peace with him and can now have assurance of final salvation through trust in his promises.

The great barrier to true spirituality is not the lack of technique in spiritual aptitude, but sin. Sin is the state of humanity in every aspect of life and personality, and the wages of sin is death. But God has dealt with our sin by the sacrifice of Christ, and has accepted us as his children. His holiness and righteousness is demonstrated in the death of Christ, our sin is atoned for and we are forgiven. We stand in his grace, and he works in us by the death and resurrection of Christ and by his Spirit to change us into the likeness of Christ. God gives us faith and obedience, transforms us and does his good works through us.

God has provided 'means' by which he works in us for his glory. We must make good use of the means provided by God, and not replace or supplement them with means we devise. The means provided by God are explained in the Bible, namely the Bible itself, the fellowship of the people of God, prayer, baptism and the Lord's Supper, and a right use of the creation. We should not neglect these means, nor use other means, such as statues, pictures, icons, silence or impressions of God's will. We should not overvalue the sacraments, those visible words of God. While we hear echoes of the Bible in our inner selves, the God-given and certain place to hear God speaking is in the Bible.

The great means is the Bible, in which we find Christ clothed in all his promises. To love God is to love his words, and to be alert to the Spirit is to receive the words of the Spirit in the Bible. In the Bible we find God's self-revelation, character, will and plan. In the Bible we find God's mystery, Christ, revealed. A corporate and personal spirituality of the Word is at the heart of biblical faith and life. We do not know everything about God and his plan, but what we do know is found in the Bible.

Prayer is an expression of our trust in God, and our dependence on him. It is gospel-shaped: we come to pray to God our Father through the power and goodness of Jesus' death on the cross. This is the means of our access to God. We pray in response to God's words in the Bible, so that we know the God to whom we pray and what he has promised. As we read these Spirit-inspired words, the Spirit also works within us, prompting us to know that God is our Father and that we may approach him with boldness because of Christ's death for us on the cross. We pray to God alone, and not to saints, because we pray as instructed by God in the Bible.

Chapter Six

Examples of spirituality: They have kept your word

In this chapter we will look at three examples of the spirituality of the Word in Christian history.

The first is the corporate spirituality of the Word that marked the early church, and is also such a feature of Reformed and Evangelical spirituality. The second is the Puritan defence of biblical spirituality against the Quaker attacks on it. The third is the practice of biblical meditation found in the writings of Richard Baxter.

Corporate spirituality of the Word in the early church

For some, Bible reading is an essentially personal and private activity, and this assumption provides the central interpretative question 'What does this say to me?' This assumption also leads to the idea that the Bible should be able to be interpreted by the individual, and that its primary aim is the edification of the individual. A moment's reflection should show that this is not the case. Most of the Bible is addressed to churches (e.g. Old Testament books, Romans, Corinthians, Galatians), to the people of God, or to leaders of churches for the benefit of the churches (Timothy, Titus). Luke wrote for Theophilus, but while Theophilus was the named recipient, Luke and Acts were written for a wider audience. Letters like Philemon are the exception, not the rule. This means that the primary question is not 'What is God saying to me?' but 'What is God saying to the church?' So therefore a 'spirituality of the Word' will primarily be a corporate or group spirituality, and the question we should ask as we hear the Bible read and preached is 'What is God saying to us?'

Similarly spirituality is often assumed to be a personal if not private matter, and spiritual growth is assumed to be individual rather than corporate. We are fundamentally members of communities, members of the body of Christ, part of the people of God; and we are affected more than we realize by the communities to which we belong. Spirituality that is personal and not corporate is sure to be unfruitful, because maturity is fundamentally corporate in the New Testament. Paul writes in Ephesians of gifts given to build up the body of Christ, 'until all of us come to the unity of the faith and of the knowledge of the Son of God, to maturity, to the measure of the full stature of Christ' (Eph. 4:13).

Paul writes in Colossians of the purpose of his ministry to proclaim Christ 'that we may present everyone mature in Christ' (Col. 1:28).

While some view the Bible as the book of the individual, or spirituality as a matter for the individual, this focus is unhelpful. The important issue is that of the corporate spirituality of the Word in a congregation or church, or 'How are the people of God responding to the Word of God?'

Remember the great scenes in the Old Testament of God's people being formed or reformed by God's word. On Mount Sinai Moses speaks and reads the words of God to God's people gathered around the mountain (Exod. 19 – 24). On the plains of Moab Moses teaches and preaches to the people the words of God (Deuteronomy). On the entry to the land God commands Joshua to meditate on the book of the law and to act in accordance with it (Josh. 1:8). At the time of the exile Baruch reads from the words of Jeremiah to the people of God (Jer. 36). On the return from exile in Babylon Ezra reads from the 'book of the law of Moses' (Neh. 8:1), and his assistants ensure that the people understand what is written (Neh. 8 – 9). It is the mark of decline among the people of God that 'The word of the Lord was rare in those days', the days of Eli (1 Sam. 3:1).

So too in the New Testament the people of God are addressed by the Word of God in the teaching and preaching of John the Baptist, Jesus and the apostles. In different ways the Gospels emphasize the preaching and teaching ministry of Jesus: Matthew by including five blocks of his teaching, Mark by pointing to his priority of preaching and of his parables (1:38; 4:1–34) and Luke by describing Jesus teaching in the temple as a child, in the Nazareth synagogue to begin his public ministry and to his disciples after his resurrection (2:46–47; 4:16–30, 24). Luke marks the progress of the gospel in Acts and the growth of the church with the following expressions: 'the word of God continued to advance and gain adherents' (Acts 12:24), 'they continued proclaiming the good news' (14:7) and 'they taught and proclaimed the word of the Lord' (15:35). Paul instructs Timothy, 'give attention to the public reading of scripture, to exhorting, to teaching' (1 Tim. 4:13), and to 'proclaim the message; be persistent whether the time is favourable or unfavourable; convince, rebuke, and encourage, with the utmost patience in teaching' (2 Tim. 4:2). In Hebrews God who once addressed his people from Mount Sinai on earth now addresses them from heaven (12:25). In Revelation the whole book is what the Spirit is saying to the churches (2:7 etc.).

This corporate spirituality is found in the life of the church in every age. Hughes Oliphant Old traces the history of the reading and preaching of the Scriptures in the church from its roots in the Old Testament, through the New Testament, and then on from the Patristic age (Old 1998a, 1998b). As one example, Old describes the centrality of the reading and preaching of the Bible recorded in the *Didache* (c. 80–110), and the high expectation of the ministry of the daily and weekly sermons for believers and for catechumens (people being discipled):

> For it is by means of the ministry of the Word that Christ is present in the congregation. Apostles and prophets are to be received as the Lord . . . This is made even more explicit when the catechumens are told to honour their teachers as the Lord, because where the things of the Lord are spoken, there the Lord is present. (Old 1998b: 264 = *Didache* 11:1–3; 4:1)

As an example of corporate spirituality of the Word we look at the ministry of Augustine (354–430), Bishop of Hippo in North Africa. Old (1998b) points to the following features of Augustine's preaching:

- He was determined to let the people hear the eloquence of God in the words of Scripture, and not to fill their minds with his own eloquence (1998b: 345).
- He practised expository preaching, that is, preaching through books of the Bible in his daily or weekly sermons (346).
- His preaching reflected the big theological themes of the Bible, the big themes of human existence (362).
- He believed in the power and effective authority of the Bible, so his aim was to let the text speak (363).
- He interpreted Scripture by Scripture, so that his hearers built up a coherent theology of God and his grace in Christ (364).
- He used biblical stories to illustrate biblical teaching (364).
- He engaged in an effective dialogue in his sermons, addressing the pastoral issues of his congregation (365).

- He used simple speech so that everyone could understand his words (366).
- He used variety to help people to listen and to see the point of what he was saying (367).
- His preaching was marked by the vitality of his personal engagement with God, with the Bible and with the congregation (368).
- His sermons were intended to convert people to Christ as well as to edify the congregation (382).

To which we add that he was intentionally training others to preach and teach the Word as well.

This practice of Augustine's ministry of the Word resulted from a deep sense of the spirituality of the Word, and of the Word as the God-given nourishment of the congregation. For God speaks through the reading and teaching of the Bible. With references provided by Polman (1961) we find that Augustine describes it as follows:

- A fire blazes in God's Word. It is the fire of the Holy Ghost. (127 = *Sermo* 22, 7)
- The Gospel is the mouth of Christ. He is in heaven, but never ceases speaking on earth. Let us not be deaf, for He calls. Let us not be dead, for He thunders. (127 = *Sermo* 85, 1)
- If He kept silent now, the Sacred Scriptures would keep silent also. His Word is read out to us, and He does not keep silent. His Word is preached, and inasmuch as the preacher speaks the truth, Christ speaks through him. He does not keep silent, and it is our duty to listen, but with the ears of our hearts. (127 = *Sermo* 17, 1)
- If we preach Christ's Word, Christ himself feeds through us. (133= *Sermo* 46, 2)
- The daily bread of the children is the Word of God, which is given them daily . . . Our daily food on this earth is the Word of God which is dispensed in the churches. (174 = *Sermo* 56, 10)

So the Bible is not only the Word of God, but is also God's own speaking to us, God's familiar speech (Polman 1961: 127). As both the Bible and the sermon are God's words to his people, they must be central to their spirituality. The congregation must come ready to hear God, and to respond with trust and obedience. Polman shows how Augustine's practice derived from his belief in the inspiration, authority, sufficiency and necessity of the Bible (39–74), and how the idea of God's Word as God's promise was fundamental to his spirituality (216–230).

The corporate spirituality of the Word was practised in the church at Hippo, and that practice is an example to churches in every age and place.

Word and Spirit in Puritan–Quaker debate

Here is an 'Anatomy' of the important theological issue that divided Puritans from Quakers in the 1650s, that of Word and Spirit. From one perspective the Quakers were Radical Puritans, and this is a helpful insight, as Geoffrey Nuttall has shown (1992).

The complementary truth is that the Quakers followed a different faith to the Puritans, and this difference resulted from opposing views on Word and Spirit. This is not an alien distinction, because both Puritans and Quakers were strongly aware of the differences between them, and regarded their battle as of fundamental and critical significance. Their sociological similarities should not blind us to their deep theological differences. The titles of their tracts indicate the strength of their controversy: *The Boasting Baptist Dismounted and the Beast Disarmed*, *The Quaker Quashed and his Quarrel Quelled* and *George Fox Digg'd out of his Burrow*. In this section I have retained original spelling.

It is also significant that many early Quakers began their life within Puritanism, often as the children of Puritan parents. They often began with a deep conviction of sin, but found no gospel relief within Puritan faith. Quakers felt frustrated with Puritans, and Puritans felt betrayed by Quakers. Richard Baxter describes those moving on from Puritanism in these words: 'I had far rather that men continued Separatists and Anabaptists than turned Quaker or plain apostates' (Baxter 1655: A4).

The success of the Quaker movement over ten years was astonishing. In the ten years from 1652 it grew from a few people to over 40,000. By 1662 there were as many Quakers as Catholics in England (Reay 1984: 141). The Quaker Stephen Crisp describes his life in his allegory *A Short History of a Long Travel from Babylon to Bethel* (Watkins 1972: 160–164) in a similar style to John Bunyan's *Pilgrim's Progress*. Crisp was dissatisfied with Puritan preachers, and discovered them to be blind guides, physicians of no value and hireling shepherds because they were paid by compulsory tithes. They were people of a book, the Bible, and so demonstrated that they themselves did not know the way of truth. Crisp then tried the Independents, then the Anabaptists, before hearing the Quaker message. Then 'the new man was made, and so peace came to be made, and so it pleased the Father to reveal his Son in me'.

Some Quakers began in meetings of Seekers, people on the edge of Puritan churches who were as yet unsatisfied, convinced that the church and ministry they knew was deficient, and searching for a deeper knowledge of God. They met to read the Scriptures, and then wait for a further direct revelation of God in silence (Barbour 1964: 31–32). The Quakers we are studying are those of the 1650s. Quaker ideas since that date have varied greatly, and modern Quakers would not all identify with their seventeenth-century antecedents.

The fundamental issue: Word and Spirit

What was their fundamental disagreement? It was about the crucial issue of the way in which God speaks to his people. The Puritans believed that God spoke through the Bible, and the Quakers believed that God spoke immediately, and not through the Bible. Both agreed that believing and obeying God's words were crucial: they disagreed about the way in which God communicated his words to his people.

The Puritans believed that the Spirit's words were the Bible. William Bridge wrote that 'the written word of God is our appointed Food, our daily Food' (McDonald 1959: 203). They regarded the Scripture as inspired by the Holy Spirit, and self-authenticating. In the words of John Arrowsmith, 'Holy men of God . . . spake as they were moved by the Holy Ghost. They wrote accordingly' (McDonald 1959: 202). According to John Ball, the Bible was inspired in both matter and form: 'to be immediately inspired is to be, as it were, breathed, and to come from the Father, by the Holy Ghost, without all means' (McDonald 1959: 202–203). So to wait on God's words in the Bible and through the preacher is a sign of humility before God. Jeremiah Burroughs reminded his congregation, 'you come to tender up your homage to God, to sit at God's feet and there to profess your submission to him' (Burroughs 1990: 197).

In Margaret Fell's account of her conversion to Quaker experience, we find the Quaker distinction between what God has said through Christ and the apostles, and what God is now saying to the Child of Light inwardly:

> And then he [George Fox] went on, and opened the Scriptures, and said The Scriptures were the prophets' words, and Christ's,

> and the apostles' words, and what as they spoke they enjoyed and possessed and had it from the Lord. And said, 'Then what had any to do with the scriptures but as they came to the Spirit that gave them forth? You will say, Christ saith this, and the apostles say this, but what canst thou say? Are thou a Child of Light, and hast thou walked in the Light, and what thou speakest is it inwardly from God?' I cried in my spirit to the Lord, 'We are all thieves, we are all thieves, we have taken the scriptures in words, and know nothing of them in ourselves.' (Braithwaite 1912: 101)

So George Fox, in his anti-Puritan tract *The Great Mistery Of The Great Whore Unfolded, and Antichrist's Kingdom revealed unto destruction* claimed that having the Scriptures was no use without the Spirit: 'And who have the Spirit of God, have that which is infallible . . . Now many may have the scriptures, and if they have not the Spirit that gave them forth, they do not worship God in the Spirit' (1659: 28).

The Quakers also called the indwelling Spirit the Light of Christ. They believed that God gave the Light of Christ to everyone, and identified that Light with salvation in Christ. The Puritans believed that it was important to distinguish between the light of general revelation that God gave to all, and the saving light of Christ found in the gospel. So Baxter wrote about this inner Light:

> [Do] you mean it is sufficient to leave men without excuse (that we maintain as well as you), or is every man's light sufficient to his salvation? Or is it now sufficient to all who have never heard the gospel? If so, is not the gospel a vain a needless thing? If the world has sufficient light, what need they your teaching, of discourse, or conviction? If all have sufficient light within them, what need they any converting grace? (1655: 8)

The Quakers claimed that the saving Light of Christ came to everyone directly from God, and was not limited to those who had heard the gospel of Christ by hearing or reading the Bible.

The debate also turned on whether Puritans believed in personal and immediate revelations. So Baxter claimed:

> I own all divine revelations, and disown all diabolical ones, so far as I know them. I own all those blessed revelations contained in the Holy Scriptures, for they were infallibly sealed by

multitudes of uncontrolled miracles and a spirit of holiness. I believe that the scriptures or laws of Christ being finished and sealed (1 Tim. 6: 13,14), and that these are able to make men wise to salvation without any more additions, and therefore no more is to be expected. But yet I believe:

1. That God has not tied himself from revealing particular matters in subserviency to scripture extraordinarily, as divers murders have been revealed, and the like matters of fact.
2. And I believe that all true Christians have the illuminating, sanctifying spirit of Christ to help them to know all the meaning of scripture which is of flat necessity to salvation. (1655: 12, 13)

The Quakers did not make use of what the Spirit had said to others in times past in the Bible, and would only use what God was saying to them in the present age. They objected to believers saying David's psalms, because these were the Spirit's words to David, not to people today. Baxter replied, 'If all scripture is written for our use and learning, why may we not speak to God in the words of David's psalms as well as any other scripture?' (1655: 13).

The distinction between them was in their use of the Bible. John Knott describes the Digger Winstanley's use of Scripture in words that also describe that of the Quakers:

- Where the orthodox Puritan divine, instructed by Perkins, painstakingly collected parallel texts and tested his interpretations by the analogy of faith, Winstanley followed his intuitions of the Spirit in rendering what he saw as the truth behind the letter, not so much expounding scripture as re-creating it by fashioning his own highly individual version of the Fall and redemption of Man.
- He approached the Bible as a poet might, alive to the power of images and the symbolic force of names . . .
- Winstanley could let his imagination range freely over Scripture because the words of the text had no fixed meaning for him. (1980: 96, 97)

In fact the words and messages the Quakers received and passed on to others were frequently in words that originated in the Scriptures. They had learned enough from the Scriptures to know that, in the words of Barbour, 'the Bible was the Spirit's characteristic vocabulary' (1964: 121). Over 70 per cent of their writings used biblical language (157). Their Puritan background meant that in many cases the Bible formed an unconscious safeguard to their understanding of what God was saying to them. Quaker leaders were so immersed in the Scriptures as a result of their Puritan upbringing that the manifestation of the Spirit to which they bore witness was tested by the written Word in ways of which they were not conscious (McDonald 1959: 178).

There was however a dark side to this use of biblical words and phrases. It concealed the wide gap between Puritan faith and Quaker experience. For the use of biblical phrases does not ensure that the Bible's message is being communicated. Indeed the use of biblical phrases may have obscured the fact that the Quaker message was a radical departure from Puritan faith. For the Quakers' use of the Bible was of course selective. They sensed vitality in those passages that corresponded to their own vivid experience and felt coldness when Puritans expounded them (Knott 1980: 157). The twentieth-century Quaker Harold Loukes makes a revealing point when he writes that 'Quaker propaganda was full of Biblical quotation, but not by way of appeal to authority so much as a persuasive device. Those who listened took the Bible as authority. [Quakers] appealed to it to destroy its authority' (1965: 28).

The Puritan objections to the Quaker view were matched by Luther and Calvin's objections to the prophets of their times. So Luther said of the Zwickau prophets that he would not believe them 'though they had swallowed the Holy Ghost, feathers and all', or 'even if it snow miracles everyday'.

The Quakers did not expect that the Spirit would contradict his past revelations in the Bible, but denied that the Spirit spoke through the Bible today. Ironically, though they would assert that God spoke to all, they would not accept the Puritan witness that God spoke to them through the Bible.

Consequences and clarifications

If revelation is immediate, as the Quakers claimed, then we should note the following consequences and clarifications.

Revelation is immediate, so the Bible is obsolete

The Puritan Francis Higginson wrote *The Irreligion of the Northern Quakers* in 1653. The Quaker movement grew initially in the north of

England, and attracted many from Puritan congregations. Higginson attacked the attitude to Scripture that resulted from the Quaker conviction that revelation is immediate:

1. They hold that the holy scripture, the writings of the prophets, evangelists, and apostles, are not the word of God, and that there is no written word of God; but they say, using a foolish distinction of their own coining, that they are a declaration of the word only in those that have the faith.
2. They hold that their own speakings are a declaration of the word (Christ) in them, thereby making them, though they be for the most part full of impiety and nonsense, to be of equal authority with the holy scriptures.
3. They hold that no exposition ought to be given of the holy scripture, and that all such exposition of scripture is an adding to it, and that God will add to such a one all the plagues written in that book. Opening, and applying the scripture, is one thing they mainly declaim against, wherever they come.
4. They teach poor people that whosoever takes a text of scripture and makes a sermon of it or from it is a conjurer, and that his preaching is conjuration. (1653: 4)

When Higginson mentions 'conjuration', he is replying to the language Quakers used to attack exegetical preaching, for example George Fox's words in *Saul's Errand to Damascus* of 1653:

> All that study to raise a living thing out of a dead, to raise the spirit out of the letter, are conjurers, and draw points and reasons, and so speak a divination out of their own brain. They are conjurers and diviners, and their teaching is from conjuration, which is not spoken from the mouth of the Lord, and the Lord is against all such, and who are of God are against all such. (Fox and Nayler 1653: 7)

Fox is claiming that the Scripture is dead, and that it represents the letter rather than the spirit. He describes exegesis of the Scripture as conjuring and divination, so clearly forbidden in the Old Testament.

William Dell makes the point even clearer: 'the believer is now the only book in which God writes his new testament'. As Barbara Siddall said of the Bible, 'not the Word of God but onely a dead letter' (Reay 1984: 146). The Quakers regarded the Bible as valid for its time, as the record of how God spoke to the people who wrote it. But it was now obsolete, and a distraction from hearing God's words at the present time. As George Fox wrote:

> The Spirit that gave forth the Scriptures teaches us how to pray, sing, fast, give thanks, to praise and worship, and how to honour and glorify God. And so the Spirit of Truth, which gave forth the Scriptures is our director, guide, leader and comforter. (Fryer 1991: 225)

The Puritans recognized the danger of this attitude to Scripture. It was, in the words of Thomas Shepherd, 'the precipice of all delusion [to] forsake the scriptures and wait for a spirit to suggest immediately God's inmost thought toward me' (Spurr 1998: 7). The orthodox response to both attitudes has been to assert the authority and effectiveness of the more objective revelation in Scripture. This was certainly the response of the Puritans. So John Owen asserted authority and origin of Scripture: Scripture is from God, and he speaks in it and by it. The work of the Spirit is found in the Scriptures: the Spirit never speaks to us *of* the Word, but *by* the Word and through it (Ferguson 1987: 195). Because the Holy Spirit is Christ's Spirit, there can be no separation between what is found in Christ and what is found in the Spirit's Scripture (Trueman 1998: 78).

The Quakers believed that the Scripture was inspired but is now obsolete, and that only present and immediate revelation is valid, while the Puritans believed that the inspired Scripture remains the effective Word of God. The Quakers believed in the sufficiency of the Light within, while the Puritans believed in the sufficiency of the Scriptures.

Revelation is immediate, so salvation history occurs now

Another consequence of immediate revelation is that as the present replaces the past in verbal revelation, it does also in salvation history. God's works as well as God's words become contemporary. It is this present aspect of saving history that lay behind the often inflated language used of the early Quaker leaders Fox and Nayler. Here are some examples of the language used to address George Fox:

- let not that beastly power which keeps us in bondage seperate thy bodyly presence from us, who reigns as king above it & would reioyce to see thy kingly power here triumph over it.

- Grant that I may live with thee for ever & be cload with thy righteousnesse. (Watkins 1972: 147)

In 1656 James Nayler rode into Bristol welcomed by his followers with shouts of 'Hosanna to the Son of David!' These actions of the Quakers were inspired by the Scriptures, but meant that the focus of attention was on the progress of God's kingdom through them now, rather than through salvation history recorded in the Scriptures. The immediacy of verbal revelation was matched by the immediacy of salvation history.

Geoffrey Nuttall wrote that Fox 'so "telescopes" the divine processes of creation and redemption as inevitably to reduce the significance of the coming of Christ and His Holy Spirit in history' (1992: 159). In the words of the twentieth-century Quaker H. G. Wood, there are three defects within Quakerism from its beginning. These are 'the tendency to distrust the intellect, to suspect the outward, and to neglect the historical' (Flew 1968: 290). If the past has been caught up into the present, so too the future has also been made present in the Quaker experience.

John Owen noted the vital connection between the historical revelation in Christ and the Holy Scriptures in his reply to the Quakers. He pointed out that Christ and Scripture have the same formal content, that is, the saving will of God (Trueman 1998: 70–75). Christ sends the Spirit, so the message of the Spirit will be that of Christ. As Christ is sufficient for salvation, so the Scriptures are sufficient for knowledge of salvation. As God's saving work in Christ is found in history, so God's revelation of the meaning of that work is also found in that same history.

Revelation is immediate, so Christ's saving work is internal, not historical

It was not just that the Quakers' focus on God's immediate saving work resulted in a lack of regard for the saving work of Christ on the cross. They believed that the Puritan emphasis on the atoning work of Christ on the cross was an evasion of personal responsibility, a way of excusing sin, and an avoidance of costly moral perfection. So the Quakers saw the great Puritan doctrines of imputed righteousness and substitutionary atonement as an evasion of the agony of facing personal sin, repenting of it and becoming perfect (Barbour 1964: 106). So although the Puritans had a reputation for demanding great moral change in believers, from the perspective of the Quakers their trust in the atoning work of Christ on the Cross meant in practice that they accepted continued sinning too easily. Their message could be ridiculed as 'Christ died outside the gates of Jerusalem, and then all is well' (Watkins 1972: 162).

So in Fox's *Saul's Errand to Damascus*, the answer to the question 'Whether a believer be justified by Christ's righteousness imputed, yea, or no?' is that '"He that believeth is born of God"; and he that is born of God, is justified by Christ alone without imputation' (Fox and Nayler 1653: 12). And in Edward Burrough's *Declaration to All the World of our Faith* there is no mention of the atoning work of Christ, even though he asserts that 'salvation, justification and sanctification are only in (Christ)' (Barbour and Roberts 1973: 299). Newton Flew comments, 'Fox knows, like his later followers, that the Cross is no "dead fact, stranded on the shore of the oblivious years", but an inward living experience in the heart of the believer, refashioning his life into perfect love' (1968: 291).

For the Puritan, the cross derives its internal power to transform from its external reality in the history of salvation.[1] Fox however did later assert his belief in the historic saving work of Christ: 'Christ gave himself, his body for the life of the world: he was the offering for the sins of the whole world, and paid the debt, and made satisfaction' (Fox 1659: *Response to Jeremy Ives*). In general Fox and his associates were more radical in their assessment of the atoning death of Christ in the 1650s. They reverted to more orthodox views by the 1670s, as is demonstrated in Robert Barclay's *Catechism and Confession of Faith* of 1673 (Barbour and Roberts 1973: 314–349).

Barbour comments on the Quakers, 'The effect was to make the actual historical events of Jesus' life mainly an example, at times only a symbol or type, of the recurring events on every Christian's pilgrimage' (1964: 146).

Revelation is immediate, so the Golden Age is now

The Quaker experience was so vivid and powerful for those involved that they assumed that they were living in a Golden Age. This view is characteristic of those living in a time of revival of religion. The Puritan Richard Sibbes spoke of 'these latter times' in which there was 'a reformation of religion, after our recovery out of popery . . . a second spring of the gospel [through] the revelation of Christ by the

[1] See Trueman 2002 for an explanation of the link between valuing history and the Reformed tradition.

Spirit, which hath the Spirit accompanying it' (Nuttall 1992: 104). Arthur Dent in 1603 thought that his was the last age, that of the war between the armies of Christ and the Antichrist (Hill 1988: 94). In the words of John Milton, 'God is decreeing to begin some new and great period in His Church, even to the reforming of the Reformation itself: what does He then but reveal Himself to His Servants, and as His manner is, first to His Englishmen [*sic!*]' (Nuttall 1992: 121).

If there were a revival of the first days, could it be that revelations should continue? Puritans believed that extraordinary revelations that happened in the days of the apostles should not be expected today. They believed that God's saving works, words and signs were all tied to salvation history. Quakers asserted that God's saving work was immediate and in the present, and that signs should accompany this revelation.

William Erbury wrote of his Quaker age in terms of the third age, that of the Spirit:

> God under the Law and to the Fathers before, was known, as the Father. In the Gospel, God was known, as the Son; of the knowledge of the Son was peculiar to the Gospel-dispensation. The third will be pure Spirit, when nothing but Spirit and power shall appear, when God shall be all in all . . . the presence of the Lord, and his power, was more spiritual, in inward and eternal things . . . Therefore the third dispensation . . . will be more spiritual yet. (Nuttall 1992: 106)

Of course the idea of the third age of the Spirit was immensely attractive to the Quakers, because it enabled them to dismiss obsolete features of the first two ages, and to help to shape the new age in which they lived. It necessarily meant that they devalued the Puritans and others who went before them.

No wonder Baxter complained in *The Quakers Catechism*:

> And yet more unmatchable pride and impious infidelity is it, to damn all the church and people of God for this 1600 years at least . . . who can believe that Christ hath no church until now, and that all the ministers of the gospel for 1600 years were the ministers of the Devil? (1655: C1)

Revelation is immediate, so God is unity, not Trinity

Why did the Quakers tend towards Unitarianism? The reasons

included the following: the loss of historical revelation and the Bible meant that they did not pay close attention to the shape of the biblical revelation, and to the clues within it that the revelation of God's unity is only part of the story; their suspicion of clerical education meant that they were less likely to learn from the lessons of theology and church history; their concentration on the present human person as the focus of immediate divine revelation meant that they limited themselves to the economic revelation, to God as experienced, and this resulted in their undifferentiated perception of God.

In Nuttall's words, 'they identified the Logos or eternal Christ with the Spirit'; and they identified the Logos or Spirit in Christ with the Spirit within them (Nuttall 1992: 175). Thus they failed to distinguish between the presence of God in Christ and in themselves. One sign of this failure was the assumption of personal infallibility and perfection for all those indwelt by the Logos, the Light, Christ, the Spirit. Hugh Barbour comments that Fox merged Christ and the Spirit, and asserted that Christ was not distinct from the Father. For many, there was no distinction between the members of the Trinity: 'God and the Spirit hath no Person, nor cannot be truly distinguished into Persons' (Barbour 1964: 145).

For the Puritans, the Quaker views both diminished the unique incarnation of the Son of God and also elevated every believer into a Christ figure. No wonder John Owen wrote that one only needed to 'Convince any of them of the Doctrine of the Trinity, and all the rest of their Imaginations vanish into Smoak' (Nuttall 1992: 162).[2]

Revelation is immediate, and this revelation is universal

The Quakers had an extraordinarily vivid sense of a missionary call to the whole world. Their defining ideas included belief that Christ had enlightened everyone in the world, and the loss of the particularity of salvation history meant that everyone in the world had equal access to God in the Light within. So Fox's letter to Quakers in captivity included these instructions: 'get the Turks and Moors Language, that you might be the more inabled to direct them to the Grace and Spirit of God in them, which they have from God, in their hearts' (Nuttall 1992: 160). Fox firmly believed in 'that of God in every man', and so the task of the Quaker missionary was to alert

[2] See Jensen 2002: 48–49 for an explanation of the importance of words to explain the Word.

people to the God within, to encourage them to respond to this God and to learn from the witness of their internal revelation. John Woolman, Quaker missionary to the American Indians, wrote of his purpose in these words: 'That I might know and understand their life, and the Spirit they live in, if happily I might receive some instruction from them, or they be in any degree helped forward by my following the Leadings of Truth among them' (Loukes 1965: 122).

The usual Puritan response to the notion of 'that of God in every man' was to understand this to be the light of nature, the general revelation of God, or the conscience. They claimed that this was not saving knowledge of God, and they assumed that the Quakers were entirely too optimistic about the possibilities of people responding to this dim revelation. The Quakers effectively equated God's general and special revelation: the Puritans retained that useful distinction. Richard Baxter commented, 'All that come into the world of nature, he enlighteneth with the light of Nature; And all that come into the world of grace he enlighteneth with the light of supernatural revelation' (1655: 7).

For Quakers there was no such distinction, because God's saving revelation was immediate to every person in the world. Although they believed that God's revelation was universal, they would not accept the Puritan witness that God spoke to them through the Bible.

Revelation is immediate, so the believer is indwelt by the Holy Spirit and therefore infallible

The Quaker democratization of Christianity removed any distinction in roles between the human authors of Scripture and any believer. Both had the same infallible Spirit and immediate revelation. Indeed for the Quaker it was a sin to follow what the Spirit had said to a Bible writer: the Quaker call was to follow the Spirit within. Geoffrey Nuttall writes that one of the main issues of dispute between Puritans and Quakers was 'whether or no the presence of the Holy Spirit involved intellectual infallibility and moral perfectibility' (Nuttall 1992: 155).

The vital question was where the infallible Spirit was to be found: in the Bible, or in the Child of Light? So in *The Quakers Catechism* of 1655 Richard Baxter wrote:

> Your twelfth query is whether we have the same infallible spirit as the holy men of God had, who spoke forth the scriptures. But I will answer you . . . in a word.

> 1. The prophets and apostles had infallible inspirations of new matters of divine verity, not before revealed, because they were to be God's penmen and messengers of such new revelations; I have none such that I know of.
> 2. The prophets and apostles were guided infallibly in the manner as well as the matter, so that every word that they wrote to the churches was infallibly true. I have no such infallibility, nor your grandfather the Pope neither. (1655: 9, 10)

In his *An Answer to a Book Called the Quakers Catechism* James Nayler replied:

> Thou says the Prophets and Apostles were guided infallibly in the manner and matter, so that what they writ to the Church was true; but thou hast no such infallibility. I say, if thou had such a Spirit, your pulpits would have more truth, and thy book not so full of lies as it is . . . for the Spirit of God is but one, and who hath it hath an infallible guide in matter and manner, if he keep to it . . . so far as any are led by the Spirit, it guides into all truth if it be not erred from. (1655: 22)

The Quaker apologist Samuel Fisher claimed to possess infallible guidance, and sinlessness. Richard Baxter's reply was that 'I am one that is sick and have need of the Physician'.

Revelation is immediate, and only those who have responded to this immediate revelation are in Christ's church

It is important to recognize that the Quakers were not offering a complementary form of revelation to the Bible, but a *replacement*. They focused more on the process of revelation (its immediacy) than its content. For them the immediacy of the revelation was a non-negotiable fundamental. This meant that only those who responded to this internal mode of revelation belonged to Christ. Not only were they the only ones who belonged to Christ, but their task was to wage war on those who claimed any other process and source of revelation, such as the Puritans. The Quakers' battle was the Lamb's War. In Fox's words:

> And thus we became followers of the Lamb whithersoever he goes, and he hath called us to make War in righteousness for

> his names sake against Hell and death . . . against the Beast and the False Prophet . . . we war in truth, and just judgement . . . with the sword that goes out of the mouth . . . and shall slay the wicked. (1659: *To the Reader*)

The Quaker claim was an exclusive claim to be Christ's people. Richard Baxter recognized the significance of this claim, and refuted it by claiming to belong to the church of Christ, the Catholic church:

> [We are] Sincere Catholic Christians, saved from Infidelity and Impiety: Having one God, one Mediator between God and man, One Holy Spirit: being a member of that one Catholic Church, which is not confined to the sect of the Papists, or the sect of the Anabaptists, or any sect, but containeth all the true Christians in the world, though some parts of it be Reformed and pure, and others more deformed and corrupt; having one Catholic rule, the Word of God; and one Catholic love to all Christians in the world. (1657a: 1–2)

Baxter also points to the Christological significance of their claim:

> They renounce the Church that we are of: and that is the only Church on earth, containing all true believers in Christ.
>
> And if Christ had not a Catholic Church before then, and ever since his Ascension, he ceased to be Christ in Office, the Head and Saviour of the Church: For no Church, no Saviour; no Body, no Head; No School, no Teacher; No Kingdom, no King; No Wife, no Husband. (1657a: 2)

Baxter rightly recognized that the claim to be the new and true people of Christ is actually a claim to have found a new Christ. A 'new Catholic Church' means a 'new Christ'.

So the Quaker claim to be the only people of God fighting the Lamb's War not only unchurched all others who claim to be believers, but also changed their understanding of Christ and the work of the Spirit.

Revelation is immediate, so structures and 'means' are a hindrance

Francis Higginson described Quaker meetings in these words:

> They have no singing of psalms, hymns, or spiritual songs – that is an abomination. No reading or exposition of Holy Scripture, that is also an abhorrency. No teaching or preaching – that is in their opinion the only thing that is needless. No administration of sacraments – with them there is no talk of carnal things. (1653: 11)

The immediacy of revelation meant that God would not use past words, such as the Bible, and would not use what Puritans called 'means' such as the sacraments. In both private and corporate spirituality the believer must wait in silence for the immediate revelation of God within. This was in contrast with the Puritans, who greatly valued God-given 'means'.

In his biography of the Puritan pastor Richard Greenham, John Primus points out the importance of the Bible to Greenham as 'the Librarie of the holy ghost'; when quoting Scripture, Greenham's usual introduction is 'the holy Ghost here telleth us' (Primus 1998: 86–87). The Holy Spirit was the author of Scripture, but also works within us so that we not only hear 'the letter', but also 'the Spirit' (86–87). Greenham also developed a strong doctrine of 'means', which sprang naturally from his observation that God normally works through creaturely agency. For Greenham the 'means' include the Word, prayer, sacraments, discipline, affliction and the sabbath; and as God uses 'means', we should use what God has provided (126–129). We break the first commandment by 'a negligent and carelesse use of the meanes to serve God in his providence' (127). He contrasts his own view of God using 'means' with the views of the papists on the one hand, and the views of the sect the Family of Love on the other:

> Seeing the Lord hath joyned together the meanes of godlines and godlines itselfe, let us not separate them, either with the superstitious Papists, resting on the worke wrought . . . neither with frantike heretikes despise the meanes, as though without them we could live in obedience to God, or in love to our brethren. (Primus 1998: 128–129)

The 'frantike heretikes', the Family of Love, despised the 'means': so later did the Quakers. Of all the 'means', the Bible and its preaching is the chief. So preaching is the 'most principall and proper meanes to beget Faith in us' (1998: 131). Hence the Puritan critique of ministers who would not preach: 'dumb dogges that cannot barke', in William Perkins' phrase.

If the Bible is a 'means', so is the preacher: 'where a faithfull Minister is that doth sincerely and purely preach the word, it is all one as if the Lord himselfe dwelt personally among us' (Primus 1998: 137). Greenham shows us that use of God-given 'means' was crucial to Christianity.

Jane Turner gave an account of her journeys in faith, as she moved from formalism and what she called 'Legal Righteousness' as a Presbyterian to free grace as a Baptist. She then experimented with Quaker views, but moved back from them, despite their 'Angel-like appearance', partly because they did not recognize that God used 'means'. She knew that 'ordinarily [God] works by means, and leaves no ground in Scripture to expect him out of means' (Watkins 1972: 48, 88–90). So then, 'The Puritans . . . did not regard the Bible as a mere record of revelation. It is itself the revelation of God in which and through which God comes savingly to the soul' (McDonald 1959: 202).

No wonder then that the Puritans were so scandalized that the Quakers despised the 'means', especially the Bible. As we have seen, the Quakers regarded the Bible as valid for the people whose experience was recorded in it, but as a distraction for the believer today. They not only dismissed the Bible, but also the ministers who taught from it, as we have seen. Because the teaching of the Bible was not the task of the minister, and because they distrusted the use of reason and education, they therefore criticized the training that ministers received, which was one of the glories of the Puritan movement.

While the Quakers warned against Puritan and other ministers, they were of course receptive to the ministry of words of other Quakers. This ministry of words was not a ministry of teaching or preaching the Bible, but that of another Quaker speaking what God had immediately and directly put in his heart to say. In Fox's words, 'God did then speak by his Son in the days of his flesh, so the Son, Christ Jesus, doth now speak by his Spirit . . . They who neglect or refuse to hear the voice of Christ, now speaking from heaven in this his gospel day, harden their hearts' (1975: 666). For the Quaker, all the Lord's people were prophets, so believers would receive God's immediate words directly and through others, and would speak God's immediate words to others.

Revelation is immediate, and this revelation is received in the emotions

One of the crucial questions about immediate revelation is 'By what aspect or part of the human person is it received?' Possible answers include the conscience, the intellect or reason, the emotions or the will. The answer to the question has great significance for the attitudes adopted by those who are expecting the revelation.

- If revelation is mediated to and through the intellect or reason, then the attitude adopted by the believer will be one of intellectual inquiry and alertness. There may also be the use of debate and argument as part of the process of revelation.
- If revelation is mediated through the emotions, then aids to emotional receptivity will be used, and emotional intensity will signify significant revelation.
- If revelation is primarily to the conscience, then a sense of guilt will be the infallible sign of the presence of revelation, and moral transformation the sign of its long-term effects.

The Puritan Richard Sibbes spoke of the 'sweet motions' of the Spirit, but also made the point that the Holy Spirit works on the reason as well as the will. 'For though God work upon the will, it is with enlightenment of the understanding at the same time' (Knott 1980: 54). So also Baxter allows for the use of hearing and studying the scriptures, using both the 'means' of the Bible and also the use of the mind as well as the understanding: 'The Holy Spirit assisteth us in our hearing, reading, and studying the Scriptures, that we may come, by diligence, to the true understanding of it; but doth not give us that understandings, without hearing, reading, or study' (Nuttall 1992: 170).

The Quakers rejected both the Scriptures as the source of the knowledge of God and also the use of human reason in any form, because they knew that revelation was mediated through the emotions, and not through the rational mind. In George Fox's words, 'we met together often and waited upon the Lord in pure silence . . . hearkened to the voice of the Lord, and felt his word in our hearts' (Fox 1659: *To the Reader*).

So James Nayler condemned the Puritan ministers who had spent 'so many Years at Oxford and Cambridge . . . to know what unlearned men, Fishermen, Ploughmen and Herdsmen did mean when they spoke forth the Scriptures' (Barbour 1964: 157). William Bayly claimed that 'It was the Serpent who led my mind out wholly to delight in the Art of Arithmetick, and the study and practise of navigation' (Watkins 1972: 230). Even the learning of Hebrew, Latin and Greek was suspect because, as George Fox wrote, 'The tongues of Hebrew, Greek & Latin, were set up over Christ by Pilate who crucified him' (Fox 1659: *Reply to Francis Higginson*).

Whereas the Puritans believed that the Word of God that was Scripture addressed the whole person, including mind, emotions and will, the Quakers believed that the immediate revelation of God was received through the emotions, and that reason and learning were enemies of that revelation. It was not the case that Puritans were rationalists and Quakers emotionalists. The difference was that the Puritans included reason, and the Quakers excluded it.

Revelation is immediate on the emotions, and physical signs mark its presence

The presence of revelation was evident because the power of God within the human person produced 'quakings', as well as other physical signs of the internal reality. The Puritan Francis Higginson described these physical signs in these words:

> Now for their quakings, one of the most immediate notable fruits and accidents of their speakings. Though their speakings be a very chaos of words and errors, yet very often while they are speaking, so strange is the effect of them in their unblest followers, that many of them, sometimes men, but more frequently women and children, fall into quaking fits . . . those in their assemblies who are taken with these fits fall suddenly down, as it were with a swoon, as though they had been surprised with an epilepsy or apoplexy, and lie grovelling on the earth, and struggling as it were for life, and sometimes more quietly as though they were departing. While the agony of the fit is upon them their lips quiver, their flesh and joints tremble, their bellies swell as though blown up with wind, they foam at the mouth, and sometimes purge, as though they had taken physic. In this fit they continue sometimes an hour or two, sometimes longer, before they come to themselves again, and when it leaves them they roar out horribly with a voice greater than that of a man . . .
>
> The speaker, when any of them falls in this fit, will say to the rest 'Let them alone, trouble them not, the Spirit is now strug-

> gling with the flesh, if the Spirit overcomes they will quickly come out of it again, though it is sorrow now, it will be joy in the morning' . . . These quakings they maintain and in their books and papers call them the marvelous works of the Lord. (Higginson 1653: 15–16)

The Quaker Robert Barclay described the same signs with more sympathy:

> [T]here will be such a painfull travel found in the soul, that it will even work upon the outward man, so that . . . the body will be greatly shaken, and many groans, sighs and tears . . . Sometimes the Power of God will break forth into a whole meeting . . . and thereby trembling will be upon most . . . which as the power of truth prevailes, will from pangs and groans end with the sweet sound of thanksgiving and praise. (Barbour 1964: 36)

John Gilpin in his tract *The Quakers Shaken* describes being thrown from his chair during a Quaker meeting, lying on the ground all night, unable to resist the power of God that acted upon him. He later returned to the Bible and Presbyterianism (Barbour 1964: 118).

We should not imagine that these physical signs were the only evidence of the presence of Christ and the Spirit in a person. Moral change was also a necessary sign of true spiritual experience for the Quakers (Barbour 1964: 119). Quaking was taken to be a certain sign of the presence of the Light of Christ, an external and physical sign of the internal and invisible Christ.

The Puritans on the other hand did not look for physical signs: their tests were inward conviction and assurance, and gradual moral transformation. Baxter was suspicious of physical quaking as a definitive sign of the presence of God. In his *Quakers Catechism* he wrote:

> Your twenty-third query is whether do you own trembling and quaking which the scripture witnesseth? Answer: I own the fear of the Lord, which is the beginning of wisdom . . . but I think that the great quaking that was in the army of the Philistines was no virtue or blessing to them, nor any sign of God among them (1 Sam. 14:15). (Baxter 1655: 23–24)

So we can see that the Quaker view of revelation was that of immediate and direct revelation to the human person; that it was therefore in the present and not in the past; that it was within the person, and not by external means except by another Quaker; that it was received through the emotions, and not through reason or rational thought; and that the evidence of its presence was the physical sign of quaking. On the other hand the Puritan view was that revelation of Jesus Christ was given through salvation history culminating in the coming of Christ, that it was mediated through the Spirit-given Scriptures, and received by faith by the human person, in mind, emotions, understanding and will.

Reflections

Word and Spirit in the Reformers

The different attitudes of Puritans and Quakers to Spirit and Word may have their roots in an earlier difference between the Reformers about the nature of the Bible. In Luther's opinion there was a great gulf between his view of the Bible and that of Zwingli. Luther held that the Bible was the means God used to communicate his truth, whereas Zwingli held that the Bible was a sign of the truth that God communicated by the Spirit.

Luther summarized his own view in these words: 'The Word . . . is the power of God, which makes all who believe on it blessed . . . God works through His Word, which is like a vehicle or a tool whereby we learn to know Him in our heart.'

He described Zwingli and his followers' view as:

> They separate the man who preaches and teaches the Word from God who makes it effectual . . . and they mean that the Holy Spirit is given and works without the Word, which is, as it were, an external symbol, sign and mark, and meets the Spirit who is already and always waiting in the heart . . . The External Word is . . . a picture, which enlightens, witnesses and interprets . . . They reject the oral Word and the power and efficacy of the Sacraments entirely. (Parker 1947: 47, 46)

Zwingli distinguished between the external and the internal. The external Word of God is that which is read and preached, and is a sign and witness, which prompts us to attend to the internal Word, and helps us understand it. In Zwingli's words, 'What is heard is not that Word by which we believe'. G. W. Bromiley says of Zwingli's views, 'It is in the heart of the believer or unbeliever that it is decided whether at this or that point . . . the letter of Scripture is also the living

Word of God, the sign is conjoined with the thing signified' (Bromiley 1953: 36).

Here the hearing of the Bible read and preached is not an actual 'means', but an accompanying instruction. This separation between external Word and internal Spirit makes it easier to break the connection between the two. Zwingli wants to refute an automatic view of preaching, but in doing so runs the danger of failing to recognize that the Bible is God's words, 'intrinsically as well as instrumentally', in the useful phrase of J. I. Packer.

Too close an identification of Spirit and Word falls down when we reflect that the Spirit indwells believers even when they are not thinking the words of Scripture. Too radical a separation between Spirit and Word diminishes two of the 'means' God has provided and chosen to use: Bible and Bible teacher.

What Puritans believed about the Bible

They believed that the Bible was the following:

- Authoritative and powerful, an effective 'means' used by God, the present and contemporary words of God, God's words 'intrinsically as well as instrumentally'.
- The way in which God addresses every aspect of us: will, reason, emotions and character.
- To be understood in terms of God's gradual revelation of Christ, to be read in its original historical context, self-interpreting.
- Originally inspired in words as well as content, as well as Spirit-empowered in the present.
- Infallible in its teaching, sufficient and complete.
- God's word through his Spirit about his work through his Son, God's Spirit-words about his Son-work.

Quaker patterns of using the Bible

We now find the following patterns across many Christian traditions.

- *The Bible as example of process.* We should notice that for Quakers the Bible was an example of the process of immediate revelation. The believer today should follow their example and find out what God is now saying. There is a parallel to the modern belief that the Bible writers give us an example of theological reflection, and that we should follow their example by doing our own theological invention and reflection.

- *The Bible and internal spirituality.* The idea that the Bible history of salvation provides models for us to follow in our own internal spiritual journey was common to Philo and the Quakers, and is common today. The result is a preoccupation with the internal, and neglect of historical revelation.
- *The effect of the dismissal of the Bible.* While the early Quakers retained many biblical ideas because of their Puritan upbringing, the next generation moved well away from biblical faith. This move was obscured by their continued use of biblical language. People need great discernment to recognize that the use of biblical phrases does not necessarily indicate the presence of biblical faith.
- *The poetic misuse of the Bible.* Using Bible images as the raw material from which we create our own version of Christianity is as popular now as it was in the days of the Quakers, and is now defended by modern theories about the meaning of texts. Neither Quakers nor modern theorists appreciate their own texts being treated in this same way!
- *The third age of the Spirit.* The Quaker confusion about salvation history had bad effects on them, but one of the most unfortunate aspects of it was the notion that they lived in the third age, the age of the Spirit, which replaced both the age of the Father (the Old Testament) and the age of the Son (New Testament). The idea of this third age was articulated by Joachim of Fiore, and was influential from AD 1000. Of course it meant that both the Old and New Testament were now obsolete, and that Jesus was no longer the focus of God's saving activity.
- *Bible words no guarantee.* It is still possible to be bewitched by the sound of biblical words and phrases, and believe that Bible words mean Bible truth. On the contrary, Bible words can be used to convey ideas that are very far from the Bible.

Enlightenment heat and Quaker light

William Temple once wrote that the most significant moment in Western society was when René Descartes went into his stove, to emerge with the basis for all knowledge in the statement 'I think, therefore I am.' We could assert that the first Quaker who said 'I feel, therefore I know' was equally significant.

The decision to replace external authority of Bible or church by internal authority was of either great importance, whether the internal authority was that of reason or emotion. The seventeenth-century Cambridge Platonists were former Puritans who believed in the supremacy of reason, 'the candle of the Lord'; and Quakers were former Puritans who believed in emotion, 'the Light of Christ'. Both departed from the authority of the Bible. Both replaced that authority with an internal authority. Reason and emotion are perhaps closer than we might expect (McDonald 1959: 32–34, 68). Both deists and Enthusiasts followed the revelation within.

Theology necessary?

There was a profound theological disagreement between Puritans and Quakers. Ignoring theology does not work, and those who do so will be all the more effectively hindered by their unconscious theological system. The Quakers came to grief because they would not recognize the need for intellectual clarity, the good use of reason, and the benefit of informed theological thinking. The Reformers and the Puritans were strengthened because they intentionally engaged with what Alister McGrath calls 'the Great Tradition' of orthodox biblical faith (McGrath 2000: 139–158). Historic credal Christianity (Baxter's 'Catholic Faith') is a needed remedy against confusion. This does not mean that the Bible is insufficient, but that it is best understood from within the long-term history of the people of God.

God's presence and physical signs

The Quaker belief that God is most surely present when we feel that he is present is common today. The idea that God's presence is always accompanied by intense emotional awareness, or by physical signs such as quaking or falling down, is now popular in and beyond the charismatic movement. We would do well to heed the warning of Jonathan Edwards: 'Great effects on the body certainly are no sure evidences that affections are spiritual' (Edwards 1986: 59).

Christ and the Bible

I have argued that the difference between the Puritans and Quakers on the method that God uses to bring revelation to us was of fundamental importance, because the issue of the means of revelation influences all other doctrines. It leads to radically different understanding of the place where the Spirit reveals Christ, and so to radically different understanding of Christ and his work. If the historical revelation of Christ is lost because the historical revelation of that work though Christ's Spirit in Scripture is lost, then all is lost. Without the Bible the remembered Christ becomes the imagined

Christ. We must receive God's Spirit-words about his Son-work. The Bible comprises God's words through his Spirit about his work through his Son.

Richard Baxter on meditation

There is a rich tradition of Evangelical and Reformed spiritual writings, not least among the Puritans of the late sixteenth and early seventeenth centuries. They have written on many of the subjects that are also our concern. They have also written on subjects that do not concern us. Of course we can learn from both kinds of subjects. One of the advantages of studying Christian writers from a previous age is that they give us a different perspective on the matters that concern us. Another advantage is that they raise subjects that do not concern us, and are worthy of our attention. One of the best ways to escape the preoccupations and blindnesses of our own age is to find out how Christians of other ages thought about and practised their Christianity. Their reading of the Bible will always be a challenge to us. To stand somewhere else in history is a good way of seeing our own times more clearly.

Study of these writings will help Evangelical believers of today make the most of their heritage, and also mean that they will not have to adopt the spiritual practices of other traditions to fill an imagined gap in their own. And all believers of whatever tradition will benefit from this vigorous spiritual tradition.

Meditation is a common theme among the Puritans. John Owen's *Communion with God* (Owen 1965) is a celebration of our privilege in having holy and spiritual communion or fellowship with the Father, the Son and the Spirit. He describes in detail what it is to have fellowship with the Father, then with the Son and then with the Holy Spirit. As J. I. Packer explains, this notion of intentional fellowship with each person of the Trinity is also found in Thomas Goodwin: 'There is communion with all the persons, Father, Son and Holy Ghost, and their love, severally and distinctly' (Packer 2001: 113). J. Gwyn Thomas has written on the Puritan doctrine of pure joy (in Packer 2001: 119–140). He quotes Sibbes: 'Joy is the principal part of happiness in this world and in the world to come,' and 'Joy is that frame and state of soul that all who have given their names to Christ either are in, or should labour to be in' (Packer 2001: 119, 123). Or again, John Howe: 'It is plain, that it is the common duty of all to delight in God' (Packer 2001: 123).

Richard Baxter's *The Saints' Everlasting Rest*, the first book he wrote, was published in 1650, and eight more editions were published within ten years. One of the most striking features of this work is that it is an attempt to sustain present Christian living by a constant and determined expectation of our future state after the return of Christ. This expectation as a source of present spiritual comfort and encouragement seems to have disappeared from the consciousness of modern believers, even those who still firmly believe in the return of Christ. For some it has become a matter of their faith, but not a matter of their spirituality. Baxter encourages us to a spirituality of anticipation, a life based on firm Christian hope. While we focus on faith and love, hope is neglected to our peril.

In his writing Baxter made good use of the early church writers Augustine, Cyprian and Gregory. He also used the fifteenth-century writer Gerson, and his contemporaries Bishop Joseph Hall and George Herbert. He was clearly influenced by John Calvin: 'no one has made progress in the school of Christ who does not joyfully await the day of death and final resurrection' (*Institutes* 3.9.5).

Ivonwry Morgan comments that his 'discipline of godliness' recalled earlier monastic practice, but made it available for every believer, to be practised in the everyday world (Knott 1980: 66). Meditation on 'the way to heaven' was a common theme among Puritan preachers and writers. Arthur Dent wrote *The Plain Man's Pathway to Heaven* in 1605 (Dent 1994), and Robert Bolton wrote in 1638, 'Let thy soul full often soare aloft upon the wings of faith, unto the glory of the Empyrean Heaven, where God dwelleth, and bathe it selfe beforehand with many a sweet meditation in that everlasting blisse above' (Knott 1980: 68). John Bunyan used the same theme in *The Pilgrim's Progress*, written in 1678. This use of holy imagination was also popular among preachers, especially Richard Sibbes (Knott 1980: 65).

Baxter's model of meditation is based on a few words that need some explanation. It begins with 'consideration'. This means thoughtful reflection on the subject of the meditation, what we might call discerning faith. Here reason is used as spiritual discernment in the service of faith. Then comes 'soliloquy'. By this Baxter means preaching to oneself, self-exhortation. The purpose of this is to excite and engage the 'affections', or emotions. Then comes 'prayer', which in this context means addressing God with praise, thanksgiving, lament or confession.

So that Baxter can speak for himself, here are some excerpts from *The Saints' Everlasting Rest*. I am using the Fawcett summary of

1758, because this is still readily available in a reprint edition (Baxter 1981: 3–124).

Baxter begins by writing of the hope and duty of Christian meditation, and explains the motivations and theological basis for meditation on the everlasting rest that will be ours in Christ:

- May the living God, who is the portion and rest of his saints, make these our carnal minds so spiritual, and our earthly minds so heavenly, that loving him, and delighting in him, may be the work of our lives. (1981: 3)
- To stand on that mount, whence one can see the wilderness and Canaan, both at once; to stand in heaven, and look back on earth, and weigh them together in the balance of a comparing sense and judgment, how must it needs transport the soul, and make it cry out, 'Is this the purchase that cost so dear as the blood of Christ?' (7–8)
- Fellow Christians, what a day that will be, when we, who have been kept prisoners by sin, by the grave, shall be fetched out by the Lord himself! (11)
- Another thing what leads to paradise is, that great work of Jesus Christ, in raising our bodies from the dust, and uniting them again unto the soul. (11)
- Triumph now, O Christian, in these promises; thou shalt shortly triumph in their performance. (11)
- As we have been together in the labour, duty, danger and distress: so shall we be in the great recompense and deliverance. As we have been scorned and despised, so shall we be owned and honoured together. But now all our praises shall make up one melody; all our churches, one church; and all ourselves, one body: for we shall all be one in Christ. (15)
- As another property of our rest, we shall derive its joys directly from God. (16)
- Every soul that hath a title to this rest, doth place his chief happiness in God. (54)

He explains that we should not only ensure that each of us meditates in this way, but that we encourage others to do the same: 'Every good Christian is a teacher, and has a charge of his neighbour's soul' (1981: 60). He points to the advantages of this meditation:

- Afflictions likewise serve to quicken our way to our place in the way to our rest. (66)

- Hath the eternal God provided us with such a glory, and promised to take us up to dwell with himself, and is not this worth thinking upon? (73)
- A heavenly mind is the nearest and truest way to a life of comfort. What makes such frozen, uncomfortable Christians, but their living is so far from heaven? A heart in heaven will be a most excellent preservative against temptations to sin. (75)
- The frequent believing views of glory are the most precious cordials in all afflictions. (77)

He then gives practical advice on how to lead a heavenly life on earth:

- Living in any known sin, is a grand impediment to a heavenly conversation. An earthly mind is another hindrance carefully to be avoided. (1981: 82)
- Avoid frequent disputes about lesser truths, and a religion that lies only in opinions. Take heed of a proud and lofty spirit. (84)
- Labour to apprehend how near thy rest is. Let eternal rest be the subject of thy frequent serious discourse. (87)
- Be much in the angelical work of praise. Praising God is the work of angels and saints in heaven, and will be our own everlasting work; and if we were more in it now, we should be liker to what we shall be then. (89)
- Carefully observe and cherish the motions of the Spirit of God . . . that Spirit of God must be to thee as the chariot of Elijah. (90)
- The set and solemn acting of all the powers of thy soul in meditation upon thy everlasting rest. This meditation is the acting of all the powers of the soul. There is solemn meditation, when we apply ourselves to that work. (90–91)

He then gives advice the practice of meditation:

- Give it stated time. Stated time is a hedge to duty. Frequent society breeds familiarity . . . the chief end of this duty, is to have acquaintance and fellowship with God. Frequency will habituate thy heart to the work, and make it more easy and delightful. (1981: 92)
- Choose the most seasonable time. Observe the gales of the Spirit, and how the Spirit of Christ doth move thy spirit. Another peculiar season for this duty is, when thou art in a suffering, distressed, or tempted state. (93)

- The fittest place for heavenly contemplation . . . is some private retirement . . . Get thy heart as clear from the world as thou canst. Be sure to set upon this work with the greatest solemnity of heart and mind. He that trades for heaven is the only gainer, and he that neglects it is the only loser. How seriously, therefore, should this work be done! (95–96)

What then of the process of meditation? It begins with the use of the mind and theological evaluation. It is the use of reason and faith, and the ability to decide to persist in the duty of meditation:

- Consideration . . . opens the door between the head and the heart. Consideration presents to the affections those things which are most important, and brings them to eye of the soul. Consideration also presents the most important things in the most affecting way, and reasons the case with a man's own heart. Consideration is . . . the repeating God's reasons to our hearts . . . we plead with our affections to persuade them to our Father's everlasting mansion. (1981: 96–97)
- Consideration helps exalt reason to its just authority. It helps to deliver it from its captivity to the senses, and sets it again on the throne of the soul. Meditation holds reason and faith to their work, and blows the fire until it thoroughly burns. Though a sudden occasional thought of heaven will not raise our affections to any spiritual heat, yet meditation can continue our thoughts till our hearts grow warm. (96–97)

This use of consideration means not only exercising faith in God's promises, but also faith that we have a 'title' to them, because we have hoped in Christ:

- Let us see how this heavenly work is promoted by the particular exercise of the affections . . . By consideration, we have recourse to the memory, and from thence take those heavenly doctrines, which we intend to make the subject of our meditation; such as, promises of eternal life, descriptions of the saints' glory . . . we then submit them to our judgement, that it may deliberately view them over, and take an exact survey, and determine uprightly concerning the perfection of our celestial happiness. But the principal thing is to exercise . . . our faith in the truth of our everlasting rest; by which I mean, both the truth of the promises, and of our own personal interest in them, and title to them . . . Never expect to have love and joy move, when faith stands still, which must lead the way. Therefore daily exercise faith, and set before it the freeness of the promise, God's urging to accept, Christ's gracious disposition, all the evidences of the love of Christ, his faithfulness to his engagements, and the evidences of his love in ourselves. (1981: 96–97)

Baxter then explains the common order in which our affections are aroused, and gives an example of the language we might use:

- Love is the first affection to be excited in heavenly contemplation; then desire, then hope, then courage or boldness, then joy. (1863: 100–101)
- The soul that loves, ascends frequently, and runs familiarly through the streets of heavenly Jerusalem, visiting the patriarchs and prophets, saluting the apostles, and admiring the army of martyrs . . . Here must I lodge: here must I live; here must I praise; here must I love and be loved. I must shortly be one of this heavenly choir, and be better skilled in the music. Among this blessed company must I take up my place; my voice must join to take up the melody. My tears will then be wiped away; my groans be turned to another tune; my cottage of clay be turned to this palace; my prison rags to these splendid robes; and my sordid flesh shall be put off, and such a sun-like spiritual body be put on. (101–102)

There are of course other ways of achieving the same end:

- Let me here observe, that there is no necessity of exercise these affections, either exactly in this order, or all at one time . . . exercise opportunity to exercise opposite and more mixed affections: such as – hatred of sin, which would deprive thy soul of these immortal joys – godly fear, lest thou shouldst abuse thy mercy – godly shame and grief, for having abused it – unfeigned repentance – self-indignation – jealousy over thy heart – and pity for those who are in danger of losing these immortal joys. (1981: 102)

An important aid to meditation is to exhort ourselves, to use a soliloquy, to preach to ourselves:

- Consideration is not likely to affect the heart. In this respect, contemplation is like preaching, where the mere explaining of truths and duties is seldom attended with much success, as the lively application of them to the conscience; and especially when a divine blessing is earnestly sought for to accompany any such application (1981: 102).

- By soliloquy, or a pleading the case with thyself, thou must in meditation quicken thy own heart. Enter into serious debate with it. Plead with it in the most moving and affecting language, and urge it with the most powerful and weighty arguments . . . It is what holy men of God have practised in all ages. Thus David 'Why art thou cast down, O my soul . . . Hope thou in God' . . . It is a preaching to oneself . . . Do this in thy heavenly contemplation; explain to thyself the things on which thou dost meditate; confirm thy faith in them by scripture; and then apply them to thyself. (102)

Heavenly contemplation is also promoted by speaking to God in prayer:

- Thus in our meditations, to intermix soliloquy and prayer; sometimes speaking to our own hearts, and sometimes to God, is, I apprehend, the highest step we can advance in this heavenly work. The mixture of them, like music, will be more engaging. (1981: 103)

Further helps include the use of our senses:

- It will therefore be a point of spiritual prudence, to call in sense to the assistance of faith . . . Think of Christ, as in our own glorified nature. Think of glorified saints, as men made perfect. Suppose thyself a companion with John, in his survey of the New Jerusalem, and viewing the thrones, the majesty, the heavenly hosts, the shining splendour, which he saw. Do not, like the papists, draw them in pictures; but get the liveliest picture of them in thy mind that thou possible canst, by contemplating the Scripture accounts of them, till thou canst say, 'Methinks I see a glimpse of glory! Methinks I hear the shouts of joy and praise!' (1981: 103–104)

We should compare the objects of sense with the objects of faith, a series of comparisons that will excite our hope for the future:

- How sweet is this food to my taste when I am hungry . . . What delight then, must my soul have in feeding upon 'Christ, the living bread,' and in 'eating with him at his table in his kingdom'. (1981: 104)

- When we meet with some choice book. How could we read it day and night, almost forgetful of meat, drink, or sleep! What delights then are there at God's right hand, where we shall know in a moment all that is to be known. (105)
- If these things, which are but servants to sinful men, are so full of mysterious worth, what is that place where God himself dwells, and which is prepared for just men made perfect with Christ. (105)
- Compare the joys above with the comforts thou hast here received in ordinances . . . If the promise is so sweet, what will the performance be! If the testament of our Lord, and the charter of our kingdom, be so comfortable, what will be the possession of the kingdom itself! (106)
- What joy is it to have access and acceptance in prayer; that I may always go to God, and open my case and unbosom my soul to him, as to my utmost familiar friend! But this will be a more unspeakable joy, when I shall receive all my blessings without asking, and all my necessities and miseries will be removed, and when God himself will be the portion and inheritance of my soul. (106)
- If the church under her sins and enemies have so much beauty, what will she have at the marriage of the Lamb! (107)
- If we are said to be like God, when we are pressed down with a body of sin; sure we shall be much more like God, when we have no such thing as sin in us. (108)

And persistence is the key:

- Therefore stay not from the duty, till thou feelest thy love constrain thee, any more than thou wouldst stay from the fire, till thou feelest thyself warm; but engage in the work till love is excited, and then love will constrain thee to further duty. (1981: 110)
- [Continue] . . . till thou hast pleaded thyself from a clod to a flame; from a forgetful sinner and a lover of the world, to an ardent lover of God; from a fearful coward to a resolved Christian; from an unfruitful sadness to a joyful life; in a word, till thou hast pleaded thy heart from earth to heaven. (111)

Baxter knows that we cannot do what we have not seen someone else do, and so he then provides an example of that pleading (1981: 111–120).

Notice the great themes of biblical and Reformed faith that we have seen in these excerpts: the trustworthiness of God and the Scriptures, the centrality of Christ, grace and faith, the notion that this meditation is for all believers, good practical and realistic advice for ordinary believers, the engagement of mind and heart, and the hope of future glory.

This system of meditation can be used for subjects other than the 'Everlasting Rest', that is, life with God in the future. It can, for example, be used for meditation on the Incarnation, the cross of Christ, the resurrection, of life in the Spirit. The result of this meditation is not union with God, but perfect fellowship with him, not the breakdown of identity, but that intimacy that is finally fulfilled in the marriage of the Lamb with his bride, the church.

The basis of this is the truth and power of the Bible. In the original four-part version of *The Saints' Everlasting Rest* Baxter spends the second part explaining and defending the Bible as the basis for the hope on which this meditation depends. As Knott comments, if belief in the Bible promises of rest are the basis, in the third stage faith confronts the Word directly and experiences a sense of its power, for Baxter believed in 'the efficacy of the Word to stimulate the affections from love to joy by summoning scenes of heavenly joy' (Knott 1980: 71).

So there are three distinct but closely connected actions of the soul: consideration, soliloquy and prayer, all designed to engage the affections on the basis of a firm faith in the promises and power of God. Baxter drew on the tradition of soliloquy in David, Augustine and Bernard, and 'gave to the soliloquy a special importance and brought it to a new level of intensity' (Knott 1980: 72).[3]

[3] Whereas Baxter uses reason, Calvin points to the inner work and witness of the Holy Spirit. But for Baxter, reason is the servant of faith, used in spiritual discernment of the truths revealed by God in the Bible.

Conclusion: The unfolding of your words gives light

In this book I have tried to answer the question 'What does the Bible teach us about spirituality?'

I have answered this question in the light of various Christian traditions of spirituality, and shown how the Evangelical and Reformed tradition expresses biblical spirituality. My aim has been to explain the Evangelical and Reformed traditions of spirituality, because those who do know these patterns of Christian living may think that they have no spirituality, and those who follow these patterns may not know the richness that lies within their history. At the same time I have indicated the weaknesses within these two traditions, not least within their practice of spirituality. In all this I hope that I have shown how these traditions lie within 'the Great Tradition' of mainstream Christian belief and practice.

I have also shown how biblical theology helps us to make sense of the Bible's practice and teaching on spirituality, and how we can look at various books of the Bible, and find from them their particular insights into true spirituality.

I have tried to do the following:

- To show how the Bible is a rich and fruitful resource for spirituality, that is, what we can learn from the Bible about spirituality, or what spirituality it contains.
- To show the fundamental shape and structure of the 'spirituality of the Word', or, how it works.
- To show the spirituality that the Bible teaches and encourages, or what spirituality results from using the Bible.

I hope I have shown that those who participate in biblical spirituality focus on God in Christ, practise hearing the word of God by faith, experience meeting God in his Spirit-given words, and so trust in Christ and our heavenly Father.

I have also tackled some important issues for Christian spirituality, including the use of sacred times, places, objects and actions. I have shown how biblical theology helps us to make sense of these issues, and the particular perspectives of the Evangelical and Reformed traditions on these issues.

From a theological viewpoint I have expounded Calvin's theology of how we hear the word of Christ in the Bible, exemplified corporate spirituality of the Word in the early church, outlined the Puritan–Quaker debate on Word and Spirit, and described a Puritan practice of meditation.

This has been a wide-ranging exercise, as I have covered not only the history of Christian spirituality, but also Old and New Testament, church history and theology. I am well aware that I do not have specialist knowledge in all these areas, but I do hope that this wide-ranging study will be helpful for gaining an overall perspective on the subject.

I have not been autobiographical in this book, but I would like to end by saying that I have found the Bible to be a constantly rich source of true spirituality, that when I read it I hear the voice of God. The longer I live, the more I find that through it God provides the wisdom I need to understand this world and God's church, and how to live for him. On countless occasions I have been rescued from disaster by remembering words from the Bible.

Whenever I prepare a Bible study or sermon I am constantly challenged as I try to find out what God is saying through these words, rather than what I thought he was saying! I am so grateful to those who have coached me as I have listened to them preach the Word of God. I do not remember everything I have heard, but of course the purpose of coaching is to make godly change instinctive. I am also very grateful to God for opening the door for me to do the ministry of Word and sacraments. I have received this ministry with thankfulness, and it has been a blessing to me, as I hope, to others. The unfolding of God's words has given me light, and it has been a privilege to share this light with others.

Meditation

Spend some time meditating on these words, and use several of them for frequent momentary reflections over the next few weeks:

The word is very near to you; it is in your mouth and in your heart for you to obey.

(Moses)

Hear, O Israel: faith hearing the word of Christ.

(Moses and St Paul)

But this is the one to whom I will look, to the humble and contrite in spirit, who trembles at my word.

(Isaiah)

My lips overflow with praise, for you teach me your words.

(Psalms)

No one can come to me unless drawn by my Father: come to me all that are weary and I will give you rest.

(Jesus Christ)

My mother and my brothers are those who hear the word of God and do it.

(Jesus Christ)

The Spirit bears witness with our spirit that we are children of God.

(St Paul)

Our daily food on this earth is the Word of God which is dispensed in the churches.

(Augustine)

If we preach Christ's Word, Christ himself feeds through us.

(Augustine)

Jesus comforts them with his words in Holy Scripture, and gives gladness and joy to all who truly believe his promises, and humbly abide the fulfilment of his will.

(Walter Hilton)

We enjoy Christ only as we embrace Christ clad in his own promises.

(John Calvin)

God has opened his heart to us in the Bible.

(Richard Sibbes)

The Scriptures: the fairest temple of God.

(John Donne)

Bibliography

Acheson, R. J. (1990), *Radical Puritans in England 1550–1660*, London: Longman.

Adam, Peter (1981), 'The Imitation of Christ with Special Reference to the Writings of Dietrich Bonhoeffer'. PhD thesis, University of Durham.

—— (1982), *Living the Trinity*, Nottingham: Grove Books.

—— (1988), *Roots of Contemporary Evangelical Spirituality*, Nottingham: Grove Books.

—— (1992), *The Majestic Son: Reading Hebrews Today*, Sydney: AIO.

—— (1996), *Speaking God's Words*, Leicester: IVP.

—— (2001), *Word and Spirit: The Puritan–Quaker Debate*, London: St Antholin's Lectureship.

Andersen, Francis I. (1976), *Job: An Introduction and Commentary*, Leicester: IVP.

Anderson, Marvin W. (1987), *Evangelical Foundations, Religion in England 1378–1683*, New York: Peter Lang.

Arndt, Johann (1979), *True Christianity*, trans. Peter Erb, The Classics of Western Spirituality, London: SPCK.

Atkinson, David (1991), *The Message of Job*, The Bible Speaks Today, Leicester: IVP.

Augustine (1943), *The Confessions of Saint Augustine*, trans. F. J. Sheed, London: Sheed and Ward.

Baldwin, Joyce (1986), *The Message of Genesis 12–50: From Abraham to Joseph*, The Bible Speaks Today, Leicester: IVP.

Barbour, Hugh (1964), *The Quakers in Puritan England*, New Haven: Yale University Press.

Barbour, Hugh, and Arthur O. Roberts (eds.) (1973), *Early Quaker Writings 1650–1700*, Grand Rapids: Eerdmans.

Barker, Paul A. (1995), 'Faithless Israel, Faithful Yahweh in Deuteronomy'. PhD thesis, University of Bristol.

—— (1998), *Deuteronomy: The God who Keeps Promises*, Melbourne: Acorn Press.

Battles, Ford Lewis (trans. and ed.) (1978), *The Piety of John Calvin: An Anthology Illustrative of the Spirituality of the Reformer*, Grand Rapids: Baker Book House.

Baxter, Richard (1655), *The Quakers Catechism*. EEB 1641–1700, University Microfilm, Ann Arbor, MI.

—— (1657a), *One Sheet against the Quakers*. EEB 1641–1700, University Microfilm, Ann Arbor, MI.

—— (1657b), *One Sheet for the Ministry, against the Malignants of All Sorts.* EEB 1641–1700, University Microfilm, Ann Arbor, MI.

—— (1838), *A Christian Directory*, repr. Ligonier: Soli Deo Gloria Publications, 1990.

—— (1981), *The Practical Works of Richard Baxter*, repr. Grand Rapids: Baker Book House.

—— (1974), *The Autobiography of Richard Baxter* (*Reliquiae Baxterianae*), ed. N. H. Keeble, London: J. M. Dent.

Bayly, L. (1714), *The Practice of Piety*, London: Daniel Midwinter.

Beale, G. K. (1999), *The Book of Revelation*, New International Greek Testament Commentary, Grand Rapids: Eerdmans.

Bebbington, D. W. (1989), *Evangelicalism in Modern Britain*, London: Unwin Hyman.

—— (2000), *Holiness in Nineteenth-Century England*, Carlisle: Paternoster Press.

Bockmuehl, Klaus (1990), *Listening to the God who Speaks*, Colorado Springs: Helmers and Howard.

Bonhoeffer, Dietrich (1986), *Meditating on the Word*, ed. David Mcl. Gracie, Cambridge, MA: Cowley Publications.

Book of Common Prayer, Oxford: Oxford University Press.

Bosch, David J. (1979), *A Spirituality of the Road*, Scottdale, PA: Herald Press.

Braithwaite, William C. (1912), *The Beginnings of Quakerism*, London: Macmillan.

Bridge, William (1961), *A Lifting up for the Downcast*, repr. Edinburgh: Banner of Truth Trust, 1979.

Bromiley, G. W. (ed.) (1953), *Zwingli and Bullinger*, Library of Christian Classics, vol. 24, London: SCM Press.

Brooks, Thomas (1984), *Precious Remedies against Satan's Devices*, repr. Edinburgh: Banner of Truth Trust.

Brown, Callum G. (2001), *The Death of Christian Britain: Understanding Secularisation 1800–2000*, London: Routledge.

Brueggemann, Walter (1989), *Finally Comes the Poet: Daring Speech for Proclamation*, Minneapolis: Fortress Press.

—— (1997), *Cadences of Home: Preaching to Exiles*, Louisville: Westminster/John Knox Press.

Bunyan, John (1965), *Prayer*, London: Banner of Truth Trust.

—— (1966), *John Bunyan: Grace Abounding to the Chief of Sinners and The Pilgrim's Progress*, ed. Roger Sharrock, London: Oxford University Press.

Burroughs, Jeremiah (1964), *The Rare Jewel of Christian Contentment*, Edinburgh: Banner of Truth Trust.

—— (1990), *Gospel Worship*, Ligonier: Sole Deo Gloria Publications.

Callen, Barry L. (2002), *Authentic Spirituality: Moving beyond Mere Religion*, Grand Rapids: Baker Book House.

Calvin, John (1959–71), *Calvin's New Testament Commentaries*, 12 vols., eds. David W. Torrance and Thomas F. Torrance, Grand Rapids: Eerdmans.

—— (1960), *Institutes of the Christian Religion*, vols. 1 and 2, trans. Ford Lewis Battles, The Library of Christian Classics, vols. 20, 21, Philadelphia: Westminster Press.

—— (1981), *Calvin's Commentaries*, 22 vols., repr. Grand Rapids: Baker Book House.

Carmichael, Amy (1967), *Edges of his Ways*, London: SPCK.

Carson, D. A. (1996), *The Gagging of God: Christianity Confronts Pluralism*, Grand Rapids: Zondervan.

—— (1998), *For the Love of God*, Wheaton, IL: Crossway Books.

Carson, D.A., and John D. Woodbridge (1983), *Scripture and Truth*, Leicester: IVP.

Clarke, W. K. Lowther (1944), *Eighteenth Century Piety*, London: SPCK.

Clowney, Edmund P. (1988a), *The Message of 1 Peter*, The Bible Speaks Today, Leicester: IVP.

—— (1988b), *The Unfolding Mystery*, Leicester: IVP.

Coates, R. H. (1912), *Types of English Piety*, Edinburgh: T. and T. Clark.

Cockerton, John (1994), *Essentials of Evangelical Spirituality*, Nottingham: Grove Books.

Cole, Graham (1993), 'At the Heart of a Christian Spirituality', *Reformed Theological Review*, 52 (1), 49–61.

Collinson, Patrick (1967), *Puritanism and the English Church*, London: Jonathan Cape.

Craigie, P. C. (1976), *The Book of Deuteronomy*, Grand Rapids: Eerdmans.

Daane, James (1980), *Preaching with Confidence: A Theological Essay on the Power of the Pulpit*, Grand Rapids: Eerdmans.

Deere, Jack (1996), *Surprised by the Voice of God*, Grand Rapids: Zondervan.

Dent, Arthur (1994), *The Plain Man's Pathway to Heaven*, Pittsburgh, PA: Soli Deo Gloria Publications.

Dever, Mark (2000), *Richard Sibbes: Puritanism and Calvinism in Late Elizabethan and Early Stuart England*, Macon, GA: Mercer University Press.

Dhorme, Édouard (1967), *A Commentary on the Book of Job*, Nashville: Thomas Nelson.

Doddridge, P. (1977), *The Rise and Progress of Religion on the Soul*, Grand Rapids: Baker Book House.

Drummond, Henry (1899), *The Ideal Life*, London: Hodder and Stoughton.

Durston, Christopher, and Jacqueline Eales (eds.) (1996), *The Culture of English Puritanism 1560–1700*, Basingstoke: Macmillan.

Dyck, Elmer (ed.) (1996), *The Act of Bible Reading – A Multi-Disciplinary Approach to Biblical Interpretation*, Downers Grove: IVP.

Edwards, Jonathan (1986), *The Religious Affections*, repr. Edinburgh: Banner of Truth Trust.

Elliot, Elisabeth (1957), *Through Gates of Splendour*, London: Hodder and Stoughton.

Ellis, E. Earle (1966), *The Gospel of Luke*, The Century Bible, London: Nelson.

Ellul, Jacques (1973), *Prayer and Modern Man*, New York: Seabury Press.

—— (1985), *The Humiliation of the Word*, Grand Rapids: Eerdmans.

Erb, Peter C. (ed.) (1983), *Pietists – Selected Writings*, The Classics of Western Spirituality, London: SPCK.

Estes, Daniel J. (1997), *Hear, my Son: Teaching and Learning in Proverbs 1–9*, New Studies in Biblical Theology 4, Leicester: Apollos.

Farrer, Austin (1948), *The Glass of Vision*, Westminster: Dacre Press.

Fee, Gordon D. (1994), *God's Empowering Presence: The Holy Spirit in the Letters of Paul*, Peabody, MA: Hendrickson.

Fénelon, Francois de Salignac de la Mothe (1964), *Fénelon Letters*, trans. John McEwan, London: Harvill Press.

Ferguson, Sinclair B. (1985), *A Heart for God*, Colorado Springs: NavPress.

—— (1987), *John Owen on the Christian Life*, Edinburgh: Banner of Truth Trust.

Flew, R. Newton (1968), *The Idea of Perfection in Christian Theology*, New York: Humanities Press.

Foster, Richard (1998), *Streams of Living Water: Celebrating the Great Traditions of Christian Faith*, London: HarperCollins.

Fox, George (1659), *The Great Mistery of the Great Whore Unfolded*, EEB 1641–1700, University Microfilm, Ann Arbor, MI.

—— (1975), *The Journal of George Fox*, ed. John L. Nickalls, London: Religious Society of Friends.

Fox, George? and James Nayler (1653), *Saul's Errand to Damascus*, EEB 1641–1700, University Microfilm, Ann Arbor, MI.

Fryer, Jonathan (ed.) (1991), *George Fox and the Children of Light*, Journal and Epistles of George Fox, London: Kyle Cathie.

Fyall, Robert S. (2002), *Now my Eyes Have Seen you: Images of Creation and Evil in the Book of Job*, New Studies in Biblical Theology, Leicester: Apollos; Downers Grove, IL: IVP.

Gaffin, Richard B. Jr (1976), 'All I Didn't Know', *Westminster Theological Journal*, 3, 281–299.

Goldingay, John (1992), *Evangelical Spirituality in the Light of Paul's Letter to the Romans*, Nottingham: Grove Books.

—— (1994), *Models for Scripture*, Grand Rapids: Eerdmans.

Goldsworthy, Graeme (1991), *According to Plan: The Unfolding Revelation of God in the Bible*, Leicester: IVP; Homebush West: Lancer Press.

—— (1993), *The Tree of Life: Reading Proverbs Today*, Sydney: Anglican Information Office.

Goodwin, Thomas (1979), *The Work of the Holy Ghost in Our Salvation*, repr. Edinburgh: Banner of Truth Trust.

Gordon, James M. (1991), *Evangelical Spirituality: From the Wesleys to John Stott*, London: SPCK.

Gorman, Michael J. (2001), *Cruciformity: Paul's Narrative Spirituality of the Cross*, Grand Rapids: Eerdmans.

Grenz, Stanley J. (1996), *A Primer on Postmodernism*, Grand Rapids: Eerdmans.

Grudem, Wayne. A. (1983), 'Scripture's Self-Attestation', in D. A. Carson and John D. Woodbridge (eds.), *Scripture and Truth*, Leicester: IVP.

Guinness, Os (1995), 'The Word in the Age of the Image', in Melvin Tinker (ed.), *The Anglican Evangelical Crisis*, Fearn: Christian Focus Publications.

Gurnall, William (1964), *The Christian in Complete Armour*, repr. London: Banner of Truth Trust.

Harrington, Wilfred (2002), *Seeking Spiritual Growth through the Bible*, New York: Paulist Press.

—— (1973), *The Path of Biblical Theology*, Dublin: Gill and Macmillan.

Hatchett, Marion J. (1976), *Sanctifying Life, Time and Space: An Introduction to Liturgical Study*, San Francisco: Harper and Row.

Hayden, Christopher (2001), *Praying the Scriptures: A Practical Introduction to Lectio Divina*, London: St Paul's Publications.

Haykin, Michael A. G. (2000), *The Revived Puritan: The Spirituality of George Whitefield,* Dundas, ON: Joshua Press.

Heiler, Friedrich (1958), *Prayer: A Study in the History and Psychology of Religion*, New York: Galaxy/Oxford University Press.

Helm, Paul (1983), 'Faith, Evidence, and the Scriptures', in D. A. Carson and John D. Woodbridge (eds.), *Scripture and Truth*, Leicester: IVP.

Higginson, Francis (1653), *A Brief Relation of the Irreligion of the Northern Quakers.* EEB 1641–1700, University Microfilm, Ann Arbor, MI.

Hill, Christopher (1988), *A Turbulent, Seditious and Factious People: John Bunyan and his Church*, Oxford: Oxford University Press.

—— (1993), *The English Bible and the Seventeenth-Century Revolution*, London: Penguin Books.

Hindmarsh, D. Bruce (1996), *John Newton and the English Evangelical Tradition*, Grand Rapids: Eerdmans.

Hoffecker, W. Andrew (1981), *Piety and the Princeton Theologians*, Grand Rapids: Baker Book House.

Holmes, Urban T. III (2002), *A History of Christian Spirituality*, Harrisburg: Morehouse Publishing.

Houston, James M. (1996), 'Toward a Biblical Spirituality', in Elmer Dyck (ed.), *The Act of Bible Reading*, Downers Grove, IL: IVP.

Huelin, Gordon (1972), *The Cross in English Life and Devotion*, London: Faith Press.

Hügel, Friedrich von (1961), *The Mystical Element of Religion as Studied in Saint Catherine of Genoa and her Friends*, vols. 1, 2, London: J. M. Dent/James Clarke.

Hughes, Graham (1979), *Hebrews and Hermeneutics*, Society for New Testament Studies Monograph Series 36, Cambridge: Cambridge University Press.

Hume, Basil (1977) *Searching for God*, London: Hodder and Stoughton.

Huntley, Frank Livingstone (1979), *Bishop Joseph Hall*, Cambridge: D. S. Brewer.

Ignatius of Loyola (1955), *The Spiritual Exercises of Saint Ignatius of Loyola*, London: A. R. Mowbray.

Issler, Klaus (2001), *Wasting Time with God: A Christian Spirituality of Friendship with God*, Downers Grove, IL: IVP.

Jenkins, Gary (1999), *In my Place: The Spirituality of Substitution*, Grove Spirituality Series, Cambridge: Grove Books.

Jensen, Peter (1995a), 'Preaching the Whole Bible', in Christopher Green and David Jackman (eds.), *When God's Voice Is Heard*, Leicester: IVP.

—— (1995b), *Using the Shield of Faith: Puritan Attitudes to Combat with Satan*, London: St Antholin's Lectureship.

—— (2002), *The Revelation of God*, Contours of Christian Theology, Leicester: IVP.

John of the Cross, Saint (1924), *The Dark Night of the Soul*, London: Thomas Baker.

Johnson, William (1977), *Silent Music*, London: Collins Fount.

Jones, Alexander (1961), *God's Living Word*, London: Geoffrey Chapman.

Julian (1966), *Revelations of Divine Love*, Harmondsworth: Penguin.

Kempis, Thomas à (no date), *Of the Imitation of Christ*, London: T. Nelson and Sons.

Knott, John R. (1980), *The Sword of the Spirit: Puritan Responses to the Bible*, Chicago: University of Chicago Press.

Larsen, David L. (2001), *Biblical Spirituality: Discovering the Real Connection between the Bible and Life*, Grand Rapids: Kregel.

Laurence (Nicholas Herman) (1981), *The Practice of the Presence of God*, London: Hodder and Stoughton.

Law, William (1810), *A Serious Call to a Devout and Holy Life*, London: William Baynes.

—— (1948), *Selected Mystical Writings of William Law*, ed. Stephen Hobhouse, London: Rockliff.

Lefebure, Molly (1975), *Samuel Taylor Coleridge*, New York: Stein and Day.

Lindars, Barnabas (1991), *The Theology of the Letter to the Hebrews*, Cambridge: Cambridge University Press.

Lloyd-Jones, D. M. (1985), *Preaching and Preachers*, London: Hodder and Stoughton.

Longman, Tremper III (1997), *Reading the Bible with Heart and Mind*, Colorado Springs: NavPress.
Lossky, Vladimir (1957), *The Mystical Theology of the Eastern Church*, Cambridge: James Clarke.
Loukes, Harold (1965), *The Quaker Contribution*, London: SCM Press.
Lovelace, Richard F. (1979), *Dynamics of Spiritual Life: An Evangelical Theology of Renewal*, Exeter: Paternoster Press.
Lowman, Pete (2001), *Gateways to God: Seeking Spiritual Depth in a Postmodern World*, Fearn: Christian Focus Publications.
Lucas, R. C. (1980), *Fullness and Freedom: The Message of Colossians and Philemon*, The Bible Speaks Today, Downers Grove, IL: IVP.
Lull, Ramon (1978), *The Book of the Lover and the Beloved*, London: Sheldon Press.
Macaulay, Ranald, and Jerram Barrs (1978), *Being Human: The Nature of Spiritual Experience*, Downers Grove, IL: IVP.
MacCulloch, Diarmaid (2002), *The Boy King: Edward VI and the Protestant Reformation*, Berkeley: University of California Press.
Macquarrie, John (1972), *Paths in Spirituality*, London: SCM Press.
Malatesta, Edward (1974), *Jesus in Christian Devotion and Contemplation*, Weathamstead, UK: Anthony Clarke.
Manton, Thomas (1996), *The Temptation of Christ*, Fearn: Christian Focus Publications.
McConville, J. G. (1993), *Judgment and Promise: An Interpretation of the Book of Jeremiah*, Leicester: Apollos.
McDonald, H. D. (1959), *Ideas of Revelation: An Historical Study 1700 to 1860*, London: Macmillan.
—— (1986), *The God who Responds*, Cambridge: James Clarke.
McGinnis, Scott (2002), '"Subtiltie" Exposed: Pastoral Perspectives in Witch Belief in the Thought of George Gifford', *Sixteenth Century Journal*, 33 (3), 665–686.
McGrath, Alister E. (1992), *Roots that Refresh: A Celebration of Reformation Spirituality*, London: Hodder and Stoughton.
—— (1993), *Evangelical Spirituality: Past Glories, Present Hopes, Future Possibilities*, London: St Antholin's Lectureship.
—— (1995), *Beyond the Quiet Time: Practical Evangelical Spirituality*, London: SPCK.
—— (1999), *Christian Spirituality*, Oxford: Blackwell.
—— (2000), 'Engaging the Great Tradition', in John G. Stackhouse

Jr (ed.), *Evangelical Futures*, Grand Rapids: Baker Book House; Leicester: Apollos; Vancouver: Regent College Publishing.

McGrath, Gavin J. (1991), *Grace and Duty in Puritan Spirituality*, Nottingham: Grove Books.

—— (1994), *But we Preach Christ Crucified: The Cross of Christ in the Pastoral Theology of John Owen, 1616–1683*, London: St Antholin's Lectureship.

McGregor, Neil (2000), *Seeing Salvation*, a BBC video.

McKenzie, John L. (ed.) (1969–71), *The New Testament for Spiritual Reading*, London: Burns and Oates/Sheed and Ward.

Merton, Thomas (1953), *Bread in the Wilderness*, London: Catholic Book Club.

Miller, Graham (1992), *Calvin's Wisdom – An Anthology Arranged Alphabetically*, Edinburgh: Banner of Truth Trust.

Moberly, R. W. L. (1992), *From Eden to Golgotha: Essays in Biblical Theology*, Atlanta: Scholars Press.

Molinos, Michael de (1907), *The Spiritual Guide*, ed. Kathleen Lyttelton, London: Methuen.

Moore, Sebastian (1977), *The Crucified Is No Stranger*, London: Darton, Longman and Todd.

Moorman, John R. H. (1983), *The Anglican Spiritual Tradition*, London: Darton, Longman and Todd.

Motyer, Alec (1996), *Look to the Rock*, Leicester: IVP.

Murray, Andrew (1962), *Holy in Christ*, Grand Rapids: Zondervan.

Murray, Iain H. (1971), *The Puritan Hope: Revival and the Interpretation of Prophecy*, Edinburgh: Banner of Truth Trust.

Mursell, Gordon (2001a), *English Spirituality: From Earliest Times to 1700*, London: SPCK; Louisville, KY: Westminster/John Knox Press.

—— (2001b), *English Spirituality: From 1700 to Present Day*, London: SPCK; Louisville, KY: Westminster/John Knox Press.

Nayler, James (1655), *An Answer to a Book Called the Quakers Catechism*. EEB 1641–1700, University Microfilm, Ann Arbor, MI.

Nee, Watchman (1961), *The Normal Christian Life*, London: Victory Press.

Newton, John (1831), 'On Grace in the Full Corn', section 2, Letter 12, 'Letters on Religious Subjects', in *The Select Works of John Newton*, ed. R. Cecil, Edinburgh: Peter Brown/Thomas Nelson.

Niesel, Wilhelm (1962), *Reformed Symbolics*, Edinburgh: Oliver and Boyd.

Nouwen, Henri J. M. (1979), *The Wounded Healer*, New York: Image Books.

Nunes, John (2002), 'By These Means Necessary: Scriptural and Sacramental Spirituality for All Nations', *Modern Reformation*, 11 (4), 28–32.

Nuttall, Geoffrey F. (1967), *The Puritan Spirit: Essays and Addresses*, London: Epworth Press.

—— (1992), *The Holy Spirit in Puritan Faith and Experience*, Chicago: University of Chicago Press.

Old, Hughes Oliphant (1998a), *The Reading and Preaching of the Scriptures in the Worship of the Christian Church*. Vol. 1, *The Biblical Period*, Grand Rapids: Eerdmans.

—— (1998b), *The Reading and Preaching of the Scriptures in the Worship of the Christian Church.* Vol. 2, *The Patristic Age*, Grand Rapids: Eerdmans.

Ortlund, Raymond C. (1996), *God's Unfaithful Wife: A Biblical Theology of Spiritual Adultery*, New Studies in Biblical Theology, Leicester: Apollos.

Owen, John (1965), *Communion with God*, Edinburgh: Banner of Truth Trust.

Packer, J. I. (1975), *Knowing God*, Sydney: Hodder and Stoughton.

—— (1988), 'Foreword', in Edmund Clowney, *The Unfolding Mystery*, Leicester: IVP.

—— (1990a), 'An Introduction to Systematic Spirituality', *Crux*, 26 (1), 2–8.

—— (1990b), *A Quest for Godliness: The Puritan Vision of the Christian Life*, Wheaton, IL: Crossway Books.

—— (2001), *Puritan Papers*, vol. 2, 1960–2, Phillipsburg, NJ: P&R Publishing.

Parker, T. H. L. (1947), *The Oracles of God: An Introduction to the Preaching of John Calvin*, London: Lutterworth Press.

—— (1986), *Calvin's Old Testament Commentaries*, Edinburgh: T. and T. Clark.

—— (1992), *Calvin's Preaching*, Edinburgh: T. and T. Clark.

Pelikan, Jaroslav (1974), *The Spirit of Eastern Christendom (600–1700)*, Chicago: University of Chicago Press.

Peterson, David (1995), *Possessed by God*, Leicester: Apollos.

Piper, John (1989), *Desiring God*, Leicester: IVP.

Polman, A. D. R. (1961), *The Word of God according to St. Augustine*, London: Hodder and Stoughton.

Pooley, Roger, and Seddon, Philip (eds.) (1986), *The Lord of the*

Journey: A Reader in Christian Spirituality, London: Collins.

Postman, Neil (1987), *Amusing Ourselves to Death*, London: Methuen.

Primus, John H. (1998), *Richard Greenham: The Portrait of an Elizabethan Pastor*, Macon, GA: Mercer University Press.

Puckett, David L. (1995), *John Calvin's Exegesis of the Old Testament*, Columbia Series in Reformed Theology, Louisville, KY: Westminster/John Knox Press.

Raiter, Michael, (2002), 'The New Spirituality', *Kategoria* 27, 9–24.

Randall, Ian M. (1999), *Evangelical Experiences – A Study in the Spirituality of English Evangelicalism 1918–1939*, Carlisle: Paternoster Publishing.

Rattenbury, J. Ernest (1941), *The Evangelical Doctrines of Charles Wesley's Hymns*, London: Epworth Press.

Reay, B. (1984), 'Quakerism and Society', in J. F. McGregor and B. Reay (eds.), *Radical Religion in the English Revolution*, Oxford: Oxford University Press.

Reimer, Bill (2000), 'The Spirituality of Henry Venn', *Churchman* 114, 300–315.

Rice, Howard L. (1991), *Reformed Spirituality*, Louisville, KY: Westminster/John Knox Press.

Richard, Lucien Joseph (1974), *The Spirituality of John Calvin*, ed. and trans. F. L. Battles, Atlanta, GA: John Knox Press.

Roston, Murray (1965), *Prophet and Poet: The Bible and the Growth of Romanticism*, London: Faber and Faber.

Rutherford, Samuel (1984), *Letters of Samuel Rutherford*, Edinburgh: Banner of Truth Trust.

Ryle, J. C. (1956), *Holiness*, London: James Clarke.

—— (1964), *Knots Untied*, Cambridge: James Clarke.

Satterthwaite, Philip E., and David F. Wright (eds.) (1994), *A Pathway into the Holy Scripture*, Grand Rapids: Eerdmans.

Schaeffer, Francis A. (1972), *True Spirituality*, London: Hodder and Stoughton.

—— (1973), *The New Super-Spirituality*, London: Hodder and Stoughton.

Schaff, Philip (ed.) (1966), *The Creeds of Christendom*, vol. 3, 4th ed, Grand Rapids: Baker Book House.

Seddon, P., and I. H. Marshall (1994), *Spirituality: Contemporary and Biblical*, Leicester: Religious and Theological Studies Fellowship.

Senn, Frank C. (ed.) (1986), *Protestant Spiritual Traditions*, New York: Paulist Press.

Shumack, Richard (1999), 'A Few Observations on Spirituality in the Psalms'. Unpublished paper.

Simon, Ulrich (1961), *The Ascent to Heaven*, London: Barrie and Rockliff.

Smart, James (1970), *The Strange Silence of the Bible in the Church*, London: SCM Press.

Song, Choan-Seng (1999), *The Believing Heart: An Invitation to Story Theology*, Minneapolis: Fortress Press.

Sontag, Susan (1979), *On Photography*, Harmondsworth: Penguin Books.

Sproul, R. C. (1989), *Pleasing God*, Amersham-on-the-Hill: Scripture Press.

Spurr, John (1998), *English Puritanism 1603–1689*, Basingstoke: London: Macmillan.

Stein, Jock (1994), *Spirituality Today*, Edinburgh: Rutherford House.

Stevenson, H. F. (ed.) (1979), *Light upon the Word: An Anthology of Evangelical Spiritual Writing*, London: Mowbrays.

Thiselton, Anthony C. (1992), *New Horizons in Hermeneutics*, London: HarperCollins.

Thompson, J. A. (1980), *The Book of Jeremiah*, New International Commentary on the Old Testament, Grand Rapids: Eerdmans.

Thomson, J. G. S. S. (1959), *The Word of the Lord in Jeremiah*, London: Tyndale Press.

Thornton, Martin (1963), *English Spirituality*, London: SPCK.

Tiller, John (1982), *Puritan, Pietist, Pentecostalist: Three Types of Evangelical Spirituality*, Nottingham: Grove Books.

Toon, Peter (1987), *From Mind to Heart: Christian Meditation Today*, Grand Rapids: Baker Book House.

—— (1988), *Meditating upon God's Word*, London: Dartman, Longman and Todd.

Toplady, Augustus (1971), *Contemplations*, Harpenden: Gospel Standard Baptist Trust.

Trueman, Carl R. (1998), *The Claims of Truth: John Owen's Trinitarian Theology*, Carlisle: Paternoster Press.

—— (2001), 'The Importance of Being Earnest: Approaching Theological Study', *Themelios*, 26 (1), 34–47.

—— (2002), 'Reckoning with the Past in an Anti-historical Age', *Themelios*, 27 (3), 28–44.

Vanhoozer, Kevin (1994), 'God's Mighty Speech-Acts: The Doctrine of Scripture Today', in Philip E. Satterthwaite and David F. Field (eds.), *A Pathway into the Holy Scriptures*, Grand Rapids: Eerdmans.

—— (1998), *Is There a Meaning in This Text?* Leicester: Apollos.
Van Seters, Arthur (1988), *Preaching as a Social Act*, Nashville, TN: Abingdon Press.
Veith, Gene Edward Jr (1985), *Reformation Spirituality: The Religion of George Herbert*, Lewisburg: Bucknell University Press.
—— (1999), *The Spirituality of the Cross: The Way of the First Evangelicals*, Saint Louis: Concordia.
Vos, Geerhardus (1948), *Biblical Theology, Old and New Testaments*, Grand Rapids: Eerdmans.
—— (1980), *Redemptive History and Biblical Interpretation: The Shorter Writings of Geerhardus Vos*, ed. Richard B. Gaffin Jr, Phillipsburg, NJ: Presbyterian and Reformed Publishing.
Wakefield, Gordon S. (1957), *Puritan Devotion*, London: Epworth Press.
—— (ed.) (1983), *A Dictionary of Christian Spirituality*, London: SCM Press.
Wallace, Dewey D. Jr (1987), *The Spirituality of the Later English Puritans*. Macon, GA: Mercer University Press.
Wallace, Ronald S. (1953), *Calvin's Doctrine of the Word and Sacrament*, Edinburgh: Oliver and Boyd.
—— (1959), *Calvin's Doctrine of the Christian Life*, Grand Rapids: Eerdmans.
Ware, Kallistos (1979), *The Orthodox Way*, London: Mowbrays.
Watkins, Owen C. (1972), *The Puritan Experience*, London: Routledge and Kegan Paul.
Watson, Thomas (1987), *The Doctrine Of Repentance*, Edinburgh: Banner of Truth Trust.
Webb, B. G. (ed.) (1995), *Responding to the Gospel: Evangelical Perspectives on Christian Living*, Explorations 9, Adelaide: Openbook Publishers.
Webber, Robert (1985), *Evangelicals on the Canterbury Trail*, Waco, TX: Word Books.
Weil, Simone (1979), *Waiting on God*, London: Routledge and Kegan Paul.
Wesley, John (1968), *A Plain Account of Christian Perfection*, London: Epworth Press.
Westminster Confession of Faith, and the Larger and Shorter Catechisms (1958), London: Wickliffe Press.
Whelan, Michael (1994), *Living Strings: An Introduction to Biblical Spirituality*, Newtown: Australia: E. J. Dwyer.
Whitlock, Luder G. Jr (2000), *The Spiritual Quest: Pursuing Christian*

Maturity, Grand Rapids: Baker Book House.

Wilberforce, William (1997), *Real Christianity: Discerning True and False Faith*, ed. James Houston, Minneapolis: Bethany House Publishers.

Wilcox, Peter Jonathan (1993), 'Restoration, Reformation, and the Progress of the Kingdom of Christ: Evangelisation in the Thought and Practice of John Calvin, 1555–1564'. DPhil thesis, Oxford University.

Willard, Dallas (1998), *The Divine Conspiracy: Rediscovering our Hidden Life in God*, San Francisco: HarperSanFrancisco.

—— (1999), *Hearing God: Building an Intimate Relationship with the Creator*, London: Fount.

Williams, Rowan (1979), *The Wound of Knowledge: Christian Spirituality from the New Testament to St. John of the Cross*, London: Darton, Longman and Todd.

Wilson, A. N. (1992), *The Faber Book of Church and Clergy*, London: Faber and Faber.

Woolman, John (no date), *The Journal with Other Writings of John Woolman*, London: J. M. Dent.

Yeago, David S. (1997), 'The New Testament and the Nicene Dogma: A Contribution to the Recovery of Theological Exegesis', in *The Theological Interpretation of Scripture*, ed. Stephen E. Fowl, Cambridge, MA: Blackwell.

Index of authors

Index of biblical references

OLD TESTAMENT